International Construction

DEDICATION

To
Dorothy and Sudershan
Our unsung heroines

THE AUTHORS

Ernest A Stallworthy has for many years been a management consultant with his own company, Dolphin Project Management Services. He was previously a manager responsible for the cost control of large-scale projects in the petrochemical industry. He is a Fellow of the Association of Cost Engineers and a member of the American Association of Cost Engineers. Mr. Stallworthy is co-author (with O P Kharbanda and L F Williams) of *Project Cost Control in Action* and (with Dr Kharbanda) of *How to learn from Project Disasters* and *Total Project Management* – all published by Gower.

After three decades in teaching and industry in the USA, the UK and India **Dr O P Kharbanda** now runs his own consultancy advising clients in many parts of the world and across a wide range of industries. He is a Fellow of the Institution of Chemical Engineers, a Visiting Professor, and regular leader of seminars on corporate planning, cost estimating, project management and communication skills. Dr Kharbanda has published or contributed to eight books and more than 150 papers in scientific and technical journals.

International Construction

and the role of project management

E. A. Stallworthy

O. P. Kharbanda

Gower

Published by Gower Publishing Company Limited,
Gower House, Croft Road, Aldershot,
Hants GU11 3HR, England.

and

Gower Publishing Company,
Old Post Road, Brookfield,
Vermont 05036, U.S.A.

British Library Cataloguing in Publication Data

Stallworthy, E.A.
  International construction: the challenge for
  project management.
  1. Construction industry – Management
  2. Industrial project management
  I. Title   II. Kharbanda, O.P.
  624′.068′4   TH438

Library of Congress Cataloguing in Publication Data

Stallworthy, E.A. (Ernest A.)
  International Construction
  Includes bibliographies and index.
  1. Construction industry – management.
  2. Industrial project management – cast studies.
  3. Construction industry.
  I. Kharbanda, Om Prakash   II. Title
  HD9715.A2S69   1985   624′.068   84-24657

  ISBN 0-566-02546-9

Typeset in Great Britain by Saxon Printing Ltd., Derby.
Printed in Great Britain at the University Press, Cambridge.

Contents

Illustrations

Preface

Construction is big business. Its value worldwide is estimated at some US$500 billion a year and the construction industry usually constitutes the largest single sector in any country's economy. Being labour-intensive it is also the largest employer of labour. Construction is as old as history. Amongst the classics of the past may be mentioned the pyramids of Egypt and the Great Wall of China. In this book we introduce you to the Great Pyramid and to a modern classic, the Delta Works in Holland.

Over the centuries construction has been considered a craft, closely guarded by its artisans, its skills being passed on from father to son for many generations. Today it has been converted, with some measure of success, into a 'science'. Courses on construction are widespread and some are quite comprehensive. These can be of great help to those desiring to enter this fascinating industry, but the best place of all to learn is still 'on the job – in the field'. Learning is the basis of all progress and each generation should build on the experience of the previous generation. We ourselves have learnt a lot as we developed our data for presentation to you in this book. At first, we thought that we had most of the answers, but as our project (this book) slowly developed we realised how wrong we were. We are wiser now than when we began, and we hope that this will also be true of you, our readers, when you reach the end of this book.

The end of World War II saw the beginning of the construction industry as we know it today. The massive destruction, both in Europe and the Far East, called for quick and extensive reconstruction. This gave birth to the construction industry in Europe as we now know it and caused the rapid growth of that industry in the United States. Once the reconstruction of Japan was completed, Japanese construction companies, armed with the experience that

they had gained at home under the supervision of American
contractors, ventured abroad: first in the Middle and Far East and
now in Africa and elsewhere, including the US itself! The latest
entrants to this field on a major scale are the Korean, Turkish and
Mexican construction contractors, who at present have the advantage of a highly skilled workforce, low wages and high productivity. But the scene may well change yet again, since India and
China are now becoming very active in this field. This is a rapidly
changing and highly competitive industry, where the law of the
'survival of the fittest' undoubtedly prevails. Many a project has
been a disaster and many a contractor has failed because of
incompetent project management. This was indeed the main
theme of an earlier work of ours: *How to learn from project
disasters*. As we said then, there are very valuable lessons to be
learnt from a study of past projects, both successful and unsuccess-
ful. This is a theme to which we return here, by presenting you
with our analysis of yet another four 'disasters', balanced this time,
however, by four 'success stories'.

Construction is also a very specialised business, rather out of the
common run. It is labour intensive and thus has a high added
value. The capital base of the average construction company is
very small when compared with that of the average manufacturing
company. The ratio of annual turnover to capital employed with
the average construction company is of the order of ten, whereas it
is only one for the typical manufacturer. In addition, the workload
of the construction contractor can vary both widely and erratically.
It is quite common for it to range from thirty to 140 per cent of its
nominal capacity and this presents a continuing and very severe
challenge to its management. When demand is low it becomes
difficult to retain even a nucleus of key staff, whilst when demand
increases it becomes even more difficult to hire in competent
temporary staff to meet the fast-growing commitment. This issue,
amongst many others facing the construction industry, is tackled in
this book. But let's be clear. There is no magic solution to the
present problems facing the construction industry. We can only
provide guidelines developed from our own combined and extensive experience of the industry worldwide.

There are hundreds of thousands of companies around the
world engaged in construction, but once again the 20:80 rule, to
which we have drawn the attention of our readers more than once
in the past, applies. We have the 'vital few' and the 'trivial many'.
Some twenty per cent of the companies in the business contribute
more than 80 per cent of the total turnover. There are perhaps

thirty-five companies worldwide in the so-called 'billion dollar league', handling projects with a value of a billion US dollars or more yearly. The league is dominated by about twenty-five US companies. Yet several of them are still family-owned companies, where no public balance sheet is available. Typical of them, and also one of the largest, is the Bechtel Corporation, who employ some 30,000 people worldwide. At peak, their staff probably oversee the work of more than half a million people at any one time. Much of their work is in the 'management contracting' field, where their direct turnover is limited to their fees, which may be around 10 per cent of the total contracts they are thereby handling. So little information is available about such companies that until recently even their turnover figures were very much a matter for conjecture.

Much has been made by 'experts' in the construction industry of the utility of the 'critical path' approach to project management, with the use of precedence networks and other sophisticated techniques demanding extensive use of the computer and providing voluminous outputs. We, however, have always maintained that whilst such devices may well be useful they can also distort the picture. Many many times we have seen more misuse than use of the computer on a project. Voluminous printouts are produced monthly, and sometimes even weekly, but the data are most indigestible. We are firmly convinced of the value of simple, commonsense techniques such as we expounded in our first joint effort in this field, the book *Project cost control in action*, highlighted in the chapter 'Simple *is* beautiful'.

What the future holds for the construction industry is an open question. The futurists have been busy here, as elsewhere, and the Society for Long Range Planning sponsored a conference with the title: 'Construction towards 2000'. We have presented you with our own view. The point we seek to make, above all, is that the industry must continuously adapt to meet the changing demands made upon it as new technologies emerge.

We write not only for the contractor himself, directly involved in the business of construction, but also for the owner, the consultant, the financier – the other three parties also inevitably involved in every large construction project. We believe that what we have to say is of value not only to the technicians, such as the engineer, the administrator and the accountant, involved at a working level, but also to their managers, right up to the chairman. Normally these several strata each have their own 'language', and this leads to much misunderstanding. We sincerely hope, however, that our attempt at a simple, direct and straightforward approach to a most complicated subject will be understood by all who come to read it.

O. P. KHARBANDA   E. A. STALLWORTHY
Bombay   Coventry

Acknowledgements

Much of the information we have used in putting this book together has been culled from books, articles and papers in the technical press, and even news items seen in the popular press. This information is widely scattered and its source often forgotten, although we have tried to acknowledge such help in the 'References' section at the end of each chapter whenever possible. It is also our hope that the 'References' will serve a dual purpose, providing those who wish to read more about any aspect of this subject with additional sources.

It is difficult to make a specific reference when what has been written is a source of inspiration rather than of detailed fact. This is especially true of the book *Construction – a way of life – a romance* by E.E.(Gene) Halmos. His book is outstanding, we feel, in that it breathes throughout the 'life' that is lived on the construction site. He speaks continually of the challenge that construction presents and demonstrates that challenge by a multitude of stories and photographs that most certainly illustrate what he says is the motto for the whole industry:

Can do !

So there is something *we* can do: thank him for highlighting the romance that is still there, even as one wades across the site in 'wellies' that suck the mud and so 'sigh' with every footstep.

We have received information and encouragement not only from individuals, but also from leading construction engineering companies. Notable amongst these has been the Bechtel Group, whose headquarters are in San Francisco. They were well qualified to help us, with nearly a hundred major projects in 17 countries under way when we were talking to them, and a total of more than 350 project managers of various categories in their service.

This is now the fourth book that we have written jointly and had published through Gower. All in all, we have now had a working relationship with Gower for more than ten years and would like to put on record our thanks for their continuing support. Malcolm Stern, who is their Editorial Director, Management Books, has encouraged us and proffered much sage advice – some of which we have taken – whilst Ellen Keeling, our Editor, has cleaned up our text, ensured its consistency and maintained a very high standard in the format and figures.

EAS
OPK

Part One

A NEW BEGINNING

1 Where it all began

The two prime needs of man have always been food and shelter. Whilst he could use natural shelters, such as caves, these had their limitations. Caves had to be used where they were and in any event there just were not enough of them. There are no records to show us how the construction industry developed, but the earliest building work of which we have a record is 'a city and a tower' at a place called Babel. We know it as Babylon, in the state of Iraq. We have details of the building materials employed. We are told that 'they had brick for stone, and slime they had for mortar'. How they got that far we do not know, but it was very obviously a cooperative effort. It is also very apparent from our own experience that there must have been 'trial and error', this generating what we call a 'learning process'. There would have been master craftsmen, teaching others. Indeed, one such master craftsman is actually mentioned in that early record: a certain Tubal-Cain, 'an instructor of every artificer in brass and iron'.(1)

Of course, man is not the only constructor. This creative instinct is manifested in the building activities of animals of all species. There are marvels of instinct and inventiveness to be found amongst insects, fish, birds and mammals. Termites have created various systems of air conditioning, dug wells to a depth of 120 feet, built central cities and satellite suburbs, and highways to their place of work. Moles work away as mining engineers, digging trenches underground in search of privacy and food, whilst the spider, using its legs and its spinnerets, can card, pull, weave and twist the fluid silk from its glands into the right thread for the right situation far more adeptly than ever could human fingers.(2) Wasps may have taught the Indians the art of manipulating clay and shown the Chinese how to make paper. Animals from time immemorial have ingeniously used stone, wood, reeds, clay

3

and wax as building material. They use hinged doors, traps, shelters with over-hanging roofs, and cells with waterproof lining, and the precision of their architecture frequently surpasses that of human architects.(3)

But despite all this man remains unique in the way he operates. To quote:(4)

> Man is a singular creature. He has a set of gifts which make him unique among the animals: so that, unlike them, he is not a figure in the landscape – he is a *shaper* of that landscape. In body and mind he is the explorer of nature, the ubiquitous animal, who did not find but has *made his home* in every continent.

So, man is an animal, but with a difference! Man has the gift of imagination.(5) It is this *difference* that has landed man on the moon and now brings him to consider the construction of factories in space.

The importance of communication

One of the most important factors in all this is *communication*. We notice with respect to that early building work in Babylon, that once communication had been disrupted 'they left off to build the city'. We know that the animals can and do communicate with one another and do that very well indeed, perhaps better than man. They have their 'language'. So has man. But communication is not limited to speech. We realise that personal conversation is the ideal method of communication, because we not only hear the words, but also note the way in which those words are said, and the facial expressions and body movements associated with them: factors in communication which can be far more important than the words themselves. They convey the 'feeling' behind the words and it is ultimately those feelings which really matter. A mother's love for her newly-born infant can only be felt. She cannot convey the message to her child by the words she uses: only by the tone of voice.

Even amongst adults, where the words used are naturally very important, they are not all that significant in this matter of communication. Words play only a small part and that rather too slowly. It is not the words but how they are said. Psychologist Albert Mehrabian (6) expresses it thus:

Total impact of message – 7% verbal .. 38% vocal .. 55% facial

Thus, in real communication, words are the least important factor. In personal conversation there is no problem, since all three factors can play their part. In the case of a telephone conversation, however, that last important element is missing and to that extent a telephone conversation can lead to misunderstanding. Modern technology is now seeking to remedy that basic defect in communication with the introduction of phonovision, where the face of the speaker can be seen on the screen. But even this is not the same as being 'face to face'. The body movements are lost, together with the element of touching, typified by the handshake. A warm and friendly handshake can convey far more than a multitude of pleasant words. Perhaps man will eventually find a way to 'shake hands' with his friend across the other side of the world. Fiction, you think?

Well, most of our modern inventions did start as fiction. Let us give you just one example from our personal experience. The advance in worldwide communications to which we have just referred has been made possible by the introduction of the communications satellite. Yet it is less than thirty years ago that the concept of such a satellite appeared in a work of fiction written by the British physicist Arthur Clarke. It was not merely fiction. The concept was supported by a serious technical paper on the basic theory of communication satellites, published by Clarke in 1945 (7) whilst he was a Radar Officer in the RAF. He is now settled in Colombo and one of us had the pleasure of meeting him and listening to him some five years ago. He traced the background to the subject of communication satellites and confessed that when he first wrote about them he never expected them to become a reality in his own lifetime. The rest, of course, is now history. Clarke explained it by saying that whenever man has wanted something desperately enough, he gets it. According to him, it's as simple as that! That same principle will be constantly before us as we survey the construction industry. The difficulties are surmounted, the problems overcome. But at what cost? We could also pose the question: At what benefit and at what loss?

Cost is the continuing and all-important factor: probably the only limiting factor. For instance, Clarke's concept of a wrist phone, whereby one could speak to any person anywhere at any time may have sounded pure fiction when he first suggested it, even although that was less than ten years ago. But now it is a technical possibility. All the fiction has gone out of the concept:

the only question left is that of the economics. After all, 'teleconferencing' seems to be here with us to stay and the developing countries are no longer being left behind. They now 'leapfrog' over such frontiers of science and technology. Already the first International Teleconference Symposium has taken place, with live satellite video link-up via colour TV screens. Some two thousand delegates gathered in conference rooms as far apart as London, Sydney, Tokyo and Philadelphia for a three-day session. One or more groups of delegates at the four centres held two- and three-way discussions, but at one stage *all* the delegates were 'brought together' for a one-hour global session. At about the same time a medical teleconference was being held, where New Delhi was linked with some other world capitals.

All this is of great significance to the construction industry, as we shall go on to demonstrate in Chapter 22. The international contractor (or constructor), operating at various remote sites worldwide, finds his work much facilitated by ready communication. He has to communicate not only with his people on the construction site, but also with a multitude of suppliers and other agencies spread worldwide – all actively involved in this exciting business of construction.

Monuments to man's constructive ability

Man, with his ingenuity, skill and longing for immortality has built many monuments down the ages. For the moment let us take just one, the Great Pyramid of Egypt. This has been the subject of many books, articles and technical papers over the years and has been described as 'The World's most enduring wonder'. (8) It is a perfect pyramid, and was faced with white limestone polished to an almost mirror-like finish. Built around 2700 BC, the Great Pyramid still stands almost intact after nearly five thousand years, an enduring monument to man's skill and workmanship, built at a time when none of the present construction equipment and techniques was available.

The apex of the Great Pyramid is 481 feet above the ground, and each of the four sides is 756 feet long at the base. Built as the tomb of the mighty Pharaoh Cheops, and called by the Egyptians the 'Horizon of Khufu', it stands some 8 kilometres south of modern Cairo city. This colossal tomb was built by several thousands of masons, quarrymen and labourers over a period of about thirty years. Around 2.5 million stone blocks, ranging in weight from 2.5 to 15 tonnes were used in its building. How were they handled, raised and placed with such precision? The four corners of the pyramid are almost perfect right angles and its four sides face the four points of the compass with really remarkable accuracy. The limestone blocks, to judge by those still left at the base, were so smooth and so accurately finished that even a cigarette paper could not be passed between them when in place.

Judging by what we now see, the Great Pyramid must have involved tremendous organisation and careful coordination, not much different to that called for in the construction of a skyscraper in a city centre these days. Stone blocks, rough cut, came from various parts of Egypt and were shaped and polished by skilled masons using fine abrasives. The stone blocks were hauled up a great stone causeway sloping gently upwards for more than a kilometre to the lip of the plateau by sweating gangs of labourers using wooden sledges. The construction of the causeway alone took ten years. The skilled work of quarrying, stone cutting and fitting was carried out throughout the year, but the unskilled work of some 100,000 labourers was used for only three months in the year, whilst the Nile was in flood. For the rest of the year those labourers, mainly agricultural, worked on the farms.

It could be an interesting and revealing exercise to try and reconstruct the planning and scheduling that must have gone on behind the scenes as the work went ahead. Did they use Gantt charts? No records are left and we can only get ideas from the evidence left to us, such as the finely polished stones and remnants of plaited rope found in the dark tunnels of the Great Pyramid by British soldiers during the Second World War. These ropes were probably used by the quarrymen to haul the blocks up the ramp, since they are of extraordinary thickness. Made of plaited reed, they are well able to haul 15-tonne blocks.

In the heart of the structure is the King's Chamber, lined with blocks of polished granite. With thousands of tons of masonry overhead, the sense of confinement is overwhelming, and the atmosphere oppressive. It was here that Cheops' mummy was finally laid, being carried through an opening left for the purpose, through descending and ascending corridors and finally along what is known as the Grand Gallery. Here we meet yet another remarkable feat of engineering, since after the funeral procession left the building huge 'plug blocks', which had been resting on temporary timber supports, were released to slide down and completely seal the Grand Gallery. No doubt they thought that, with that operation completed, Cheops' body was safe for eternity. But no: robbers and searchers for treasure found their way in, their access route being used by the tourists of today. The

engineers amongst the latter can only marvel at this mammoth feat
of construction, completed so long ago, yet still standing.

The seven wonders of the world

This is the title of a treatise written by a Greek mathematician,
Philon of Byzantium, about 150 years before the birth of Christ.
The seven 'wonders' that he listed were:

> The Great Pyramid
> The Lighthouse at Alexandria
> The Hanging Gardens of Babylon
> The Temple of Diana at Ephesus
> Phidias' statue of Zeus at Olympia
> The Mausoleum at Halicarnassus
> The Colossus of Rhodes

Of them all, only the Great Pyramid still stands, even though it
was probably 2,000 years older than any of the others listed. Dare
we make such a list today? Consider the Sydney Opera House,
seen from the air in Figure 1.1. We are able to study the design and
construction techniques used to create that building and we do so
in Chapter 16. We also think that the Delta Works in Holland,
which we study in some detail in Chapter 19, can fairly be
described as a modern 'wonder'; but let us, for the moment, stay
with the past.

From father to son

How was the first 'monument to man' – and the next one – and the
one after that – ever brought to completion? Initially, the whole
process must have been that of 'trial and error'. The craftsman
taught himself his trade the hard way. He learnt by experience,
then and now the best teacher there is. But the craftsman, having
mastered his trade, could then teach others. He did not teach
anyone and everyone. Craft skills were closely guarded by the
artisans, since they had been learnt at the cost of much time and
effort. The normal practice was to pass the craft down from father
to son. We can picture the son beginning as a 'helper' to his father,
then an 'understudy' and finally a fully-fledged craftsman in his
own right. In due time the father retired from the scene, satisfied
that his son had learnt all the 'tricks of the trade'. Thus skills were

Figure 1.1 *The Sydney Opera House*
An aerial view, showing the beauty of the shell-like roofs to perfection. For technical details on the design of these 'shells' see Chapter 16. (Photograph by courtesy of the New South Wales Government Office.)

handed down from father to son for generations and the process has continued right down to today.

Now much of this 'know-how' has been written down and is on record in the form of books, articles and papers. What was once an 'art' has been transformed, at least to some extent, into a 'science'. Courses on construction are available worldwide and some are quite comprehensive. To list but a few, we have:

> Construction analysis – project diagnostic work
> Construction contracts
> Construction engineering and management
> Construction industrial labour relations
> Construction methods and equipment
> Construction project administration
> Construction operations – analysis and improvement
> Design of construction operations
> Field construction
> Management of construction contracts
> Management of construction projects
> Process plant construction management
> Stochastic construction estimating
> Time and money in construction control

Courses such as these can be of great help to those desiring to enter this most fascinating field of endeavour, but the best place to learn is still 'on the job'. Once on the job, it usually becomes a demanding, sometimes frustrating, but always satisfying way of life.

Modern construction industry

Construction is and always has been the largest single sector in the industry of every country in the world, once there is any degree of industrialisation with the development of an infrastructure. From then on it forms a vital sector in the country's economy and its prosperity is a measure of the economic progress of the country. The construction industry normally constitutes between 7 and 15 per cent of a country's GDP. Because the industry is still labour-intensive, despite ever-increasing mechanisation, its contribution to employment is substantially larger than such a percentage first indicates.

The modern construction industry, in the form we know it today, started at the end of World War II. Until then construction activity was almost entirely localised. Construction companies rarely operated outside their own country. However, the massive destruction caused by the war, both in Europe and the Far East, called for quick and extensive reconstruction. This demand gave birth to the construction industry in Europe as we now know it and stimulated a very rapid growth of the industry in the United States. Once the reconstruction work in Japan had been completed, Japanese construction contractors, armed with the experience that they had gained at home under the supervision of their American colleagues, ventured abroad: first to the Middle East and now in Africa. At this time we had the advent of the mega-project, where the cost of each project, still under the supervision of one contractor or consortium, ran into several billions of dollars. We introduce you later to some of these projects, for there are many lessons to learn from them. Some proved to be success stories, but others were disasters. We look at both, for disasters have as much, if not more, to teach us than the successes which are featured all too frequently in the management literature.

The latest entrants into the construction industry on a major scale are the Korean, Turkish and Mexican construction contractors, who at present have the advantage of a highly skilled workforce, low wages and high productivity, relative to their competitors elsewhere in the world. But the scene may well change yet again, since both India and China, with their enormous resources of skilled manpower, are now becoming very active in this field. This is a rapidly changing and highly competitive industry, where the law of the 'survival of the fittest' undoubtedly prevails.

The American scene

As we have just seen, the modern construction industry has been fundamentally a post-war phenomonen and in the early stages of development the American contractor predominated. This was to some extent due to the initiative of the Americans, but the fact that much of the reconstruction was financed by the US was far more significant. From a strong base the American contractors prospered both at home and overseas for twenty years or more. But from about 1970 onwards they had a setback, because of the rapid strides being made by the international engineering and construction industry in the developed world other than the US. This rapid growth was strongly encouraged by the various governments involved, in the desire to stimulate their export trade. Japanese contractors were particularly successful in this respect. Thus countries other than the US began to secure much of the new construction work overseas. While in 1976 the US construction industry ranked first in the field of overseas contracts, by the end of the decade it ranked only fifth. The leading four countries were then Japan, South Korea, West Germany and Italy, in order of volume of business done overseas. The US contractors were largely squeezed out of the lucrative Middle East business that had been fuelled mainly by the 'petrodollar surplus' resulting from the oil crisis of 1973.

One of the main reasons for this dramatic shift was that the US had lost its competitive edge in comparison with the others in the field, largely because of soaring labour costs and falling productivity. To make matters worse, government regulations and procedural requirements proliferated, extending the construction phase on some large-scale projects by years. It has been estimated (9) that between 1967 and 1980 productivity in the construction industry in the US fell by around 20 per cent.

There are now indications that the American construction contractors have taken these setbacks to heart and are doing something about it. We read an article, for instance, entitled 'Fluor rides out the hiccups', that tells us that total reorganisation is Fluor's answer to securing future expansion, following three decades of 'tempestuous growth'.(10) China is likely to become the next field for major endeavour, seeing that that country's plans for 1984 involve the purchase of up to one billion dollars' worth of Western technology and hardware, chiefly for coal mining, steel production and petrochemical processing.(11) This potential seems to be recognised, for Robert Page, Chief Executive Officer of Kellogg Rust declares:(12)

> We're bullish on the Far East ... we have been in China longer than any other foreign engineering and construction firm ... the Chinese are extremely interested in gasification.

But, with the inbuilt advantage that China has with cheap construction labour, the American and other foreign contractors will need to be flexible in their approach. Acting as managing contractors they will have to accept maximum local participation in both hardware and services.

If they approach the future with realism, having a thorough knowledge of the marketplace and its requirements, and now making a conscious effort to cut costs, the American contractors are sure to regain some of that lost ground. However, in view of the cheap labour available from India and China, it will be a tough task. But after all, is not that the very essence of the construction industry: it was, it is and it always will be a tough rough industry.

References

1   The Holy Bible. We are quoting from the Authorised (King James) Version. See, in particular, chapters 1–10 of Genesis.

2   George. J., 'Secrets of the spider's web', *Readers Digest,* Indian ed., Oct. 1965, pp.171–6.

3   Von Frisch, Karl, *Animal Architecture*, Hutchison, London, 1975, 306 pp.

4   Bronowski, J., *The Ascent of Man*, British Broadcasting Corporation, London, 1973, 448 pp.

5   Bronowski. J., 'The wondrous reach of imagination', *Readers Digest,* US ed., Sept. 1967, pp.128–31.

6   Davis, F., 'How to read body language', *Readers Digest,* US ed.,Dec. 1969, pp.127–30.

7   Clarke, Arthur C., *Voices across the sky*, Harper & Row, 1974, 228 pp.

8   Article: 'The World's most enduring wonder', *Readers Digest,* Indian ed., Aug. 1963, pp. 91–6.

9   Heckert, R.E., 'Construction's vital role in America's competitiveness'. *Chem. Eng. Progress,* 78, 11–14 Jan. 1982.

10 Article: 'Fluor rides out the hiccups', *International Construction,* June/August 1983, pp.18–19.

11 Article on China: *Wall Street Journal,* 30 Jan. 1984, p.36.

12 Article: 'The top 400 contractors', *Eng. News Record,* 212, pp.64–99, 19 April 1984.

2 Historical development

In the previous chapter we traced the origins of the construction industry from prehistoric times and saw the way in which the industry has developed and taken on the form that it has today. It is clear that throughout 'necessity has been the mother of invention'. The very real strength of the industry has been its basic resilience in the face of changing circumstances, together with the ability to move with the times and adapt to the prevailing situation. We now want to look at some of the factors, trivial and significant, which have brought the industry to the position in which it is today.

Some definitions

There are three allied but different functions in the construction industry that need definition at the outset if we are to avoid continuing confusion in your understanding of the terms we use. We have the 'consultant', the 'fabricator' and the 'contractor'. The 'contractor' could be better called a 'construction contractor' and is often so referred to in the US, but we will continue to use the term 'contractor' because of its worldwide acceptance. A simple functional definition of these three terms goes as follows:

> The CONSULTANT advises *what* (product) and *how* (which process or route).
> The FABRICATOR makes the equipment or 'hardware'.
> The CONTRACTOR carries out the work on the site.

However, the above distinction of functions is not clear-cut, nor are the three functions mutually exclusive. The main reason for this is historical. Some fabricators, in the course of time, began undertaking construction and so became contractors as well. It was thought that, for a contractor, an in-house fabrication facility would be an advantage. But that advantage was largely illusory. Ideally, the contractor should have the freedom to buy the hardware he needs from the cheapest source, worldwide, provided always that what he buys complies with the appropriate specifications. Once the contractor has an in-house fabrication facility, he will seek to maximise the use of that facility, irrespective of the cost to the project. This has proved to be a great handicap, with the result that some fabricator/contractors have eventually opted out of fabrication and confined themselves to contracting. Foster Wheeler are an example of this. Originally a fabricator, FW ventured into contracting and have now developed that to such an extent that contracting is now very much their major activity.

There is similar confusion between contractors and consultants. Some contractors do consulting work, whilst some consultants also act as contractors. But this is not a desirable development in our view, since the consultant/contractor has a vested interest, with the result that the owner, who finally has to pay for it all, may well suffer. Consulting and contracting are two distinct functions and they should always be undertaken by distinct and separate agencies. It is hoped, therefore, that those heavily involved in the consulting field, such as the World Bank and FIDIC (International Federation of Consulting Engineers) will recognise the distinction and maintain it. What is required is the adoption and application of a strict code of ethics, which would then preclude such confusion. There should be no business association, in fact or in practice, between 'consultants' and 'contractors', since that inevitably introduces the philosophy: 'you scratch my back and I'll scratch yours', a process that ultimately works to the disadvantage of the owner.

Growth of the construction industry

We noted in the previous chapter that a healthy construction industry is vital to the development of a country and in fact the expenditure on construction usually parallels the GDP of a country pretty closely. Construction activity can therefore be looked upon as a barometer of a country's economy. Figure 2.1 presents, for the UK, the USA and India (we include the latter so that you can compare developed with a developing country), the expenditure on construction for certain selected years, and their respective GDP. All the figures are in the same currency (US$) so they are comparable and we can see that with the developed countries the construction activity follows the growth in GDP. With India it is a growing percentage, demonstrating the underlying strength of the industry. These figures need to be treated with a certain amount of caution when comparisons between countries are made, since the evaluation of the scope of construction varies from country to country. Almost two-thirds of the total volume is usually housing (new construction and repair). It is also true that for most countries construction forms the largest single activity, not only in terms of expenditure, but particularly in terms of employment, since construction – in spite of increasing mechanisation – is still a labour-intensive industry.

| | India | | | UK | | | USA | | |
Year	GDP	Constr.	%	GDP	Constr.	%	GDP	Constr.	%
1960	31.5	2.9	9.2	71.5	4.3	6.0	505	25	5.0
1970	53.7	5.4	10.0	122.0	7.3	6.0	988	50	5.1
1975	88.5	10.3	11.6	231.0	16.2	7.0	1538	76	5.9
1977	103.0	12.4	12.0	249.0	15.0	6.0	1903	88	4.6
1979	134.0	20.0	15.0	402.0	20.0	5.0	2377	114	4.8

Note: All the above values are in US$ billion.
Other typical ratios for the year 1979:

Israel: 15%; Saudi Arabia: 15%; Japan: 9%; Austria: 8%; Singapore: 6%. The USSR, Poland and Czechoslovakia were all stated as 11%.

Sources: *Year Book of Construction Statistics, 1973–80; Year Book of National Accounts, 1980. (3 vols.)* (both published by the United Nations, New York)

Figure 2.1   Value of construction *vs* GDP
This table illustrates that for developed countries the relationship between the value of construction work and the Gross Domestic Product (GDP) is stable, whilst for developing countries it can grow.

Much of the normal construction activity, such as housing and roads is carried out by local contractors, whereas the more sophisticated construction work, such as airfields, harbours and docks is carried out by international contractors. These latter are essential when we come to a developing country with no background or expertise in the design and execution of such facilities.

But the local regulations in the developing countries are increasingly making it mandatory that local suppliers and services are used to the maximum extent possible. This is essential not only for the conservation of their scarce foreign exchange resources, but also to fulfil their desire to develop the local capability to handle such work.

Fierce competition in the market place

International construction as we know it today is essentially a post World War II phenomenon that developed out of the urgent need to rebuild the plants, particularly in Europe and Japan, that had been devastated by war. The concept was born in the USA, the birthplace of many commercial developments. As a nation, the USA excels in both 'borrowing' and 'buying' ideas from elsewhere and then translating them into going commercial propositions. Thereafter they export, quite often to the country of origin, the developed idea. Nylon is a typical example of this, invented in the UK but first brought to large-scale commercial application in the USA.

It was in this way that the USA set the pace for the rest of the construction industry with the result that by 1956 US contractors dominated the scene worldwide, being responsible for more than 90 per cent of the large-scale construction work going forward at that time. But their dominance did not last for long. First came Western Europe, offering comparable services at very competitive prices. A little later came Japan, who had had to start from nothing. The Japanese firms went on a 'shopping spree', importing both technology and hardware, and often buying complete plants on a 'turnkey' basis. But they usually bought only one plant, and were learning fast. They both absorbed the technology, adapting it very successfully to Japanese conditions, and then went on to improve it still further. Soon Japanese contractors were offering their services to third countries in direct competition with the American construction companies from whom they had learnt their craft. Their lower wages at that time, associated with constantly increasing productivity, made them very competitive. Their first entry was into neighbouring countries in South East Asia, but they were soon to be seen in the Middle East, despite the geographical and language advantage of European companies. We think that Japanese achievement in this area is nothing less than a 'miracle' of perseverance and endeavour.

But the 'miracle' has been re-enacted – by South Korea. This country followed closely in the path first trodden by Japan, beginning by importing 'turnkey' projects, then getting its local contractors involved, and so growing in experience. The experience thus gained finally enabled South Korea to secure important contracts in both South East Asia and the Middle East. The South Koreans followed the practice of Japanese contractors in sending out 'bachelor' teams to the project site, where they stayed until the project was completed. To save on investment in temporary housing and other facilities for their personnel, they also devised a scheme whereby their people stayed on board a ship. This suited the host country very well – particularly Saudi Arabia, who did not encourage mixing of these expatriates with the local population. As a result, South Korea had nearly 90 per cent of its overseas work in Saudi Arabia at one time.

A constantly changing scene

The construction boom in the Middle East following on from the postwar reconstruction work was fuelled by the surplus petrodollars that accrued to the oil producers in this region as a result of the four- to five-fold advance in the price of crude oil in 1973, followed by a further doubling of the price in 1979. The objective was to use the petrodollars for the development of their countries whilst their 'treasure', their oil reserves, lasted. In 1981 the Middle East market, consisting of around 21 Arab nations, totalled some US$82 billion.(1) This was about half of the total world construction work, excluding the USA. Over 70 per cent of this volume of work was concentrated in three countries, thus:

Country	Volume – billion US$	
	1981	1980
Iraq:	23.0	12.6
Saudi Arabia:	22.0	15.7
Libya:	15.0	3.5

The remarkable growth is immediately apparent. Other countries, such as Egypt, Kuwait, Jordan and Algeria, were spending very little by comparison.

The constantly changing scene is typified by a statement in a survey of overseas construction,(2) likening the situation for the contractor to that of a football team which must win the World Cup year after year if it is to make its mark. A 'one off' win would be a fluke, soon forgotten. Also, to win in this particular game you must have a 'plus point'. For example, South Korea stormed into this very competitive field by quoting prices up to 25 per cent lower than their competitors, whilst their productivity was comparable. Others have specialised in certain specific fields and so have been particularly competitive in that area. For instance, Italian contractors lead in the field of tunnelling and earth dams, whilst the Dutch lead in dredging.

Another factor of significance is religious or political affinity. Thus Turkey made a breakthrough by virtue of its close links with its Muslim neighbours and India may well gain in the near future because of its old friendship with Egypt, which now promises to become an important market. These are intangible factors but they can play a decisive role when contracts are being let.

Much also depends in this area upon what is called the 'personal equation'. Sir John Buckley, then Chairman of the Davy Corporation, the largest process plant contractor outside the US, once summed up his experience in China thus:(3)

> ... in this business where lots of money is being spent ... the customer likes to look the top man in the eye from time to time to say '*You* are going to stand by me, aren't you?'

This 'personal equation' can obviously be of crucial importance with small jobs, but apparently it still plays a significant role in 'mega-projects': presumably because even in the biggest project work is finally done via personal relationships at the operating level.

'Dash' it

Let us now look at some of the 'pecularities' of the construction industry. One is that, whilst the total workload in any country may well be fairly stable, the workload of an individual contractor can oscillate widely. Work from one year to the next can be halved or doubled. For instance, in Figure 2.2 we present the variation in job manhours in the London Office of a leading international contractor over the years.(4) The manhours per month varied from 12,000 to 75,000 over a period of three years. The causes of this are many and varied, but probably the biggest factor is pricing policy: each contractor in turn reacts to under- or overemployment of his workforce and so takes the lead in winning contracts.

An interesting factor in the winning of contracts is what is called

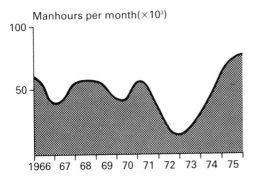

Figure 2.2   Engineering manhours year by year
This graph illustrates the violent fluctuations that can occur in
engineering manhours in a design office. (With acknowledgements
to Mr H.W. Dean – see Ref. 4)

'dash'. This is an integral part of local social customs in countries
such as Nigeria.(5) Dash is, to put it simply, a tip 'in anticipation of
services about to be rendered', presumably as an inducement to
hasten the process. Mr Peter Enaharo, in his guidebook *How to be
a Nigerian*, is quite blunt on the subject.

> Tipping for services rendered is quite repugnant to the
> Nigerian ... [he] thinks it is vulgar that good service should
> be rewarded *after* the deed is done. Even when a Nigerian
> negotiates or demands a gift which is sure to influence his
> judgment, he does not accept the interpretation that this is a
> *bribe*. It is for him not corruption, but merely a fee or a price
> for doing you a favour.

Such expenses are not insignificant. Currently ranging between 7
and 10 per cent of contract value, depending upon the country and
the nature of the 'favour' being granted, they are an integral part
of the cost of every contract in those countries where it is the
custom and *must* be allowed for in the estimate if the construction
contractor is not to work at a loss.

Another illustration of the very distinctive character of the
construction industry is presented in Figure 2.3.(6) This table
illustrates the contrast between an engineering contractor and his
main market, the process industry. We see that the construction
industry is labour-intensive and that for a contractor the turnover/
capital ratio is very high, some ten times that of the process
industry he serves. He thus has a very small capital base, compared with his turnover, and is vulnerable. Even a relatively small

	Process industry	Process plant industry
Nature of business:	Product (hardware)	Service (software)
Price:	Fixed	Negotiable
Specification:	Clear	Vague
Scope:	Fixed	Negotiable
Turnover, US$ billion/yr.: (Total industry, US)	1,000	130
Turnover/capital ratio:	1	10
Turnover/employee:	1	4
Focus:	Capital – intensive	Labour – intensive
Load:	Even	Erratic
Utilisation:	70–90%	30–140%
Turnover per company: (US$ billion per year)		
Largest, US only:	20	10
25 largest, US only:	200	90

Figure 2.3   A study in contrasts
This table presents the stark contrast between the work done by the
contractor in the process industry and his client.

loss on one contract – small, that is, in relation to the size of the
contract – can land a contractor in deep trouble and even bring
him to bankruptcy, as we have demonstrated elsewhere.(7)

Since the construction industry is a service industry, with little
influence on its market, the contractor has to learn to live with the
peculiarities of his business. This can be a challenging task, but the
successful contractor thrives on such challenges.

Construction management

This is a comparatively recent development, born out of the risks
inherent in situations where the scope of the work cannot be
precisely defined before the contract is let, or we have a mega-
project whose cost runs to billions of dollars. In such circumstances a lump sum bid just is not feasible, yet the 'cost-plus'
contract puts the owner at a disadvantage. This led to the 'fixed fee
plus reimbursable cost' contract, and the contractor receiving the
fee became a managing contractor, acting on behalf of the owner.
The managing contractor thus became a specialist in construction
management.

Construction management became widespread with the construction 'boom' in the Middle East in the 1970s, and was in effect
a 'marriage' between the owner, the contractor and the
designer.(8) The function of the construction manager is to
reconcile the objectives of these three disparate groups in order to
serve the best interests of the owner. Leading construction companies such as Bechtel pioneered this concept, particularly in the
Middle East. Judging by results it has been quite successful and is
here to stay. But how are we to assess the workload and the
turnover of the construction manager, or managing contractor?
His fee will be, most usually, between 5 and 10 per cent of the total
cost of the project. Is his workload the full cost of the project or
only ten per cent of it? This just adds to the confusion when one
tries to assess the volume of business being undertaken. We have a
chain: managing contractor – contractor – subcontractor. Thus
when contract awards are being totalled, it is quite possible for the
same work to be counted twice, if not three times on occasion.

London – the Mecca for contractors

With the rapid expansion of the construction industry on an
international basis after World War II, the need arose for a central
'headquarters' to facilitate negotiation. Probably purely by accident this has turned out to be London. It began when leading
American contractors established branch offices in London, to
give them access to the European and Asian markets from a base
with whom they had a common language. Contractors worldwide
watch one another very closely, so the establishment of such
branch offices in London steadily gathered momentum. Finally
most of the major international contractors, not only American but
Japanese, French, Italian and others, had a London Office, often
with a full complement of engineering staff. Because of the
transport problems occasioned by the size of London, many of
these firms have now moved out of Central London to the
suburbs, or nearby towns such as Reading and Northampton. On a
somewhat smaller scale, The Hague in The Netherlands also
experienced an influx of process plant contractors operating
worldwide. Once again language played an important role: the
average Dutch engineer *has* to have a command of English.

Project financing

The growth in the size and cost of projects over the years has brought a new dimension to the construction industry: international project financing. Contractors have now quite often to offer a 'financial package' as part of their tender for a project. As a result, there is now a wide range of articles and papers offering guidance on the best way to handle it. (For example, references 9, 10, 11, 12.)

It seems that an attractive financial package can tip the scales in favour of an otherwise uncompetitive tenderer. To take but one example to let us see the way it works, the case can be cited (13) of bidding for two 2500 TPSD methanol plants for the USSR. In terms of price, the West German contractor Lurgi were the obvious winner, their quotation being some £20 million (US$30 million) lower than the runner-up, the British company Davy McKee (then Davy Powergas). However, the availability of British credit and a 0.75 per cent improvement in their offer by switching the British tender, made in pounds sterling, to US dollars, immediately tipped the scales in favour of Davy McKee and they secured the contract. All this required very close and in-depth liaison between the British consortium making the bid, their financial advisers, the bankers Morgan Grenfell, and various Government agencies, such as the Export Credits Guarantee Department. Further, the fact that the British group had a West German partner, their subsidiary Klöckner, also helped to swing the decision in their favour.

Thus you can see that considerable flexibility and much ingenuity is required if one is to excel in this newest of disciplines, financial engineering. Countries such as Italy, France, Japan and lately South Korea have excelled in this field, with the full backing of their respective governments. The United States and Canada do not normally offer interest subsidies, but they can offer long credit periods, up to 30 years. There is no doubt that 'financial engineering' is a highly specialised and complex subject, but it is one which the contractor must learn to handle if he wishes to operate on a worldwide basis.

The 'new boys'

We have already commented on the fact that the international scene is steadily changing, in that the biggest contractors, once exclusively from the United States and the industrialised countries of Western Europe, are being replaced by contractors from the developing countries. South Korea and Turkey are the most recent examples of this movement. But they are not alone. They are now being joined by others: notably Mexico, China and India.

Just twenty years ago Mexico was totally dependent upon foreign technology and contractors. Yet today she has emerged as an important supplier of engineering services and construction know-how to the Third World – particularly the Latin American countries. Mexican contractors have pooled their resources to work as a team in undertaking projects overseas.(14) ConstruMexico, a consortium of 42 national firms, have bid since 1973 for nearly US$3 billion of overseas contracts and won about 20 per cent of this against stiff competition. China is rich in manpower and its workers are highly skilled, but as yet it has barely set foot on the first rung of the ladder of international construction.(15) The Chinese are well aware that they are weak in management techniques but they are willing to absorb technology from the foreigner and so learn. India is perhaps a little further ahead. Having vast manpower resources and considerable construction expertise, the Indian contractors have already taken advantage of the Middle East construction 'boom' and are undoubtedly capable of both maintaining and improving their position in the international market.

References

1   Supplement: 'International Construction', *Financial Times,* London, 9 Nov. 1982, pp.177–22.
2   Supplement: 'Overseas Construction', *Financial Times,* London, 4 March 1977, pp.15–26.
3   Feature article: 'We try to find ways of disorganising ourselves', *Worldwide Projects,* September 1980, pp.41–9. (In an interview with Sir John Buckley, of Davy International)
4   Dean, H.W., 'The problems of cyclical investment', *Chem. & Ind.,* 15 April 1978, pp.249–53.
5   Article: 'The "dash" – becoming a stampede?', *Diogenes Africanus,* September 1982.

6 Kharbanda, O.P., 'Process industry with and vs. the Engineering Contractor', *Chemtech*, 13, November 1983, pp.668–9.
7 Kharbanda, O.P. and Stallworthy, E.A., *How to learn from project disasters'*, Gower, Aldershot, UK, 1983, 274 pp.
8 Kavanagh, T.C., Muller, F. and O'Brien, J.J. *Construction Management*, McGraw-Hill, 1978, 399 pp.
9 Brochure: *International Project Financing*, issued by M.W. Kellogg, Houston, Texas.
10 James, J.L. and Martin, P.R., 'Financing Constraints', paper presented at a symposium organised by the Institution of Chemical Engineers at Nottingham University, 27 Sept. 1978.
11 Sterling, P., 'What Engineers should know about Project Finance', *Eng. & Proc. Econ.* 2, pp.127–32, 1977.
12 Flowers, E.B. and Lawson, S.J., 'Financial Technology', *Asian National Development*, May 1983, pp. 9–10.
13 Kharbanda, O.P., 'Financial Engineering in Construction', *Chem. & Ind. News*, March 1984, pp.860–2.
14 Prescott, R., 'The Mexicans abroad – a strong new international competitor for Third World Projects', *Worldwide Projects*, Aug/Sept. 1980, pp.27–30.
15 Green, E.C., 'China's moves into international construction', *Worldwide Projects*, Dec./Jan. 1981, pp.61–7.

3   Where we are today

The construction boom first set in motion by the devastation of World War II persisted till the early 1970s. Then, when the rest of industry began to go into decline because of the oil crisis, that same crisis brought a further boom, now in the Middle East. This secondary boom was fuelled by the very petrodollars that were bringing depression worldwide. The price of crude oil went up rapidly from US$3 to US$ 30 or more per barrel and the resultant flood of petrodollars was used by the oil producers for extensive industrial development.

Has the boom ended?

Well, we think it has, for the time being at least. The boom years from 1975 to 1981 reached a peak in terms of the volume of work carried out that we believe will never be reached again. The boom collapsed due to the financial restraints finally imposed by the depression elsewhere in the world. The demand for oil fell drastically and with it the petrodollar income. Hence the very ambitious capital investment programmes initiated a few years earlier had to be drastically curtailed. Many projects were cancelled and others postponed and rescheduled. The impact with respect to plans for ethylene plants in the Middle East is graphically illustrated in Figure 3.1.

Third World projects – the human realities

As we have just seen, there was a boom in construction over ten

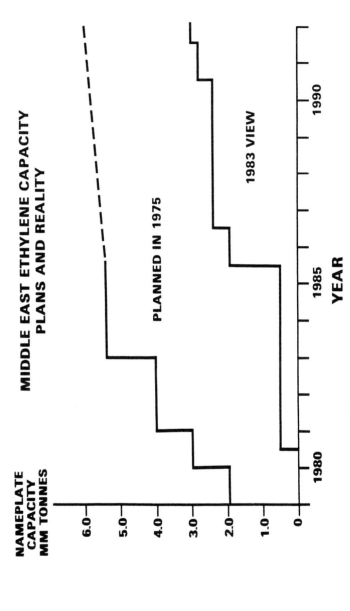

Figure 3.1 The plan compared with the reality
This chart illustrates the change that has taken place in planned ethylene capacity since 1975. (With acknowledgements to Mr Alan Plaistowe, Chem Systems International, London)

27

years or more throughout the developing world and particularly in the oil producing countries. Many large projects were initiated that were carried out by multinational corporations, who provided the technology, management, design and construction and even sometimes offered a market for the final product from the plants they were building. Such international collaboration was not always successful. The problems that arose were generated in the main by the enormous gulf in social and cultural values between the parties involved.(1) One study reviewed more than 1,600 projects, valued at more than US$ 1,000 billion in all, over a wide range of work, such as chemical processing, power plants, metals manufacture, transport, communication facilities and the like. These projects were those announced for construction in ten developing countries over the past decade. An analysis showed:

Project size, US$ mill.:	100–249	250–499	500–999	1,000+
No. of projects as %:*	49	22	16	13
Value as %:*	10	12	17	61
Trouble rate, %:†	21	28	38	47
Average escalation, %:	30	70	106	109

*As a percentage of the total value of the 1,614 projects analysed.
†Percentage of the total number of projects in the size range that had cost escalation, completion delays, postponements and/or suspensions.

The above table demonstrates, as one would expect, that the larger the project the more troublesome it is. Pitfalls are strewn all along the path to completion and their avoidance and mitigation demands effective leadership that will both coordinate and direct the responsibilities and duties of the several participants. Above all, it is vital that the gap be bridged that exists between the expatriates involved in the execution of the project and their hosts: the owners of the project.

It is best, we feel, to illustrate by example. So let us take the case of a large aluminium smelter and associated hydroelectric power plant to be built in Sumatra, a joint venture between the Japanese and the Indonesians. The equity was 90 per cent Japanese- and 10% Indonesian-owned, with the Japanese providing the technology and the finance. The Japanese also agreed to purchase the entire output of the plant on a long-term basis. Fine!

It was when the two nationalities began working together that the trouble started. Their food was different, their language was different, even their concept of time was different. The Japanese were always punctual, whereas the Indonesians operated according to what is called 'rubber time'. In addition, there were basic cultural differences and communication problems. The Japanese were absolutely loyal to their management and reached decisions by consensus, both concepts foreign to Indonesian thinking. On the other hand the Indonesians were intensely religious, in contrast to the Japanese materialism. All this led to misunderstanding and then conflict.

These potential hazards are the responsibility of the owner, since he is the 'host'. A competent owner will actively manage and direct the project, establishing his own project team to audit the actions of his contractors. He must ensure that they have a correct perception of the project, that their standards are acceptable and that the right staff have been assigned to the project. Due allowance needs to be made for the skills and productivity of local labour and training facilities set up as necessary.

Emergent trends

In Chapter 2 we considered at some length the changing international scene, with first this country and then that taking a major share of the market. We saw that Japan, South Korea and later Turkey and Mexico had entered into what was previously the domain of the American and European contractors. We expect this type of transition to continue, with China and India picking up more and more contracts in the international field. This means that the international contractors already in the field are faced with a shrinking market. They have, therefore, been looking for fresh fields to conquer. So we see France's master builder, the firm of Francis Bouygues, who have been competing quite successfully with such giants as Bechtel and Brown & Root in the countries of the Third World, now turning their attention to the world's largest market of all – the United States itself.(2) Ranking number 21 in the 'billion dollar league' for foreign contracts, the firm of Bouygues secured their biggest coup when they won the contract, worth some US$2 billion, to build the King Saud University at Riyadh in Saudi Arabia. We are told that this promises to be 'the greatest project the world has ever seen'. To secure an entry into the US market, the company are seeking to purchase an American construction firm.

But French companies are not alone in trying to enter the American market. Some Japanese companies are also reported to be active there.(3) Whilst their share of that market at the moment is a mere 0.1 per cent, they have every confidence that it will grow.

Yet another trend has to be faced by contractors working internationally. There is increasing emphasis on local control (4) and the ultimate goal is clear: the replacement of every foreigner by a national. International contractors will have to adapt their policies and their operations to meet this trend. In some countries, of which Saudi Arabia is a good example, the shortage of local labour and other resources may be such that the trend is not yet visible, but the *desire* is still there. In 1980 expatriate labour working in Saudi Arabia was probably four times the local workforce and may well have increased further since then (5), but the objective remains and will be achieved in due course.

The size and hence the cost of projects has increased over the years. This increases the risk and has led to the creation of consortia and other devices to spread that risk. We see the smaller companies being purchased by the larger companies: we even see a growing degree of 'East-West' cooperation. Typical of the latter is a turnkey cellulose plant for the Cameroons. Here engineers of the firm Vöest-Alpine of Austria worked not only with the French (Stein Industries) and the Swedes (ASEA and Sunds) but also with the Poles (Polimex-Cekop) and the East Germans (Invest-Industrie Export).(6) Such cooperation is obviously advantageous for all concerned. This trend is undoubtedly on the increase, since several East-West joint venture companies have gone so far as to set up permanent offices in the US and some countries in Western Europe. Whilst there are the obvious problems of coordination, financing and protracted negotiations, these are counterbalanced by advantages such as reduced costs and a wider range of technology. Such arrangements can therefore offer profitable opportunities, apart from the increase in international goodwill. This latter aspect has meant that such cooperation has found strong support from international organisations such as UNIDO and UNCTAD.

The four Rs

Another feature in construction activity that is now clearly of ever-growing importance is the modification of existing facilities. This has been motivated both by the growing cost of new facilities, the need to increase the efficiency of existing operations, particularly in the area of energy conservation and the current worldwide overcapacity for many products. These activities have been grouped together under four heads, or four 'Rs':(7)

Retrofitting
Revamping
Restructuring
Rationalisation

Both restructuring and rationalisation refer to the reorganisation of a company's business, with changes in product portfolio, in order to increase profitability. In the chemical process industry, to take an example, rationalisation could involve a switch from a commodity product, such as plastics, to speciality chemicals with quite small markets. Chemical giants such as DuPont, Dow and Hercules have followed this route, seeking to make speciality chemicals some 50 per cent of their total turnover and have achieved a measure of success. Their profitability has certainly improved.

The construction industry, however, is much more concerned with retrofitting and revamping. The objective is to increase capacity at minimum cost. The demands of such operations have tapped a whole new technology and 'know-how' resource amongst contractors. The contractor is confronted with what is called 'live site working' on a grand scale and the load on his resources is very different to that imposed by a 'greenfield' project. There is much more 'software', with intensive preplanning and complex design problems, since each case has to be tailored to meet the specific requirements of the project and there can be no 'off the shelf' solution. Whilst intrinsically costly, in terms of the effort that has to be made, it is economically viable in that the final cost in terms of $/tonne of additional capacity is very competitive.

There are many examples we could take to illustrate the way the construction industry has to move to meet this changing demand. In the case of the ethylene cracker, for instance, retrofit technology results in the plant being designed to operate on a wide range of feedstocks. Such inbuilt flexibility means that the plant can utilise the most economic feedstock, whichever that happens to be at a particular point in time. Whilst the provision of this flexibility demands an increase in the initial investment, this can usually be recovered within the year through the ability to use the cheapest feedstock. Had the plant been designed for one feedstock only, it would have to shut down once use of that particular feedstock resulted in the plant running at a loss.

A good example of revamping is brought to us by a break-through in process technology that can result in substantial savings in the cost of manufacturing low density polyethylene (LDPE). For instance, Union Carbide claim savings of 90 per cent in terms of space, 50 per cent in capital cost and 75 per cent in energy consumption through the use of their UNIPOL process. The process has now been taken up by some 20 licensees in 14 countries (8) and the company are earning substantial revenue from their royalties. Everybody benefits. The construction contractor gets work, the owner improves his profits, the consumer gets a cheaper product and the licenser receives his royalties. Just to illustrate the order of magnitude of this one example, the savings in operating cost are said to be of the order of 5-6 US cents per pound. Union Carbide receive an initial fee and then 50 per cent of the savings under a ten- or fifteen-year contract. The process is proving so popular that they may well achieve their target of US$60 million of additional earnings in 1985.(9)

The floating factory

It is interesting to see the way in which process design, construction techniques and the transport facilities go forward hand in hand, as it were. We have just mentioned the outstanding savings that can be achieved by the adoption of the UNIPOL process. See how quickly the specific advantages of the new process are applied, utilising all the latest construction techniques. We receive a brochure from Union Carbide Europe SA of Switzerland, describing the construction of 'world-scale polyethylene plants' on ocean-going barges. Such plants can be delivered as a 'turnkey unit' anywhere in the world accessible by deep water. The brochure carries the title 'The W Plant Option', the 'W' standing for 'waterborne'.

The plant is constructed in a shipyard, this offering a host of advantages over conventional on-site construction, particularly for those areas of the world that lack the appropriate technological infrastructure. The specialised fabrication shops and equipment available in a shipyard, together with the highly skilled and experienced workforce that is constantly available, mean that construction can be supervised and controlled much more closely than in the field. Since site conditions do not have to be taken into account, design can be standardised and innovative modular construction techniques can be utilised to the full.

The first 'W' Plant has been completed. It was built for Ipako SA of Argentina, using the shipbuilding facilities of Ishikawajima-Harima Heavy Industries (IHI) near Nagoya, in Japan. The plant had a design capacity of some 135,000 tonnes per year of low-pressure low-density polyethylene. The plant was erected on a

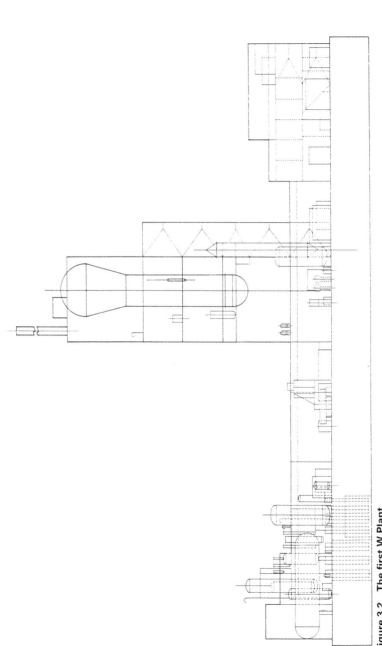

Figure 3.2 The first W Plant
This is an outline elevation drawing of the first 'W' (Waterborne) Plant, completely erected on a barge approximately 89 by 22.5 metres. It was built in Japan and then shipped to Bahia Bianca, Argentina, for operation at a waterside site. (With acknowledgements to Union Carbide Europe SA, Geneva, Switzerland)

barge approximately 89 metres long by 22.5 metres wide and construction, from keel-laying to shipyard commissioning, took just eight months. We present an outline of the unit in its totality in Figure 3.2. It includes a raw materials storage and handling system, an onboard nitrogen plant, a purification system and fresh and salt water cooling systems. Amidships, and standing out boldly in our sketch,is the all-important gas-phase reactor system and product recovery system. In the bow, to the right in Figure 3.2, is a personnel area, with a laboratory,the electrical substation and switchroom facility. The completed plant was loaded onto a carrier ship to cross the Pacific, making a 15,000 mile voyage from Japan to Argentina.

Here we see project management transferred almost completely from the site to the fabricator's yard. The benefits to the owner are considerable. He can expect a fixed price contract; the plant will be in commercial production perhaps a year earlier than normal, whilst the complete plant can be fully warranted by the licenser. The plant is purchased almost 'off the shelf', with all the advantages thereby implied.

The modular concept

The 'W' Plant is, we think, a supreme example of the modular concept in action. But the use of prefabricated buildings and plants – that is, items assembled in a factory and only joined together on site – has been developing widely over the years and has radically changed the style of the construction industry. The concept began with buildings. The design was standardised and the various components both manufactured and assembled into major units at the factory, thus minimising the work to be done on site.

Typical of what is currently on offer today are the Modular Building Systems manufactured by Glasdon.(10) These are made of glass-reinforced polyester in modular panel form, as illustrated in Figure 3.3. From these standard panels utility buildings both for temporary and permanent use are rapidly assembled on site. They are most usually the first thing you see as you seek to enter the site, since they are very popular as security posts and gatehouses, but they also find wide application for housing plant such as generators, compressors and switchgear.

More recently the concept has been applied to industrial plants

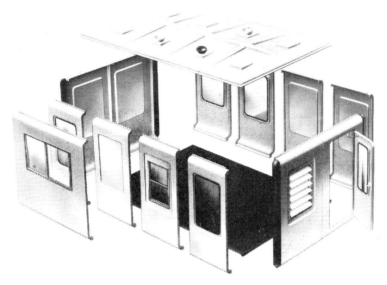

Figure 3.3 A typical modular building design
This view of the major modules in the Olympic range manufactured by Glasdon illustrates the way in which they can be assembled to form a building. (Photograph by courtesy of Glasdon Limited, International Division, Blackpool FY4 4UR)

of various types in the process industries. A number of construction contractors, notably CE Lummus in the US, Hitachi of Japan and Constructors John Brown (CJB) of the UK, have pioneered in this field and have been using it successfully for a period of years. The size of module has grown steadily so that it is now possible to offer a complete plant as one unit, requiring only to be connected to the various services in order to come into operation.

What is modular construction? Let us quote a definition 'straight from the horse's mouth':(11)

> The concept of modular construction or pre-assembly is the division of a plant into large transportable units or modules, which are fabricated and assembled at Works remote from the construction site. These units are then transported to the site, where they are connected together to complete the installation.

The approach is particularly valuable where the site is remote and it becomes extremely costly to bring labour to the site for

Figure 3.4   Arco's Seawater Treatment Plant
The plant brought by sea from Korea, now rests inside the hook at the end of
the causeway, which also includes unloading facilities for equipment – and
module-laden barges. (Photograph by courtesy of Bechtel Power Corporation,
San Francisco)

construction purposes. Typical of the use of this technique in this way is the provision of a seawater treatment plant that represented a series of 'firsts' in relation to Arctic oil production. The plant was a single huge barge-mounted facility that arrived at Alaska's North Slope during the brief summer sea-lift – the only time when Prudhoe Bay is free of ice. It was berthed in the Beaufort Sea, just offshore of Prudhoe Bay: you see it in place in Figure 3.4. The largest piece of equipment ever transported to the Prudhoe Bay oilfield, it is also the largest seawater treating plant in the United States and the first offshore plant to operate in the Arctic. The 26,000-ton, 610-foot long plant will treat two million barrels of seawater a day, which will then be pumped into the oil reservoir to 'waterflood' the formation and maintain its pressure. The plant was assembled at the huge Okpo, Korea, shipyard of Daewoo Shipbuilding & Heavy Machinery Ltd. The location of the ship-yard was determined in part by the fact that, at 150 feet wide, the barge was too large to go through the Panama Canal.(12)

We have dwelt at some length on this particular trend – towards modular construction – because we believe that it is going to have a profound influence on the course of the construction industry over the next few years. One contractor experienced in this field, CE Lummus, has published a brochure (13) which offers a number of valuable 'tips' to those interested in this development, under the heading 'Keys to the success of the Modular Approach'. These are:

> Think modular from the start
> Select the module fabricators early
> Enquiries to module fabricators should include dimensions, weight and applicable codes
> Make no compromise in plant design from a process view-point
> Assess the 'trade-off' between module dimensions and weight

The brochure includes a number of examples of modular applications as carried out by this particular company and they conclude with this firm forecast:

> There is very little doubt that greater use of barge-mounted

plants is part of the 1980s that will soon be heard about in more and more commercial installations, just as the modular concept has already done today.

On that optimistic note let us bring this assessment of the construction industry today to a close.

References

1 Murphy, K.J., 'Third World Macroprojects in the 1970's – Human Realities – Managerial Responses', *Technology in Science,* 4, 1982, pp.131–4.
2 Article: 'France's Master Builder is on the march', *Fortune,* 2 May 1983, pp.210–24.
3 *Wall Street Journal,* 24 March, 1984, p.32.
4 Whelan, J., 'Winds of change along the Gulf', *Worldwide Projects,* Dec/Jan. 1981, pp.49–53.
5 Article: 'Saudi Arabia's dilemma – Too much, too fast', *Business Week,* 8 Dec. 1980, p.53.
6 Goffin, Michel, 'East-West collaboration on Third World Projects', *Worldwide Projects,* Aug/Sept. 1980, pp.16–24.
7 Chowdbury, J., 'Retrofitting gives CPI a boost', *Chem. Eng.,* 90, 14 Nov. 1983, pp.55–61. The term 'CPI' means 'Chemical Plant Industry'.
8 Hyde, M., *Chemical Insight,* no.2723, 1983. (*Chemical Insight,* published twice monthly, presents Mike Hyde's perspective on the international chemical industry.)
9 Hyde, M., *Chemical Insight,* no.223, 1981.
10 Brochure: *Modular Building Systems*, published by Glasdon Limited, Preston New Road, Blackpool, FY4 4UR, UK.
11 Brochure: *Modular Construction – the pre-assembly of process plants*, published by Constructors John Brown, London, 14 pp.
12 Article: 'The billion barrel boost'. *Bechtel Briefs,* Jan.–Feb. 1984, pp.4–6. Published for their employees by the Public Relations Department, Bechtel, PO Box 3965, San Fancisco, CA 94119.
13 Glaser, L.B., Causey, E.D. and Kramer, J., *What are the practical aspects of modular plants and barge-mounted plants?*, published by CE Lummus, 1979, 22 pp.

4 The changing scene

As we have seen, the construction industry made a 'new begin-ning' as the Second World War came to an end. It had to meet a whole new series of challenges. Of these challenges, the greatest at that time, and even now, is that of working in the hostile environment of the seas and oceans. The construction industry has always faced the sea, building breakwaters and harbours, but now it had to work in and under the sea. This is called by those in the trade 'working in a marine environment'. It all began back in 1947, when the search for oil and gas led to the building of the first platform offshore in 20 feet of water in the Gulf of Mexico.(1) But things have changed since then!

The offshore challenge

It is some twenty years now since the UK Government first licensed 75 drilling sites to Shell/Esso in the North Sea. Since then around US$30 billion (at 1981 prices) has been invested in exploring and developing Britain's oil and gas resources. The marshalling of resources for North Sea oil development can be compared to the effort which went into the building of Britain's railway system in the last century, the building of its canals a century earlier or, in recent times, the US space programme. Just as those important developments have had a worldwide impact, bringing many benefits both to industry and to society as a whole, so have the demands that construction in the hostile environment of the North Sea has made on those engaged in it resulted in increased expertise and wide-ranging technological development. These installations way out in the sea are tremendous in concep-tion, majestic in execution. The scale of the undertaking is difficult to comprehend. The output of many of the platforms matches the throughput of a refinery, whilst the power requirements of a single platform can involve generating on the platform enough electricity to supply a town with a population of 200,000 people. What is happening in the North Sea is going on all over the world – offshore in the Gulf of Mexico by both the US and Mexico, off the coast of India and shortly, no doubt, off the coast of China.

On the grand scale

It is indeed a changing scene. The areas of the world where large-scale construction work is being carried out have most certainly changed over the last twenty years. We meet the phrase 'the world's largest' or 'the world's first' in the developing world, rather than in the industrialised countries. The place names are unfamiliar. For instance. we are told that 'the largest NGL storage facility in the world' is at Ju'aymah, Saudi Arabia.(2) We are told that the 'world's *first* totally offshore NGL Recovery Plant' is located in the Ardjun field in Indonesia's North Java Sea.(2)

Saudi Arabia has been planning a series of important projects for many years; during the 1970s these projects seemed to stagnate, but they are now moving ahead strongly. Three major complexes – two at Jubail and one at Yanbu, with a total ethylene capacity of some 1.6 million tonnes per year – should be on stream by 1986.(3) The table, Figure 4.1, presents the status of ethylene plants throughout the Middle East, all the figures being expressed as 'hundred thousand' tonnes per annum. Thus the Middle East has presented a picture of growth and expansion, with all that that means to the construction industry, in terms not only of the petrochemical plants themselves, but also the related infrastructure – complete new towns, airports and major roads. But the growth will not last for ever and is already in decline. Whilst the six major Middle East countries placed some US$60 billion of new contracts in 1980, this has fallen to US$26 billion in 1984. Back in the industrialised world, however, the picture has been one of contraction rather than expansion for a much longer period.

South Korea storms its way through

South Korea has been active worldwide in the field of engineering design and construction for some years now and seems to have caught up with and perhaps have now beaten its peers, the

MIDDLE EAST ETHYLENE PROJECTS

ALGERIA	**120**	**OPERATING**
QATAR	**280**	**OPERATING**
IRAQ	**130**	**DAMAGED**
LIBYA	**300**	**NEARLY COMPLETE**
SAUDI ARABIA		
SADAF	**650**	**CONSTRUCTION**
PETROKEMYA	**500**	**CONSTRUCTION**
YANPET	**450**	**CONSTRUCTION**
IRAN	**300**	**DAMAGED**
KUWAIT	**350**	**DEFERRED**

Figure 4.1   Status of Middle East ethylene projects
This table sets out the present (1984) status of the several projects for the manufacture of ethylene from 'associated gas' or gas wells, in the Middle East. (With acknowledgements to Mr Alan Plaistowe, Chem Systems International Limited, London)

Japanese. This has been achieved through low prices associated with a hard-working and well disciplined workforce that has a very high productivity. The work teams who are sent abroad to work on the construction site have a clear target: complete the project as quickly as possible, within the budget. It seems that a major incentive is the desire to be back home once again with their families, since they always operate on construction sites at 'bachelor' status, as it is called. There are also attractive bonus incentives, tied into the bonus clauses in the contract with the owner.

The Koreans got their first big breakthrough into worldwide construction with the building of a dry dock at Bahrain in 1977. They did such a good job that they earned a handsome compliment from the Bahrain Deputy Industries Minister. He was an engineer himself, so we can trust his judgement. He said: 'These South Koreans are disciplined, correct and technically sound'. This approach to their projects brought them rich dividends. There is, for instance, a story concerning the late King Khalid of Saudi Arabia. Whilst hunting in the desert he camped out for the

night and saw lights in the distance. This turned out to be on a
project where the South Koreans were working through the night
under searchlights. The King was much impressed, declaring: 'I
can't believe that the Germans, the English or the Americans
would work at night in the desert in the same way.' Thus began a
long and enduring working relationship between Saudi Arabia and
the construction contractors from South Korea.(4)

To illustrate the growth of their activities over the past decade,
we list below the orders booked per annum, expressed in US$
billion. The data are compared with those for Turkey and India,
since we shall consider these new entrants into the worldwide
construction market in a moment. Thus:

Orders booked

Year:	1975	1976	1977	1978	1979	1980	1981	1982	1983
S. Korea:	0.8	2.5	3.5	8.1	6.4	8.3	13.6	13.4	10.4
Turkey:				0.2	0.5	1.4	5.6	3.5	
India:						1.1	0.8	0.4	0.5

But competition from the 'new entrants' has been putting severe
pressure on their profit margins, which have fallen from some 15
per cent in 1976 to about 5 per cent in 1983. They have also had
problems in collecting their money, largely due to the falling oil
revenues of their main clients. For instance, about US$3 billion,
payment for work done in Iraq, has been deferred to 1985.
Advance payments have also been sharply reduced. Once 20 per
cent, they are now down to 5 per cent. This change in market
conditions has posed serious liquidity problems to South Korean
contractors and some have even been driven into bankruptcy.(5)
The Government have been standing firm, not being willing to
'bail out' the firms in trouble, who in their keenness to win
contracts have made 'suicidal' bids. In general they do not favour
joint ventures as a method for getting additional business. Their
philosophy is expressed in the thought: 'Even if the margin is a
mere 1 per cent, why share it?'

The Middle East was the main market for South Korea, but the
volume of business there is steadily declining. However, the
demand in South East Asia is picking up, so the South Koreans are
now seeking to expand their activities there.

New entrants

As we have just indicated, the search for new markets is made the

more difficult because of the new entrants on the international
scene, such as Turkey, India and Mexico. This is a good illustration of the 'learning process'. For instance, many of Turkey's
domestic development projects have been funded in the recent
past from foreign sources and, as usual, the construction contractors of the lending nations were largely involved in the work that
resulted. Turkish contractors, also as usual, were employed as
subcontractors, grew up in the process, learnt fast, and were soon
competitive with the outside firms. Now the Turkish contractors
are described as 'an emerging force in international
construction'.(6)

The story is thus a familiar one. The Turkish adventure into
overseas construction apparently began in Libya. To quote Ali
Riza Carmikli, Chairman of Libas:

> We arrived in Libya in early 1975 with nothing more than our
> curiosity and a tourist visa ... We returned with US$200
> million worth of orders.

Now, some eight years later, more than 200 Turkish firms are
active overseas, working predominantly in Libya, Saudi Arabia
and Iraq. Of course, the Turkish contractors sit next door to one of
the most important construction markets in the world – the Middle
East. This gives them a clear advantage: the inefficiencies of
distance are eliminated. They have another telling asset: highly
skilled engineers and labourers who work for less than any
equally-skilled counterparts from other nations. The Chairman of
Tekfen dares to assert that 'a first-rate Turkish engineer costs the
same as a third-rate American engineer'.(6) It is considered that
Turkish contractors can make attractive joint-venture partners.
Indeed, it can pay to have the Turkish contractor 'up front', as
they say. There are certain countries that would prefer to see a
Turkish firm leading a joint-venture group. If Western contractors
were to link up with their Turkish counterparts in this way, they
could well have an edge in the Middle East and North African
markets, simply because of the Turks' greater ethnic and cultural
acceptability there.

It would appear that these contractors in no way lag behind the
rest of the world in their competence and skills. Enka, another
leading company in the field, have been using computers for
project management for ten years and are now looking at a
satellite link so that all their overseas work can be coordinated
from Istanbul. To conclude this picture of the Turkish contractors,
yet another element in the changing scene, let us quote from an

advertisement by Betrek Engineering & Construction Company Limited:

> To our colleagues worldwide ... For your next Middle East project ... we make a strong ally ... our capabilities can give you the competitive edge.

> For your next Middle East project ... talk to us. We'll help you avoid potential problems. You'll gain speed, economy and local competence.

Another example of this process of development is given by India's premier design and engineering organisation, Engineers India Limited.(7) Typical of a project well executed on their home ground is a critical shutdown project at the Barauni Refinery.(8) This involved the removal of four existing reactor vessels and their replacement by four new reactors, each 4.6 metres in diameter and 28 metres long and each weighing 100 tonnes. Altogether some 1,500 tonnes of equipment, structures, pipework and the like had to be handled at levels up to 72 metres above ground, with severe limitations on the space available. Scheduled for completion in 90 days, it was all completed in 75 days, teams working round the clock with determination, following a detailed plan, with constant monitoring and detailed supervision. Such a project had never been undertaken before in India. Its satisfactory completion, 15 days ahead of schedule, avoided a production loss of more than US$7 million in petroleum products.

But EIL have been equally effective abroad. They secured a contract for the construction of a 150-km pipeline from Umm-Al-Nar to Al-Ain in Qatar against stiff global competition. Yet they secured the maximum bonus permissible under the contract for early completion and successful commissioning. They have added another 'feather to their cap' (7) by securing several prestigious contracts in the past five years from the Algerian state organisation SONATRACH for LNG and LPG products. This was previously the exclusive domain of the large American contractors. Why do we use the word 'prestigious'? Because they were acting as the owner's 'right arm', as we go on to discuss in detail in Chapter 5. Their work involved the review of the process design, engineering, procurement, inspection, construction and startup supervision. These are the very same functions that India, until recently, used to hire in from abroad. Indeed the tables have been turned!

Based on its achievements both at home and abroad, EIL has emerged as one of the largest contracting and engineering organisations in South East Asia: a force to be reckoned with on the international scene. With lower salaries but comparable productivity with its international competitors, EIL has a distinct advantage in the world markets. In mid-1983 EIL, with a staff of more than 3,000, were working at 33 sites in India and three sites abroad. The sites range from Abu Dhabi to Visakahapatnam and the projects from aromatics production to a zinc smelter.

The recession hits construction

With the growing impact of the 'new entrants' and the continuing recession, the construction contractors throughout the developed world have been striving to cope with 'overcapacity'. They seek to promote their specific areas of expertise, whilst continually watching for new opportunities. The current situation can be demonstrated by noting the way in which the permanent staff of the main contractors has fallen over the past few years. Thus:

	Peak (1978-81)	1984 (approx.)
Bechtel:	45,000	36,000
Brown & Root:	70,000	40,000
Davy International:	20,000	12,000
Parsons:	10,000	5,000

Impact of research

One way that the construction industry strives to keep ahead and so win work is by having its own Research Engineering Departments, and then offering their services to clients. This has the twofold result of keeping the engineering organisation at the spearhead of the latest developments and bringing them work because of their ability to bring the appropriate experience to bear. To quote from one of the brochures:(9)

> We serve our clients by maintaining a leading position in emerging technologies as diverse as solar energy, fusion power, and oil shale. Our goal is to 'keep Bechtel positioned for the future' by anticipating new developments and establishing the company's presence in promising growth areas through entrepreneurial activities.

We deal in a little detail with one such project, a solar facility in the Hawaiian Islands, in Chapter 24, when we try to see where the construction industry is heading, and what it has to face, in the future.

Plant maintenance

Another area holding prospects for the construction industry is plant maintenance. A great many plant installations these days operate 24 hours a day, 168 hours a week, and 52 weeks in the year. Such plants need the most rigorous maintenance if they are to continue in full production. This is achieved by what is called 'preventive maintenance', but the day still comes when the plant has to be shut down for a complete overhaul. This may happen every eighteen months or two years. In view of the loss of production whilst the plant is shut down, every effort is made to minimise this shutdown period. That calls for the most meticulous planning and detailed organisation.

The operating company does not normally have the staff to cope with such shutdowns, so it has to call in contractors. This has led to the birth of construction companies specialising in this 'turn around' operation. Whilst the work is cyclical, proper planning and the staggering of shutdowns by their clients can ensure that such firms have a reasonably smooth workload. A typical company working in this field has been set up by two of the world's leading contractors, Fluor and Daniel International. It is called International Maintenance Organisation Ltd (IMO). The company draws upon the combined resources of its parents, with staff drawn from both companies, thus combining the best of Fluor management and the Daniel maintenance expertise. A brochure describing their activities (10) says that they –

> ... offer a dynamic approach to plant maintenance based on almost half a century of worldwide experience. Our advanced maintenance management techniques provided through our Maintenance Assurance Program (MAP) will lower your operating costs while protecting your plant investment. This comprehensive plant maintenance system includes maintenance program planning and control functions

and can be tailored to fit your needs. Programs to utilise the on-line computer or manual systems can be adapted to your facility while applying maintenance planning, engineering and control techniques. Our program's goal is to assist you in achieving optimum utilisation of resources.

Construction companies have always found work in the maintenance field, but we see the operation becoming highly organised, the services being offered worldwide.

References

1   Lee, Griff C., 'Twenty years of platform development', paper presented at Offshore Exploration Conference, New Orleans, 14–16 Feb. 1968.
2   Brochure: *Gas Processing*, published by Fluor Engineers and Constructors, Inc., Irvine, Cal., USA.
3   Plaistowe, Alan D., 'Development of Petrochemical Projects in the Middle East', paper presented at an open meeting organised by the London & Kent Centre and the SCI on 26 April 1984. Mr Plaistowe is Chairman of Chem Systems International Ltd, London.
4   Report in *Far Eastern & Economic Review*, 120, 78, 2 June 1983. See also 120, 68, 26 May 1983.
5   Feature article: 'Construction – suicidal cut-throat competition abroad', *FEER*, 125, 9 July 1984, pp.68–9.
6   Special Supplement: 'Turkish Contracting '83', *Worldwide Projects*, June/July 1983, pp. S1-S23.
7   Kharbanda, O.P., 'Pride of India – Engineers India Ltd', *Swagat,* August 1984.
8   Anon., 'Speed Thrills', *Hamara*, September 1983. *Hamara* is the Newsletter of Engineers India Ltd.
9   Brochure: *Research and Engineering at Bechtel*, published by Bechtel Group, Inc., San Francisco, Cal., USA.
10 Brochure: *IMO – A Fluor-Daniel Company*, published by Fluor of San Francisco, US.

Part Two

CONSULTANTS AND CONTRACTORS

5 The owner's right arm

The development and then execution of a project is both a mission and an adventure. A project, in its broadest sense, is any task which has to be accomplished within a scheduled time and within a defined budget. This implies that every project has its stated objectives and there are always three that are basic:

1 The completed facility, complying with the appropriate specifications.
2 The budgeted or target cost.
3 The time required to completion.

Three lead 'players' can be involved in all such projects, each having their specific role if the objectives outlined above are to be achieved. This trio are: (a) owner (or client) (b) consultant and (c) contractor. Their specific functions can well vary from case to case. No two projects are ever the same, even when they may appear to be. Each and every project is *unique* and so, therefore, are the roles played in each project by our respective players. Here in Chapter 5 we define the role of the consultant, going on in Chapter 6 to study the role of the contractor.

Once the owner has decided to proceed with a project he always has to first establish feasibility, then initiate design and construction, and finally commission and operate. When he begins he has a variety of choices open to him, his choice being determined to some extent by his own capability – or, more often, his own *judgement* as to his capability, which may well be at fault. He can:

1 Do it all himself
2 Seek the services of a consultant
3 Seek the services of a contractor

4   Seek the services of both consultant and contractor

It is the last course that we most strongly recommend, where each of the two 'players' can take his proper part in this most exciting 'project game'.

The lines of demarcation

In the concept of project management that we are now developing, the three key participants that we have just introduced have three distinct and separate roles to play, thus:

1   The owner – oversees and pays
2   The consultant – advises
3   The contractor – does the job

The boundary between consultant and contractor is somewhat blurred these days and there are many – too many – contractors who feel that they are quite competent to play 'consultant' and so combine items 2 and 3 above, but we do not agree. We shall enter into our reasons for this later. For the moment, let us assume that the owner takes the course of employing a consultant and see where that concept takes us in terms of project management. So far, we have said nothing about the size of project, chiefly because that has so little to do with it. Even the smallest of projects may well merit the treatment which we have outlined above. There are few projects these days, we believe, where the owner is wise to 'go it alone'.

Getting in early

The other significant aspect is that the consultant should be brought in at the very earliest stage. All too often he is brought in after the owner has gone some way along the road. This has the inevitable result that certain aspects of the project become 'fixed', to the later detriment of profitability, but it will be the consultant, not the owner, who finally has to carry the blame. Few realise the powerful influence that the earliest of the actions taken with respect to a project, in what is called the pre-design, or feasibility study stage, can have upon the ultimate cost and profitability of a project. We have set this out graphically in a very simple diagram, Figure 5.1, in the hope that this diagrammatic representation may bring the relationship home to our readers – and particularly the prospective 'owners' amongst our readers – really vividly. We wish to emphasise, as we hope Figure 5.1 emphasises, that the pre-design stage in a project is *the* time for *action*. That is the time of maximum influence on cost, when the opportunities for cost reduction are real and substantial.

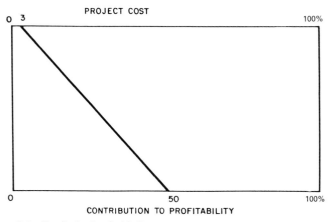

Figure 5.1   Catch the 'early bird'
Early studies, though costing less than 3% of the total project cost, can contribute 50% or more to the ultimate profitability of the project. (Diagram based on an idea presented in *'Management of Snowdon Engineering Projects',* – Newnes-Butterworth, 1977)

There is, of course, more than one way of bringing this most crucial lesson home. Consider also the diagram we present as Figure 5.2. The subject is project cost control and the diagram demonstrates that, as a project progresses, the number and detail of the cost control reports increase in inverse ratio to the effect that such reports can have on the final cost of a project. It is as a project is conceived that changes in concept and approach can be made easily and therefore cheaply. To quote:(1)

> One must take the time to do a proper job of basic design while the project is still pliable and capable of change at a low cost whilst time is still cheap. On the other hand, in the engineering and construction phase, every effort must be made to move fast and expeditiously. People work better under some pressure: this is the time for production, not deliberation.
>   At this stage, the owner is locked into an irreversible position, and every day the fixed charges are mounting

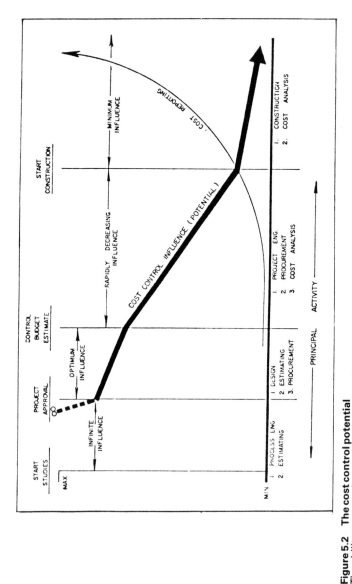

Figure 5.2   The cost control potential
The ability to control costs diminishes rapidly over the life of the project, as the volume and number of cost control reports increase. (Originally reproduced from a paper 'Owners CAN control costs', included in the 1969 Transactions of the American Association of Cost Engineers, by permission of the author, Mr G. Azud)

higher and higher. Too often, too little time is taken to do a thorough job in the basic design phase. Too often, too much time is taken to do the detailed engineering and construction work. Such disregard for priorities may well prove disastrous.

That is a consultant speaking. The point being made is that time is cheap at the beginning of a project and dear at the end because of the impact of fixed charges, the growing investment in plant and equipment, together with the vast growth in the numbers of people employed on the project, whose time is wasted if there is hesitation and change. The impact of this basic fact, that the cost of time climbs rapidly as a project progresses, emphasises the great savings in cost that will undoubtedly be achieved if a sound design basis and project organisation are established right at the beginning when time is relatively cheap. The consultant has the experience to ensure that this will happen.

The choice of a consultant

We have already made it clear that the very first decision that the prospective owner has to make is whether to use a consultant or to 'go it alone': that is, do the preliminary work in-house, with his own staff. There is a great temptation to do this, since there is always the feeling that 'we know all about it'. There is also considerable reluctance to explain it all to a third party. But it is that very discipline that is so valuable, apart from the fact that that third party comes to everything with a fresh eye.

There is an enormous literature on the way in which a consultant should be selected. There are dire warnings given, introduced by articles carrying titles such as: 'Why projects fail – the wrong way to choose a consultant'.(2) Here what is known as Murphy's Law is invoked. Mr Murphy's maxim was said to be: 'If anything can go wrong, the chances are it will!' Maybe, but why blame consultants? No, let us take a more positive approach, as brought to us by a thoughtful article which we strongly recommend to anyone thinking of employing a consultant: 'How to get a good consultant'.(3)

Beginning with the assumption that a consultant is needed, the article asks questions such as: When we seek a consulting firm, what characteristics and qualities should we look for? What size? How will we know its fee is fair? It starts out with the rather brutal statement:

Management consultants are generally hired for the wrong reasons. Once hired, they are generally poorly employed and loosely supervised. The result is, more often than not, a final report that decorates an executive's bookshelf with as much usefulness as *The Life and Mores of the Pluvius Aegiptius* would decorate his coffee table – and at considerably more cost.

But of course, by no means all consulting engagements result in such unsatisfactory results. The article goes on to set the prospective user on the right road by discussing in detail such topics as 'When to hire', 'Whom to hire' and 'How much to pay'. It is a great temptation to quote from this particular article at length, but we must restrain ourselves. The point is made that the greatest contribution a consultant can make is his experience. He has seen the problem now being presented, or a variant thereof, in other situations. He has devised solutions to it or absorbed solutions implemented by previous clients. He should be, therefore, a living compendium of case studies.

He has seen the problem now being presented ... that thought introduces us to the most important aspect of the role that the owner plays, and *must* play if the work of the consultant is to be effective. To quote once again:

> A consultant's effectiveness is closely related to the client's ability to express his needs, understand the results, and implement the recommendations.

Does size matter?

Consultants and consulting organisations can be arbitrarily separated into three categories: individual specialists, small firms with staffs of specialists, and large, multidisciplinary companies. Each presents advantages and drawbacks to the potential user. We shall be considering a little later the way in which some of the large contractors seek to carry out consultancy work. The large multidisciplinary consulting companies seek to add areas of work, especially in the domain of detailed engineering, that more properly are within the province of the contractor.

Some large consulting firms claim that they offer greater expertise in more fields than their small competitors. But the respected, successful large firms severely limit the number of fields in which they seek business and on which they stake their reputations. The average client does not come to the consultant with a motley 'bag' of requirements. He comes with very specific, limited requirements and looks for a specialist in the specific field that is his concern at the time. So the specialist consultant is far more likely to succeed than the 'generalist'. Each consulting project is usually a 'one-off' affair and the expertise has to be sold in the face of fierce competition. That moves us to say something about the professional fees that consultants charge. Rates are usually very competitive and depend heavily on reputation and experience. When you are dealing, in particular, with an individual specialist consultant, the 'one man' firm – and there are a great many of them, his fee may strike you as very high, since you know that he will be the sole beneficiary of that income. But do not forget that he will be fortunate indeed to work more than six months in the year. The rest of the time he is prospecting for work or educating himself about prospective work. Of course, consulting firms have their overheads like any other business.

To sum up, the decision to hire a consultant should be made with circumspection, even reluctance, and with the conviction that you can expect sensible recommendations. You must also have the further conviction that you are going to use or act upon his recommendations, however unpalatable they may be. When you *do* decide to proceed, select carefully to fit your needs, your company and your staff. Remember always that, unlike consumer goods, consulting services carry no warranty. They cannot!

Finding a consultant

The interests of consultants are well looked after by both national and international associations. Typical of the latter is FIDIC, the international federation of consulting engineers' which affiliates with the national associations of a number of countries including certain developing countries. The main objective of FIDIC is declared to be 'to enhance the stature and opportunities of the profession' and it does so through dialogue, seminars and publications. This theme has been elaborated upon by the then President (4), but one wonders whether these various associations are going the right way about it. There seems to be too much 'politicking' in such associations, with the result that what should be their basic objective, the provision of a service to their ultimate paymasters, their clients, is lost sight of. However, the prospective user, in the absence of any recommendation to a specific consultant, can safely approach such an association for a listing of suitable individuals or firms.

Part of the problem here is that consultants are not supposed to advertise their services. Nevertheless, their selling costs are reported to be quite high, running to about 20 per cent of their turnover. (5) Such is the fierce competition that consultants have to go out and canvass for work: very rarely does the work come to their doorstep. This leads to substantial expense, indeed to costs that sometimes reach absurd proportions. For instance, it is quite common for some 30 to 40 consultants to respond to a tender announcement, submitting elaborate offers on 'glossy' paper. In one extreme case 140 firms responded to an invitation to prepare a feasibility study. Not only does this lead to a proliferation of costs for the consultant, but how is the prospective purchaser going to select his consultant? The services of a consultant cannot easily be reduced to numbers. All their rates will be much the same and, as we have said already, their prime qualification is experience. A seasoned owner can circumvent this problem, in part, by prequalifying prospective bidders and thus reducing the original listing down to a more sensible four or five bidders. For us, as consultants – but perhaps we are biased – competitive bidding is irrelevant. A consultant is rather like the doctor or surgeon. The average patient does not go around comparing their fees: all that he is concerned with is their degree of skill and expertise.

From the other side of the fence, as it were, some consultants tend to be too exclusive. This is typified by the attitude of Swedish consultants, who adopt a selective marketing strategy rather than compete in the international market. But Sweden is too small for that, so they seek to overcome the handicap by developing very advanced design techniques. Once they offer their services abroad they have to have something very special to offer, since their fees are among the highest in the world. Nevertheless Sweden and the other Scandinavian countries have established a pre-eminent position in highly specialised fields such as dairy farming and dairy processing.(6) Their overall variety, high quality and particularly their flexibility, seen in their ability to tailor their services to their clients' requirements, have enabled Scandinavian consultancy firms to make a considerable impact on project development in the Middle East.

British consultants also do very well abroad: largely, we believe, due to the way in which they always show regard and concern for the interests of the owner. As a result, members of the Association of Consulting Engineers, their UK organisation, were involved in the design and supervision of overseas work totalling some

US$75,000 million during 1981, providing net 'invisible earnings' for the UK of about £450 million (US$800 million).(7)

The owner–consultant relationship

The owner has an idea. But is it feasible? That is the very question and it leads us – and the consultant – straight to the

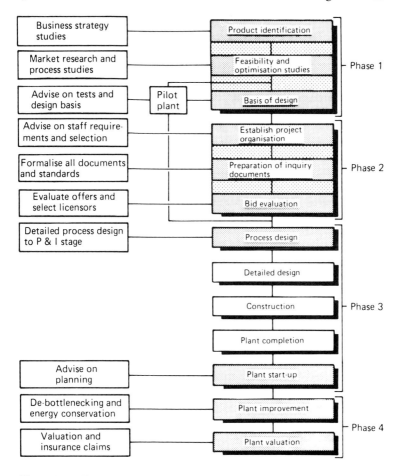

Figure 5.3   The role of the consultant
The steps in project development where the consultant can and should have a role are emphasised by being shaded. (Developed from data provided by Tri-Chem Consultants Limited, London)

feasibility study. Looking ahead, we see a path strewn with 'go/no go' decisions, each to be taken by the owner upon the advice of his consultant. Each stage of project development leads to such a decision and it should be a matter of policy by the owner never to spend more money than is strictly necessary to reach the next stage. The feasibility study stage can itself be divided into two: firstly the 'pre-feasibility study' to establish feasibility; then a detailed 'feasibility study' to establish the parameters within which the owner must operate if the project is to remain feasible.

To illustrate this, we have divided the whole process of project development to completion into a series of phases, four in all, as illustrated in Figure 5.3. Phase 1 can be divided into two as we have just said: pre-feasibility and feasibility studies, each followed by a 'go/no go' decision. Phase 2 proceeds on the strength of a decision to 'go', but there still remains the possibility of cancellation if the detailed 'firming up' discloses unacceptable features. Once, however, Phase 3 has been entered upon, cancellation can be very expensive indeed, although it may still be cheaper than continuing to the 'bitter end', as we demonstrate when we take the petrochemical complex being built in Iran as a case study, in Chapter 14. It is to get through Phase 1 that we first turn to the consultant. A working relationship has to be established that can last from three months to a year: rarely longer.

The subject of owner-consultant relations is so important that it was the main theme of a conference held in Florence, Italy during 1983 under the auspices of FIDIC, the international federation of consulting engineers referred to earlier. The relationship *must* be based on trust and mutual understanding.(8) This can only be achieved if the main causes of misunderstanding and friction between owner and consultant are spelt out. This is not the place for that. Let us just sum up and bring this chapter to a close by saying that good communications and sound human relations are the key to success here.

References

1   King, R.A., 'How to achieve effective cost control', *Chem. Eng.*, July 1977, pp.117–21.

2   Simplicimus, J.T., 'Why projects fail – The wrong way to

choose a consultant', *Worldwide Projects*, Dec. 1981/Jan. 1982, pp. 26–33.

3 Frankenhuis, J.P., 'How to get a good consultant', *Harvard Business Review*, Nov/Dec. 1977. pp.133–9. We qualify Mr Frankenhuis by stating that he is an independent consultant based in Paris who has worked for industry as well as for large consulting firms on four continents. His clients have included multinational manufacturers and banks as well as state and national governments and agencies.

4 Frijlink, H.C., 'Role of the consulting engineer in Today's World', *Chem. Econ & Eng. Rev. 11,* 20–4. March 1979.

5 Norman, V., 'It's not good enough to be engineers, we have to be good businessmen as well', *Worldwide Projects*, Dec.1980/Jan. 1981, pp.39–47.

6 Roberst, J., 'Design consultancy spearheads Scandinavia's Middle East presence', *Middle East Economic Digest,* 22–3, 19 Feb. 1982.

7 Anon., 'All abroad – UK's architects, engineers and surveyors overseas', *British Business*, 20 Aug. 1982, pp.686–92.

8 Anon., 'Client-consultant relations', *Intl. Consulting Engr.,* No. 1, pp.5–8, 1983.

6 It's a love/hate relationship

Our theme is the construction industry and more particularly the international construction industry, so we are directing our attention, above all, to the activities of 'constructors' – or 'contractors', as they are more usually called. In the last chapter we turned aside, as it were, to consider the consultant, seeing the consultant as the owner's 'right arm'. The contractor has to work for the owner. The owner keeps him in being. And because the owner employs consultants, the contractor has also to work with them. If the consultant is the owner's 'right arm', the objective of the contractor should be to be the owner's 'left arm'. We have illustrated this arrangement diagrammatically in Figure 6.1. There we distinguish between the 'managing contractor' and 'subcontractors' so that if we push our analogy to the limit, whilst the managing contractor acts as a representative of the owner and on behalf of the owner, the sub-contractors should not be wholly divorced from the relationship. They should see themselves as yet further extensions: 'fingers', if you like. It is when contractors lose sight of the cooperative relationship that *should* exist between them, other contractors, the managing contractor if there is one and the owner, that all the trouble starts. All should be working in harmony to one common goal, that of completing the project for an economic cost, within an economic time.

Conditions of Contract

The owner, acting on the advice of his consultant, finally reaches the point where he decides to proceed with his project in real earnest. He has then to enter into a contract or contracts. By this time he should have a project specification, defining what he

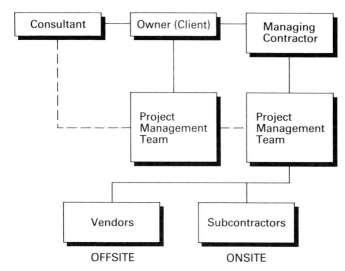

Figure 6.1   The basic relationship
Here we see the relationship between the main parties involved in a project as it develops.

wishes to have done, together with 'conditions of contract', which define the relationships between and the responsibilities of the various parties involved in, or related to, the contract that is to be made. If we assume an arrangement such as that outlined in Figure 6.1, where a 'managing contractor' is to be used by the owner to look after the project for him – and this is the most common arrangement these days with a project of any size – then the 'conditions of contract' should – *must* – define with precision the scope of work to be undertaken by each party and the contractual relationship between all the various parties who are ultimately going to have to work together, usually for a period of years.

In the conditions of contract the managing contractor is usually referred to as the *contractor*. In addition to the contractor, who is then the main party to the contract, we can also have a number of third parties, such as a *subcontractor*, a *manufacturer*, an *erection contractor*, a *technical adviser*, and so on. All these parties will be involved directly or indirectly in the project and the relationships that should exist between them have to be precisely defined. Also, their respective duties and responsibilities have to be outlined.

The contract document can be very simple or very elaborate. We have even known well-executed contracts that have been successfully completed without – at least initially – a formal contract at all. To save time the contractor gets his 'instructions to proceed' before a formal contract is concluded (in fact, the issue of 'instructions to proceed' creates a contract between the two parties) and the terms and conditions of contract are negotiated whilst work is proceeding. This approach can only be adopted where there is *trust* between the two parties. In a situation where the two parties have faith in one another and are prepared to trust one another, the contract can be a simple, straightforward document, and that is the type of document we much prefer. Why? Because the spirit of a contract is far more important than the letter, yet it is impossible to set down the spirit of a contract in words. We are not alone in our liking for simple and brief contracts. The Chinese, it seems, share our viewpoint.(1) Judging by the experience of Sir John Buckley, Chairman of the Davy Corporation, one of the biggest international engineering and construction companies, the Chinese seem to say: 'There's nothing in the world you can't get into three pages ... if we don't *trust* you, we won't do business with you.' In their eyes a long, complex document demonstrates a basic lack of *trust* between the two parties. The emphasis on *trust* is ours: notice that we thought it necessary to use this word repeatedly whilst discussing 'conditions of contract'. In dramatic contrast to the Chinese approach, American practice favours very elaborate contracts. We do not need to tell you which approach brings more disputes and litigation. The complex contract creates a legal jungle full of pitfalls for the unwary, an aspect we discuss in detail in Chapter 10.

So an enquiry document is prepared and issued to a range of prospective contractors, and the bids come in. How does our owner then go about selecting and appointing his contractor or contractors?

Appointment of the Contractor

When the various offers come in, what is the predominant requirement? Not necessarily a low price. Of equal, if not of greater, importance to the owner is the quality and competence of the contractor, reflected above all in the project management team that he puts forward. That is why, in Figure 6.1, we have indicated the presence of the 'project management team' within our typical organogram.

If we go 'over the fence' for a moment, as it were, to look at all this from the point of view of the contractor, he realises well enough that it is his project management that is going to be the key to success in winning the contract. We shall come to the problem of project management in detail in Chapter 8, but let us for the moment just look at the matter in broad outline. The contractor, in response to the enquiry from the owner, proposes to set up for the specific project now the subject of enquiry a project management team headed by a project manager exclusively devoted to the interests of this particular project. The project manager will be made responsible, within the contractor's organisation, for every aspect of the project. Listen to what one contractor says of him:(2)

> He is responsible for every aspect of the job from inception to completion. He is responsible for every service required to carry out the work: planning, scheduling, costing, designing, engineering, purchasing, inspection, shipping, construction and commissioning. And he is responsible to you, our client. He is your direct contact. And you will know him personally. His position calls for wide experience, broad knowledge of every group within the organisation, the ability to control progress and make decisions.

So the project manager is going to run the project, is he?

Who runs what?

The proverb says: 'he who pays the piper calls the tune.' The owner is ultimately responsible, but he has inevitably to delegate a large proportion of his responsibilities to his managing contractor. The larger the project, the more he has to delegate. Delegation is achieved through the contract. Once the responsibility *has been* delegated, it should be so left. The owner should not interfere. Rather he should see the organisation of the managing contractor – and indeed, those of *all* his contractors – as an extension of his own, all mutually working toward a common goal.

Truly the owner is in ultimate control – or should be. That is why we propose, in Figure 6.1, that he too should have a project management team. But that project management team should be working *alongside* the project management team set up by the managing contractor, not *over* them. Let us illustrate that diagrammatically, as Figure 6.2. We then see very clearly that the owner and the managing contractor should be mutually supportive. This is indeed the way in which the relationship is seen by the managing contractor himself, since the layout shown in Figure 6.2 has been copied faithfully from a brochure illustrating the project team as proposed by one such contractor.(3) The interrelationship shown in light rule is from the brochure. We have added the heavy rule and will explain why in a moment.

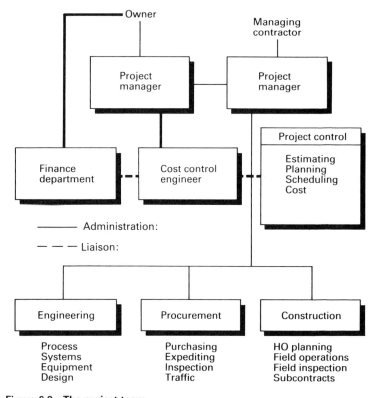

Figure 6.2   The project team
This chart shows (in light rule) a typical project team (with acknowledgements to the M.W. Kellogg Company, Houston). Added in heavy rule are the key functions that afford the owner control.

There is no doubt that this method of working both alongside and in parallel, just like a team of horses 'in harness', is highly successful and should therefore be completely acceptable to all the parties involved. How does it work? Let us quote once again from that brochure issued by a contractor:

> The Project Control Team [refer to Figure 6.2] under the direction of the Project Manager sets the control guidelines for the project. On major projects a Project Control Manager heads the Project Control Team. Each supervisor within

the Engineering, Procurement and Construction areas is involved in the development of the project controls which affect his area of work. Thereafter, he is responsible for the execution of the project within the control plans and budget established for his area of work. The Project Manager, the Project Control Manager and his Project Control Team constantly monitor performance, making adjustments as may be required to plans as they may affect the interfaces between the specialty groups.

It is very clear that this contractor knows the road he has to follow. But the owner also has a role to play and we have sought to demonstrate this as well in Figure 6.2. That is why we have elaborated on the original organogram produced by the contractor. We have indicated the two key functions which should be exercised by the owner, both functions that he should have or should establish within his own organisation. These are the finance department and the cost control engineer. They will have to work *alongside* the managing contractor's personnel day in, day out for the next three years – or however long it takes not only to bring the project to completion and commission it, but to pay the very last invoice. They will still be busy when the managing contractor's team has packed up, left the site and gone off to the next project.

Team work

We have said very firmly that both owner and contractor should work alongside one another as a *team*. This is the beginning of their relationship: they are 'in love', to take the word from the heading of our chapter. That 'love' should *not* turn to 'hate'. This is very simple and all very obvious. But it is *the* aspect that needs to be fostered and encouraged. If this cooperative spirit is there, then all the other problems inevitably encountered on the project will be solved without strain. We shall be introducing you in Chapter 12, when we discuss project cost control, to our 'KISS' concept: 'keep it stupid simple'. Here you see another way of looking at it: our two parties should 'KISS' one another, so closely should they work together.

The seasoned contractor knows this well enough. Let us take by way of illustration the way in which Lummus Canada handled a project they had from Esso Chemical Canada. The project ran over the years 1981 to 1983. During construction in the field the two companies developed what was considered to be a unique integration of their field staffs.(4) The Esso personnel on the site constituted some 30 per cent of the total site administration, Lummus personnel the other 70 per cent. But they *all* reported to the Lummus Canada Construction Manager. This integration was not the result of some grand design but evolved from a series of *small* steps taken on site.

Now that it is all over, Esso are on record as saying that this integration, with single (not dual) reporting to management, saved some eighteen manyears, or about 15 per cent of the total supervisory and technical manpower that had been estimated to be required for the project. The integration, it seems, was brought about primarily by the pressure of circumstances. Truly, it brought better site relations and speeded completion, but it was originally necessitated by a shortage of technical manpower as construction began on site. The decision to overcome the staff shortage by integrating the two staffs was taken in January 1982 and the final organisational plan was approved by both owner and contractor by June, when the first staff nucleus was also agreed. This carefully detailed plan, developed over a period of some six months, was then transferred from the 'blueprint' to the field.

There were initial problems, largely psychological and ego-related. But once they had traded in their respective 'hard hats' (Esso wore blue and Lummus white), uniting in their common objective to complete the project on time and within budget, these hurdles were crossed and success ensued. Commissioning time was also shortened quite considerably, since Esso personnel were themselves involved throughout and therefore fully familiar with all aspects of the plant as it had been built. Time was also saved in the area of quality control, since this was carried out simultaneously rather than consecutively – first by the contractor and then by the owner, as is normally the case.

We are told that everyone on the site, irrespective of the hat they wore, had the same basic attitudes and objectives. As a result of the good personal relations between the two teams, now merged together, the work progressed smoothly and was completed successfully. Yet, in spite of the success achieved on this occasion, an Esso executive cautions:

> … integration can be implemented only on an individual project basis, and it requires total owner and contractor commitment to the concept.

In addition, and as a bonus, the project set up an all-time record for safety in Canada, with more than one million construction manhours without a lost-time accident. According to the Lummus construction manager this was achieved by Esso having 'total commitment to safety and giving its complete support to the program in a very visible way – awarding tokens of appreciation to the workers'. The tokens included belt buckles which were custom-made of pewter, showed a portion of the plant under construction and were individually numbered. This gave them the prestige of a 'limited edition' design. The men in the field were very proud of their record and the effects were contagious. The attitude towards safety that prevailed throughout the site had a salutary effect on the maintenance crews, who kept the site extremely neat. This was a secondary result of team effort, being induced rather than directed.

The end of the road

It is to be hoped that both parties to the project we have just been looking at entered into yet another project quite happily, and shortly afterwards, with an equally successful outcome. All too often, it seems, the initial working relationship sours as a project proceeds. Claims are made, disputes result, and argument drags on long after the project itself has been 'put to bed', as they say. That is why we called this chapter 'It's a love/hate relationship'. It almost always is. For most owners, the last big contractor they employed was the 'world's worst', whilst the contractor they propose to employ on their next project, whom they probably employed and fell out with perhaps two big projects ago, is now everything that is desirable.

To illustrate this uneasy relationship, yet hopefully in somewhat lighter vein, we have extracted a few metaphors from an article on this subject.(5) We are not quoting precisely, since we have adapted from the ideas presented in the article.

TOPIC	OWNER'S THOUGHTS	CONTRACTOR'S THOUGHTS
Owner	A dog's life	A necessary evil
Contractor	A necessary evil	It's a dog's life
Bid document	Fair, objective and complete	6 weeks to read, 2 to design and 1 to quote
Job lost	Objective decision	We have been 'robbed'

| Job won | Objective decision | Won, but hope we don't lose a packet |
| Project abandoned | Objective decision | Income nil, outlay $100,000 |

The above may well seem somewhat cynical, but nevertheless most projects are completed without a lawsuit at the end of the day. Given faith, trust and goodwill, all the problems that inevitably arise between owner and contractor *can* be solved around the table. This happens the more readily if the contract document, once signed, can be filed away until the project is completed. Let us not forget that these parties both *need* one another.

References

1 Editorial report: 'We try to find ways of disorganising ourselves', interview with Sir John Buckley, Chairman of the Davy Corporation, *Worldwide Projects*, Aug./Sept. 1980, pp.41–50.
2 Brochure: *Foster Wheeler expertise*, issued by Foster Wheeler Limited, Reading, Berkshire, UK, 1981.
3 Brochure: *Project control as practised by M.W. Kellogg*, issued by the M.W. Kellogg Company, Houston, Texas, USA, 1981.
4 Anon., 'Esso Chemical projects set new high in client/ contractor relations', *Canadian Update*, Spring 1984, pp.12–13. Magazine published by Lummus Crest, Bloomfield, NJ, USA.
5 Bidder, J., 'Client/Contractor Relationship – Mutual Metaphors', *Eng. Costs & Prod. Econ.*, 15, 1980, p.2.

7 They should complement: not compete

If you are an owner, you will be habituated to thinking in terms of ten or fifteen years ahead about the way in which you deploy your very large, but rather immobile, resources of manpower. If you are a contractor, your horizon is never more than some five years away, but your manpower resources are very flexible. If you are a consultant, you carry your resources about with you and you probably live from day to day. We speak from the heart! These different attitudes are crucial and must be recognised when it comes to developing the synergy that would make the mutual existence of the three parties we have before us – owner, consultant and contractor – mutually profitable. Synergy is a combined effect that exceeds the sum of the individual effects (*Oxford English Dictionary*). Synergy *should* result from their cooperation.

In Chapter 5 we considered the relationship between the owner and his consultant, whilst in Chapter 6 we turned to the relationship between our owner and his contractor (or contractors). Now we should assess the situation that exists between consultant and contractor. We treat these three parties as equals and in the area of activity in which we are interested – project management – they *are* equals. This is illustrated by the membership of their qualified staff in the appropriate associations. For instance, the Association of Cost Engineers in the UK has broken down its membership thus:(1)

	%
Contractor-type organisations:	39
Client-type organisations:	20
Consultants and Quantity Surveyors:	31
Process equipment manufacturers:	7
Academics:	3

This is probably typical not only of the UK, but of the situation worldwide. The relative financial strengths of the several parties are obviously vastly different, but at the technical level the three we are interested in – owner, contractor and consultant – are equals.

We have seen that owner and consultant need each other – and usually recognise that this is so. The same is true of the relationship between owner and contractor. When, however, we come to consider the relationship between consultant and contractor, whilst it is very true that they too need one another, neither of them think so for a moment.

One consultant once put his view thus:(2)

> Hungry contractors are quite prepared to steal crumbs from starving consultants, in the hope that the rest of the cake will follow. They compete for business strategy studies too, though with less success because they are less credible, and our own experience is that the contractors themselves are a small but interesting market: usually for advice on how to get into consultancy!

How does the contractor go about picking up those 'crumbs'? Let us quote from one of their 'glossies'.(3) This particular contractor says that he can offer expertise –

> for the plant you want to build
> for the part you want us to play
> *in venture study*
> in project management
> in engineering design
> in procurement and shipping
> in construction
> in management services
> in finance
> in any size of plant, anywhere

The venture study

Notice the activity we have highlighted. A 'venture study' they call it, carefully avoiding the more popular and well-known term, 'feasibility study'. The contractor hopes, via such a 'venture study', to 'get in on the ground floor': to be in a very advantageous position when the project is approved and gets under way. Let us assume that our owner is attracted to that offer and decides to use a contractor, rather than a consultant, at this point in time. If he is wise, he will only commit himself to the 'venture study': nothing more. Our advice earlier, in Chapter 5, when discussing the owner-consultant relationship, was exactly this. We saw a series of 'go/no go' decisions, and said that it should be a matter of policy for the owner never to spend more money than is strictly necessary to reach the next stage. So what should happen next?

Our owner receives his venture study from the contractor and decides to go ahead with the next stage. He decides to implement the project. He goes out to tender – and puts the contractor who has prepared the venture study on the tender list – perhaps. He is under no obligation to do so. But let's say he does. Where, then, is the 'follow-up' advantage to that contractor? He only stands on equal terms with all the others who submit an offer. But he *thinks* he has an advantage. He knows a lot about the project. He has what is called 'inside knowledge'. This, in fact, is the reason why some owners refuse to go back to the contractor who prepared the study. It can also work very much to the disadvantage of the contractor when he submits his tender for the work to be done. He automatically fills in the gaps in the tender specification that he happens to be aware of and so prices himself out of a job. The volume of work that such a contractor gets from such studies is trivial compared with his main workload and he will quite possibly lose money, since his people are likely to be working in an area where they operate less efficiently. So we assert once again that he would do better to leave it to the specialist, the consultant.

This is to see the matter from the contractor's point of view. Let us now look at it from the owner's point of view. This trend for contractors to 'wear a consultant's hat' on occasion is full of risks to the owner. The contractor has a vested interest in the project going ahead, for he hopes it will bring him a substantial volume of work. In view of this, he may well offer his 'consultancy' services free, or at a nominal charge. His main interest is to see the plant or facility built. But this very fact can inhibit him from offering unbiased advice. The consultant, on the other hand, can take a detached view, since if the project does go ahead it means very little more work for him. His work is basically finished once the project is 'go'. An impartial consultant can well advise, on occasion, that the project be abandoned: a most difficult recommendation for a contractor to put forward.

The growing pressures

It seems that in this changing world most of the large scale projects coming forward in the future are likely to be built in remote areas, with little in the way of infrastructure, but much in the way of complexity, such as multiple ownership, involved financial provisions and political ideology. These projects will be difficult to manage and it is the risks, rather than the rewards, that are most likely to increase for those who undertake them.

Of the various factors likely to affect the work available, the financial-cum-political factors are the most potent. We see government departments becoming ever more heavily involved in the contract between the owner and his consultant or contractor. Governments involved in financing a project seek to maximise the benefits to themselves, usually the volume of work that comes to their country. The government behind the 'owner' is equally concerned, but in an entirely opposite direction. There the anxiety is to maximise the work done in the country where the plant is going to be built. At the moment, there are practical limitations: local people do not have the necessary expertise. But they are learning all the time. These continuing pressures will eventually reshape the form that the contract between owner and contractor takes: that is already happening. What are called 'management contracts' are already becoming increasingly popular with buyer governments and their agencies, with the result that the contractor finds himself mostly concerned with the provision of what is called the 'front end' design, technical supervision and training. Most of the manhours that he would wish to sell for detailed design and drafting will now be provided by the buyer country. So the contractor's role is steadily being reduced to that of a 'consultant', at least in the international sphere.

Consultant resources

We have just been looking at the way in which the contractor appears to be invading the domain of the consultant. Let us now look at the matter the other way round. Let us see what a firm of consultants has on offer. Consultants, in terms of staff levels, go from one man only on up. We have deliberately chosen a large organisation as an example since such an organisation best demonstrates the point we wish to make. But of course we only mention their name because we are quoting from their 'glossy': that does *not* mean that we are recommending them.

We are told that the human resources available to this particular consultancy group (4) include well over 1,400 professionally or technically qualified permanent staff located in their various offices, together with many more on sites the world over. So that is the size of organisation we have before us. What do they offer to do? We quote, putting them in alphabetical order:(5)

Administration
Budgeting
Commissioning
Construction supervision
Contract documentation
Contract law and administration
Cost management
Estimating
Expediting
Feasibility studies
Financial appraisal
Inspection
Procurement
Project management
Project planning
Project procedures and systems
Quantity surveying
Tender evaluation
Translations

Would you care to put a cross against any of the items in the above list that you consider to be more properly the domain of the contractor? It is a subtle list, because whilst many of the activities listed above are indeed carried out by the contractor as part of his function to design, procure and construct, they are at the same time activities which the owner might well share with him in certain circumstances.

It is clear that the consultant at this level is seeking the role of 'project management' on behalf of the owner and it may well be that it is a role that he can play well where the owner has neither the experience nor the resources to provide such a team. But then, of course, consultant and contractor have to work *together* in real earnest. It seems that there is indeed scope for this. Quoting from the brochure again:

> ... we have considerable experience in managing a large number of diverse projects. We have also been asked to advise on projects already in progress and it is apparent that a large number of the problems encountered arise from factors normally considered external to the project. On any project there are many diverse parties involved and each

party requires to be identified and his interests and motivation clearly understood. Only then will the relationships between these parties be managed and balanced and a successful project achieved.

It is certainly more difficult than it looks. Owners, beware!

The eternal triangle

We have now looked at each corner of the triangle. We have said that it is in the interests of each of the three parties to cooperate one with the other, but that unfortunately does not always happen. Contractors seem to have the most complaints. They say, for instance, that both owners and consultants act at times like 'warlords', bullying small contractors in particular and throwing their weight around.(6) The remedy lies in the hands of the owners. It was the Ministei for National Development in Singapore who, recognising the problem,(7) urged government departments and statutory boards dealing with contractors to stop watching them 'like hawks, ready to pounce on them for any little misgivings'.

It should not be forgotten that it is the contractor who almost invariably has the most at stake and the most to lose. He is most often working against a lump-sum tender that he has submitted, and is vulnerable. The consultant, acting on behalf of the owner, is required to administer the contract fairly and impartially, but some consultants seem to act arrogantly and authoritatively. It is essential that the contractor's legitimate interests are properly safeguarded and his business risk minimised. His financial resources are usually limited and it is only right that he should receive his progress payments promptly.

The owner has a duty here. He is the only one who can curb the power of the consultant. As the 'owner's right arm' (our Chapter 5) the consultant is required to approve the quality of workmanship, issue instructions for contract variations and approve prices. There is normally no mechanism within the contract whereby these decisions can be challenged and the contractor can well suffer hardship as a consequence of delayed and unjust decisions by the consultant. The owner must recognise that, particularly on large and sophisticated contracts, there can be issues where genuine disagreements exist, which he should resolve with all speed. The contractor sometimes seeks to protect his own interests by engaging his *own* consultant, but we doubt the efficacy of this particular solution. It introduces a fourth party into the arena and can well contribute to a free-for-all. We feel that it is far better for the three parties to get together round the table, with the owner taking an active part and playing arbitrator.

As we survey the scene in the construction industry worldwide, it is apparent that in the present context, with fierce international competition for a falling volume of work, disputes between our three parties, and particularly between owners and contractors, have increased considerably. Yet no one wants disputes, for no one benefits. Disputes are both time-consuming and costly. The contractor is almost invariably the loser and he, desperate for work and a profit, may well underbid his next project, face a further loss and so enter a vicious spiral of contractual contests.

This type of situation has led to the establishment of a new breed of consultant, the 'international claims consultant', who counsels the parties to such disputes both before and afterwards. One such consultant has gone so far as to suggest the formation of an Owners' Association to look after their interests.(8) There certainly seems a need for such an association on an international scale, since both contractors and consultants are organised into associations of various sorts not only nationally but international-ly. It is, indeed, this lacuna that caused us, in writing our earlier work, *Total Project Management*, to look at project management from the point of view of the owner. To quote:(9)

> Unlike most books on project management, this one is written primarily from the point of view of the prospective owner of a new manufacturing facility.

Our next chapter deals with the subject of project management in some detail, so suffice it to say here that practically all the literature on this subject is written by those working for contrac-tors and presents their point of view. Of course it is a completely legitimate point of view but the owner, after all, is the most important 'third party' in our triangle. The formation of an association should contribute to the 'learning process' so far as owners are concerned and so minimise disputes which have at times had the most tragic results. Whilst contractors may well contribute to their own failures, they are often helped on their way by an ignorant owner. Serious disputes can lead, for instance, to a change of contractor, as occurred with the Algerian LNG project (10) or the collapse of an otherwise viable and desirable project whilst in the course of construction, such as Iran's petrochemical project, which we deal with in Chapter 14.

Let us conclude by putting in a word once again for the contractor in the construction industry. He *always* has the most at risk: he is the most likely to go bankrupt: he is fighting to live in an industry where the competition is growing ever greater. He *has* to make a profit. Let him.

References

1 Harris, D.P.M.,'The Cost Engineer and the 7th International Cost Engineering Congress', *Proc.Econ.Int.*, 3-3, 1982, pp.10–11.

2 Dingle, John, 'Contractors, consultants and the chemical industry', speech given at the European Chemical Marketing Research Association Conference, Oslo, 11-13 October, 1982. (Mr Dingle is a Director of Double L Consultants Ltd, London.)

3 Brochure: *Foster Wheeler Expertise*, issued by Foster Wheeler Energy Limited, Foster Wheeler House, Station Road, Reading, Berks., RG1 1LX, UK.

4 Brochure: *WS Atkins Group*, issued by WS Atkins Group from Woodcore Grove, Ashley Road, Epsom, Surrey, KT18 5BW, UK.

5 Brochure: *Project Management Services*, issued by WS Atkins and Partners, address as above.

6 Lim, W.S.W., 'Improving Contractor's Lot', *Singapore Business*, October 1982, p.27.

7 News item: *Business Times*, Singapore, 3 Aug. 1982.

8 Fairweather, W., 'Construction Disputes', an editorial in *Asian National Development*, August 1983, p.3.

9 Stallworthy, E.A. and Kharbanda, O.P., *Total Project Management*, Gower, Aldershot, UK, 1983, 329 pp.

10 Kharbanda, O.P. and Stallworthy, E.A., *How to learn from project disasters*, Gower, Aldershot, UK, 1983, 274 pp.

8   Project management

Construction, national or international, stands or falls by the quality of its project management. A project that is not properly managed can quickly head for disaster. So important indeed is the subject of project management that hundreds of books have been written about it, from almost all possible angles. When we dealt with the subject,(1) rather than deal with the mechanics of project management, we sought to provide the prospective owner with a 'cradle to the grave' view of the important considerations that he has to face and cope with at each stage of project development. We did this because, whilst it is the owner who has the greatest financial stake in any and every project, very little of the literature is directed towards him and his needs.

In Chapter 6 we dealt with the basic relationship that has to be established between owner and contractor and we saw there (refer back to Figure 6.1) that both owner and contractor should have their own 'project team'. Figure 6.2 goes on to illustrate the key elements of each project team and you will have noticed that *both* have a project manager and a cost control engineer. The project manager is there to 'manage' and a vital part of project management is cost control.

Project management *is* cost control

Yes, effective project cost control is only possible with effective project management. But it is equally true – dare we say it – that effective project management is only possible with effective project cost control. Yet, despite its crucial importance, cost control remains a much neglected subject, in that it is preached far more than it is practised. More often than not cost monitoring is accepted and passed off as cost *control* and *that* exercise only starts in earnest *after* construction starts on site, which is far too late. Cost control should start with the conception of the project, since from then on, as the project takes shape, the ability to *control* costs steadily diminishes – although the actual cost of exercising that control steadily increases, as is illustrated in Figure 8.1. The relationship of cost to time in the project might perhaps be illustrated by a simple analogy. If we liken our project to a taxi and project cost to the sum on the taxi meter, we can say that once a project is approved the taxi is hired and the meter set in motion. Thereafter, until you reach your final destination, costs climb, whether the taxi is in motion or standing still at traffic lights. So with our project. Even if no progress is being made, costs will still be incurred, possibly unseen, but inexorably. The key to proper project management is therefore a sound approach to project cost: the control of cost, rather than the monitoring of cost. To manage, one must look ahead. But if the project team fails to look ahead, the consequences are most unpleasant. Let us quote an owner:

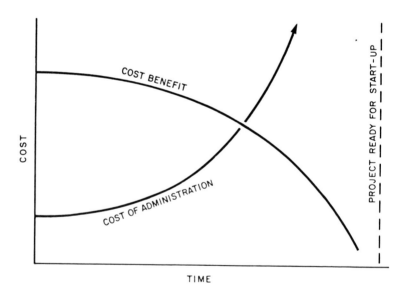

TIME

Figure 8.1 The cost benefit related to time
Figure 5.2 demonstrated the ability to control cost diminishes rapidly over time. At the same time, the cost of such control will escalate, as we see here, unless the futility of further effort is realised.

Great is the grief of one who is deeply entrenched in a capital spending program and *suddenly learns* [our emphasis] that the cost will exceed expectations.

It is quite obvious from this 'cry from the heart' that the most meaningful of all the information that becomes available in relation to cost is the *trend* – where we are going. Management never likes to learn suddenly that the budget is going to be exceeded. Much, much better to know ahead of time if that is going to be the case. Data that contribute to the early assessment of the cost trend are therefore very valuable indeed, since they can provide an early warning in relation to the estimates of both time and cost.

The trend is everything

We do not propose to go into any detail with respect to the technique of project cost control, having once emphasised the importance of looking ahead and seeing where the project is going: assessing the trend. But just to show how that *should* work, let us consider a project about a year from authorisation. This is the point in time when, in any project of substance, work is just beginning on the site. With the appropriate forecasting procedures, one could make a study at Month 11, say, as illustrated below.

PROJECT PROGRESS: VALUE OF WORK DONE (in US$ × 1,000)

MONTH	FORECAST		ACTUAL	
	In month	Cumulative	In month	Cumulative
7	900	3,800	794	4,533
8	900	4,700	495	5,028
9	900	5,600	402	5,430
10	1,630	7,230	641	6,071
			REFORECAST	
11	1,630	8,860	1,000	7,071
12	1,630	10,490	1,360	8,431
13	2,000	12,490	1,410	9,841
14	2,000	14,490	1,410	11,251
15	2,000	16,490	1,410	12,661

Actual lag in value of work done is about one month's work at Month 10.

Reforecast is on the basis of a 3-month delay in the completion date.

Studying the progress being made, it was obvious that it was falling behind the forecast. At Month 10 there was a lag of about $1,159,000. This was roughly one month's progress at that time in the project, but the delay is in fact more serious than at first appears, because progress is not going to pick up overnight – things do not proceed by leaps and bounds. That means that we have to anticipate a continuing reduced level of progress for some while yet.

This is illustrated by the 'reforecast' also shown in the table above, which was made on the assumption of a 3-month delay in completion. The actual value of work done for month 11 was $1,000,000, a first indication – and an *immediate* indication – that the reforecast was realistic.

We have presented just one example of the way in which cost data should be analysed by the cost engineer in order that he may give 'early warning' to his project manager. But let us remember that the cost engineer cannot *control* cost. He can only advise his project manager where he thinks the project is going in terms of cost and time. It is the project manager who must seek to take preventive action. That leads us to consider the role of the project manager in some detail.

The project manager is vital

A project manager has to live day in, day out, with the realities of life. Construction projects are built on the earth, not in space – although that stage may not be *so* far away. He has to be 'down to earth', as the saying goes. He must be a pragmatist, with his feet very firmly on the ground where his projects are – most of them, anyway.

We can and have likened our project manager to the captain of a ship or the commander of an aircraft. Whilst at sea or in the air the immediate need is for quick, firm decisions. Those decisions will have to be based, quite often, on incomplete data, yet the crew must implement them forthwith, without question, or else disaster could result. Similarly the project manager must react with decision on the receipt of early warning signals such as we have referred to above. This requires, above all, a wealth of experience.

All this means that the project manager's primary contribution to a project is *not* technical, although his technical background can be helpful. His contribution is *mainly* in the area of what is loosely called *human relations*: his ability to handle people rather than things. This leads us to another analogy. Likening our project manager to the conductor of an orchestra, we realise that the best results are obtained when all the musicians play in unison, following the lead (baton) of the conductor. The conductor achieves harmony by being in direct and instant communication with his orchestra. He stands where every eye can see him. For harmony – success – the project manager, in like manner, must maintain clear, direct and instant communication with his project team and they must respond.

Perhaps we have already said enough to demonstrate that a good project manager is hard to find. What is the stuff that good project managers are made of? Once again, this is a subject dealt with at length in the many hundreds of books on project management. Indeed there is one book with the simple title *Project Manager*. But the following paragraph drives home the point that we wish to make:(2)

> I remember a project manager, working in a very remote and hostile location, who received a very attractive offer of a new job, in a very civilised location and with many 'perks'. To his pleading wife and son, his first thoughts expressed were – 'But I can't leave – the reservoir has not been filled, and the penstock hasn't been tested. The turbine check is not due for six months.' Of such materials one makes a project manager. No wonder they are hard to find.

The role of the project manager

How do project managers themselves see their role? Talking of the project manager as the conductor of an orchestra, as we have just done above, one seasoned veteran is quoted as saying:(3)

> A project manager should not try to do the work of his team members, however proficient he may be at it, just as a conductor does not play any of the instruments while he is directing the orchestra.

His boss on his first job described the project manager whom we have just quoted as 'long on judgement and foresight, unfazed by totally new situations and able to establish credibility with people quickly'. To do so he starts his daily schedule thus:

> ... I usually talk to the client's project manager to get his perception of current problems, provide my own and discuss project status. Then I try to talk to key members of my team to update myself on their activities.

Notice that he is 'talking', not 'writing' to them. Do you remember our initial emphasis in Chapter 1 on the need to communicate 'face to face'?

Should the project manager hold a tight rein on his team? Let us quote another project manager:(4)

> I think the worst thing a project manager can do is to hold such a tight rein on his people that they're paralysed from making decisions, because they are not effective. You've got to give them some leeway to be able to do the job. Now that doesn't mean you just let everybody do his own thing. You need appropriate controls and overviews and monitoring to see that the work is progressing as it should. But you've got to let people have some elbow room.

Is the client always right? He would like to think so, but let us quote our project manager once more:(4)

> Sometimes we can best serve our client by disagreeing with him. There's a very fine line. One doesn't want to be uncooperative, or difficult, but you have to recognise that they are hiring us for our advice and expertise. We need to tell them when we think a course of action may be the right one, or a wrong one, then work with them to come up with the best decision.

The project manager, then, must be honest and have the courage to tell his client what he really thinks.

Well, have we said enough to give you an idea as to what project management is all about? We have quoted 'straight from the horse's mouth' by giving you the views of successful project managers. We could multiply such examples, but we have made our point if we have demonstrated that the role of the project manager is vital in the successful completion of the project. He is the focal point: all the project data are directed to him. His project team look to him for encouragement and inspiration. He is the *one* person who, however large or difficult the project, *must* retain a *feel* for the project as a whole. He *has* to lead. Whilst this quality of leadership is most difficult to define in words, one can recognise it immediately when it is present.

Communications: the link

We have just been demonstrating, through the mouths of project managers, the vital importance of communications in successful project management. To get things done, the project manager has to ensure a constant and prompt flow of information and instructions through his project team to the entire workforce – a workforce that can range from a few hundred to several thousand on a large-scale project. Effective communication, therefore, whether written or verbal, is absolutely essential. That is why we introduced this subject in our very first chapter under the heading 'The importance of communication' and have gone on to devote a whole chapter to it later (Chapter 22 – 'Communications world-wide').

In spite of the research that has gone into the subject of communications, the skills of most people in this respect are poor indeed. Peter Drucker, in a foreword to a book on the subject,(5) states quite bluntly that poor communication is the direct result of ignorance. He says that we do not know –

1 What to say
2 When to say it
3 How to say it
4 To whom to say it

Need we say more? Results of numerous surveys (1) confirm that communication both at the project site and in the home office are usually very inefficient. One reason for this, we believe, is that the communicator tends to concentrate on only one of the four steps in communication. We have:

1 The communicator
2 The medium of communication
3 The message
4 The recipient

A survey based on interviews and returned questionnaires among some 400 project engineering personnel (6) proved that nearly 80 per cent of a project manager's time is spent in face-to-face interpersonal interaction with his co-workers. It was further found that, although the substance of the oral message was important, the style and credibility of the communicator was the key to the impact of that message on its recipient.

With the poor communicator, all the attention becomes focused on the message, the other three equally vital components to successful communication being largely ignored. This leads to a complete breakdown in communication.

When we come to consider international construction, there are additional complications, such as language and cultural barriers that also hinder effective communication. These can have the further damaging result that they distort the message that *is* received. Those involved in international construction need to appreciate national traits not only with respect to language but also to gestures. For instance, when a Japanese says 'yes', you might well think that he is agreeing with you, but what he really means is that he *understands* what you have said: no more than that. An Indian may move his head from side to side, giving you the impression of 'no', but what he could mean is 'yes' – although the real intent may vary, depending upon which part of the subcontinent he comes from. The language of gestures is considered further in Chapter 22, in the section headed 'Lucky and unlucky days', in the light of some recent psychological research on the subject.

Manage by wandering around

The description provided by one of our project managers above of his daily routine makes it clear that he is busy, not at his desk, but going the rounds talking to people. A book on the subject of management that has become a bestseller (7) uses the phrase we have placed at the heading of this section: Manage by wandering around. Its meaning is self-evident and the adoption of this style of management has led, it is said, to the success of leading companies in the USA. The technique is styled MBWA.

The project manager at the construction site should also MBWA. If he will but walk around the site, observing what is going on, asking simple straightforward questions, he will get a real feel for the status of his project. It is truly amazing how much one can learn by asking simple innocent questions, sometimes even bordering on the silly. At the end of such a walk, lasting perhaps half an hour or an hour at the most, he can confidently say 'the job is going well', or perhaps 'I sense trouble'. This 'gut' emotion is far more valuable than all the progress reports or the piles of computer printouts that he has left behind on his desk.

Although the theme of this chapter is project management, we have focused much of our attention on the central figure at every construction site – the project manager. This is as it should be. We have done it by design: it was no accident. We have said before and will now say it again: The project manager is the *one single person* who can make or mar the project. It really does all rest with him.

Knowing this, the owner should let his choice of a contractor be very powerfully influenced by the character, qualities and experience of the project manager proposed for the project.

References

1 Stallworthy, E.A. and Kharbanda, O.P, *Total Project Management*, Gower, Aldershot, UK, 1983, 329 pp.
2 Lucas, C.L., 'A good project manager is hard to find', *Worldwide Projects*, Aug/Sept. 1981, p.30.
3 Feature article: 'Michael Kappaz: A knowledge of engineering – and of people', *Bechtel Briefs*, June 1982, pp.13–15. *Bechtel Briefs* is the house magazine of the Bechtel Power Corporation, PO Box 3965, San Francisco, CA94119.
4 Feature article: 'Daniel A. Greenburg: Balancing free rein and enterprise', *Bechtel Briefs*, Nov. 1982, pp.16–17.
5 Parkinson, C.N. and Rowe, N., *Communicate – Parkinson's formula for business survival*, Prentice-Hall, 1977, 205 pp.
6. Klaus, R. and Bates, B.M., *Interpersonal Communications in Organisations*, Academic Press Inc., New York, 1978.
7 Peters, T.J. and Waterman, R.H., *In search of excellence – Lessons from America's best-run companies*, Harper & Row, New York, 1982.

Part Three

LET'S GET UP AND GO!

9 Site administration

Where shall we begin? When we come to look at 'site administration' the first thing that we have to realise is that the 'site' can be anywhere in the world – absolutely anywhere. It can be in the centre of a busy city or far, far away in the depths of the jungle. And not only that: it does not have to be on the ground. These days it can be deep under the sea or even in space, where some repair work on a moving 'site' has already been successfully accomplished.

Construction contractors advertise their skills, their experience and their competence in their continuing search for work. We still await the day when the brochures they issue make reference to their experience in the construction of factories on satellites, but that is the only area of activity that they do *not* mention. Such publications read almost like a holiday travel brochure. In a sense it is invidious to quote, since we can only refer to one or two such brochures from the thousands that have been issued proclaiming the merits of the construction contractors who issue them. Yet the best way to give you an impression of all that lies behind site administration is to do just that.

One company, said to be in the 'top ten', offers 'engineering, construction and development ... anywhere in the world' – this may be revised in due course to 'anywhere in the universe'! At any one time, they say, they may be engineering new roads in remote regions, fabricating offshore platforms for tropical waters, undertaking turnkey projects in arid climates and erecting complex buildings in congested urban areas. The company speak of more than one hundred years of experience in construction, spread over 60 countries in five continents, handling contracts with values ranging from US$0.5 million to over US$1,000 million.(1) Another company in their brochure speak of engineering services,

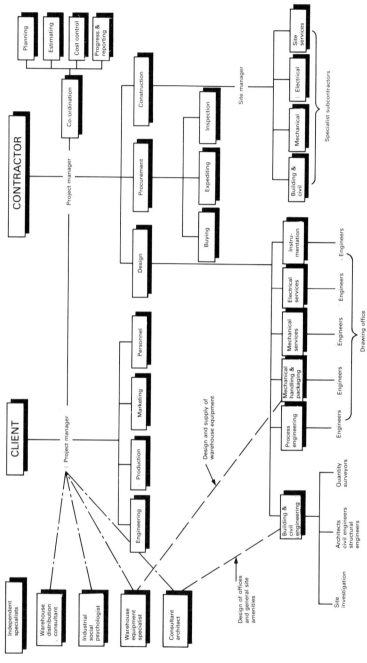

Figure 9.1 Typical project organisation
Here we see the framework for project management as established by the contractor, showing the relationship between him, his client and the independent specialists.

92

procurement services, financing services, and finally construction services.(2) This sets the site activities in context, so perhaps before we look at site administration in any detail, we should first look at the management structure into which the site administration is integrated.

Project organisation

The disciplines involved in the development, design and construction of almost any project are many and various. Perhaps the scope of the possible requirements can best be illustrated by considering the most complex case, where we have a contractor engaged by and working alongside the client, who also seeks the support of specialist consultants. This is illustrated diagrammatically in Figure 9.1. The term 'contractor' in the diagram covers any of the possibilities open to the client. He can engage a 'main contractor', perhaps a 'managing contractor', perhaps a 'construction contractor'. The terminology varies from country to country. What we wish to demonstrate is that the contractor has three main streams of activity:

- Design
- Procurement
- Construction

All these three activities operate in parallel to a very large extent and whilst the diagram illustrates the 'line of command' it does not show the way in which all the various departments within the organisation of the 'contractor' interrelate. We indicate the basic interrelationship that must exist between the two project managers, and we show, with a few lines at an angle, the further possibilities that can exist, but that is only the beginning, as we shall see. We shall look in detail at the complexities of site administration; the primary lesson, we feel, that comes from a study of Figure 9.1 is that site construction is wholly dependent upon the activities and the support of a wide range of other disciplines. Indeed, we finish up with 'specialist subcontractors'.

The subcontractor

To demonstrate what is involved, let us first of all provide more detail of the activities coming under 'Construction' in Figure 9.1. That brings us to Figure 9.2, where we see that the site manager

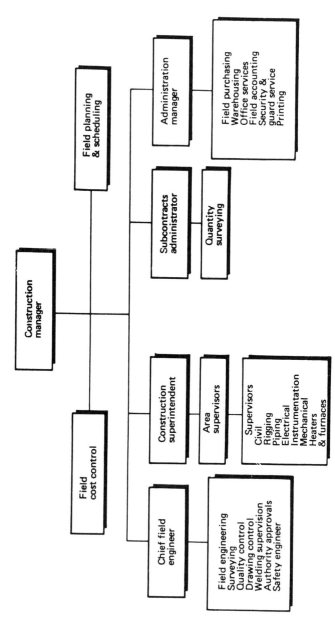

Figure 9.2 Typical construction site organisation
The number of personnel covered by this organogram will vary according to the size and complexity of the project.

94

(or construction manager) has four principal areas of activity to administer. The diagram provides for the possibility that his company will undertake part of the work on site with his own 'direct labour' – this is the responsibility of the construction superintendent – whilst part will be carried out by various subcontractors under the direction of the subcontracts administrator.

The management organisation behind the site activities will be responsible for getting all the materials that are required on site, supervising the employment of staff and the 'direct labour' and entering into the various contracts that will be required to bring the subcontractors to the site. The administration procedures designed to achieve this will vary from company to company. The work of getting proposals from subcontractors and then placing contracts is a procurement activity, but not all companies place this work under the control of their procurement manager. Quite often it will be the exclusive province of the director of construction and the merits of either approach can be the subject of much debate.

Construction manpower

Despite the extensive and growing use of larger, more complex and sometimes highly specialised machinery, the construction industry remains one of the most labour-intensive operations in the world. This is, of course, in part the reason why there is constant effort to maximise the amount of work done 'off site': effort that has led to the prefabrication off-site of larger and larger units, using 'skids' or 'modules'. Perhaps we should just explain those two terms before we go any further, seeing they will crop up time and again from now on, as we go on from chapter to chapter, following plant and equipment from one side of the world to the other.

Briefly, a 'skid' is a flat steel frame upon which equipment is mounted. The skid is so designed that the several items of equipment, together with the related interconnecting piping, valves, instrumentation and electrics, form one integrated unit which can be transported to site for final installation. The skid has to be rigid enough to ensure that it does not flex whilst being transported from workshop to site. A 'module' is somewhat different, in that all the equipment and other facilities are within a structural frame, assembled and tested under factory conditions, for eventual transportation and use elsewhere. However, the two terms seem to be interchangeable to some extent. The impact of modularisation on site construction has been summed up as follows:(3)

> Modularisation has the benefit of reducing the time required to bring the plant onstream. Once the plant arrives and is placed on its prepared foundations it can be hooked up and be in operation in a relatively short time. On a large construction project the selected use of modularised plant can involve a reduction of 10–15 per cent of site manhours, although no actual time saving is likely to result. This is because the time will be transferred to the vendor's works where a greater control over the finished product will result. A point however to be borne in mind is that unless carefully planned the late arrival of a large modular section can sterilise an area of the site. Late delivery can as a result negate the intended advantages.

So, whilst such an approach will certainly reduce the total number of men required on the site, they are still required in their hundreds, and sometimes in their thousands. Where do they all come from?

Let us quote from yet another brochure:(4)

> When a large process plant construction project recently called for a skilled workforce of approximately 5,000 and only a handful could be hired locally ... the construction craft training program made up the difference.

We are told that on large construction projects in remote or developing areas, where there is almost invariably a critical shortage of the skilled manpower required to see a project through, the necessary skilled craft labour, such as welders, pipefitters and electricians, has been provided in such locations by an 'on-the-job' training programme. This particular company claims to be the first to go into the field with construction training back in 1948, to have trained Eskimos for the trans-Alaska pipeline project (5), to have site-trained more than 12,000 on a syn-fuels project in South Africa.(6) In all, more than 100,000 craftsmen have been trained in this way in over 30 countries around the world. Of course, there are many other construction companies with similar programmes. So the manpower requirement on construction projects is built up and maintained. Every large-scale construction project, even in the industrialised countries, is likely to have its training centre for the support of the construction workforce, and also to provide operations training for the plant technicians who will run the installation once it has been commissioned.

Now – go to work

So there are men at work. Men working in crews, men working with 'mates', men working alone. They require a safe place from which to work, so scaffolding and other access structures have to be built. They need to be protected, this calling for safety equipment which ranges from the safety helmet and the safety boot to ear and nose masks. First aid facilities must be to hand, and they will also require certain comforts – a place to eat, rest rooms, changing rooms and the like. They must have transport, not only to the site, but all over the site, both horizontally and vertically. They must have communications, whether that be the telephone, the portable radio, or a site postal system. They must have power, to operate all their tools and equipment. All this requires site administration: nothing will happen on its own.

We took the heading for this section from a book on construction which enumerates all the things that have to be thought of when a site is opened up for construction in great detail.(7) We are reminded of the need to establish traffic patterns both within and immediately outside the construction site. Stockpiles and storage areas have to be organised as close to the point of use as possible. Thought has to be given to providing access for the main items of equipment and the needs of what is often called the 'heavy lift' programme. We enter into that aspect in more detail in Chapter 11 – The 'sky hook'. But, as Mr Halmos reminds us, this aspect of construction causes us to recognise that we may well have traffic problems hundreds of miles away from the site. Such equipment may well require intricate arrangements for its movement under police escort, with careful routing to ensure that it can reach the site. Obstacles on the way may have to be removed and later replaced; bridges may have to be strengthened.

Finally such equipment arrives and is offloaded. Men have been at work. This moved us to select the view of a lifting operation given in Figure 9.3. The vessel, on a low loader, has now to be lifted into place. The shackle is to hand. The man has to remove the pin, negotiate the shackle into place across the 'eye' provided on the vessel for lifting purposes, and then replace the pin. The man, a rigger, is signalling to the crane driver to lift the shackle slightly. Once the shackle is fast, the operation will have to be

Figure 9.3   Men at work
Here we see a dewatering bunker being prepared for hoisting onto the
concrete superstructure which will be its final resting place, below the reactor,
all part of a 'needle coke' plant. See also Figure 11.4 and the related text, where
the crane is described. (Photograph by courtesy of Shell Nederland BV,
Rotterdam, The Netherlands)

repeated on the other side of the vessel. After that will come the lift.

The challenge

To quote Jimmy Knox, a Project Executive for Essochem Olefins Inc.:(8)

> The Fife Ethylene Plant is the largest privately financed onshore process plant currently (1984) under construction in the U.K. ...
>
> It is a huge challenge to start with nothing more than words and numbers on a piece of paper and translate them into an operating plant; to take a green field site and construct under it and on it the complex of equipment, buildings, structures, machinery, electricals, and instrumentation required for a modern process plant.

We have always felt that the best way to drive a lesson home is by practical example, so once again we have chosen to take a few lessons on site administration from a real life situation.

We have said, of the relationship between owner and managing contractor, that *both* should see the managing contractor as an extension of the efforts and activities of the owner. It *has* to be a cooperative effort if they are to be successful. Mr Knox goes on to say of *their* managing contractor, The Lummus Company, that:

> *Together*, we are putting the highest priority on making sure that everyone has the right facilities, the right information, the right equipment, the right materials and in the right order at the right time.

Together! The emphasis is ours.

It was as early as 1977 that Lummus were retained to carry out preliminary design work for an ethane cracker at Mossmorran. Some two years later planning permission was granted. Then, with Lummus as managing contractors, site preparation began in 1981, with the objective of bringing a world-scale petrochemical project on stream by 1985, at a total cost of some US$600 million.

Impact on the region

The surrounding countryside at Mossmorran is very attractive and every step is being taken to safeguard the environment. The Mossmorran site covers in all some 260 hectares, of which 40 hectares will be occupied by the Fife Ethylene Plant. But more important than the impact of the plant on the environment is its impact on people.

This plant was being built in an area of high unemployment and Essochem have made every effort to employ suitably qualified local residents wherever they could meet the requirements. We have already mentioned above the matter of construction training. On this project, to help ensure construction working practices of the highest standard, Lummus awarded a training contract to the Centre for Industrial Studies at Glenrothes and Buckhaven Technical College. These are courses for first line supervisors and comprise the biggest programme of its kind ever introduced into the United Kingdom construction industry. All foremen receive four weeks' training prior to having a work crew assigned to them. In addition, every person coming on the site is also required to attend an introductory course at the Prior Lane Centre in Dunfermline, where the purpose and objectives of the project are explained, along with other items of importance, such as safety, site arrangements and working practices. This is, we believe, an aspect of employee training which is absolutely vital to the success of a project. All involved in construction will appreciate the truism involved in the story of a workman who, on being asked what he was doing, replied: 'Just laying bricks'. But beside him was another who replied: 'Building a great building'! We need say no more, surely, on the importance of informing all who work on a project of the objective in view.

The prospective operators on the plant also need training. A 10,000 sq. ft. temporary building has been erected on the site to act as the training centre for about 200 trainee plant technicians. There is a formal nine-month programme, after which training continues 'on the job'.

The largest lift ever in the UK

Let us demonstrate another aspect of site administration by considering the steps that led up to the 'largest lift of its kind' ever undertaken in the UK.(9) The item of equipment finally lifted was a fractionation column over 100 metres high and weighing 780 tonnes. This lift was the culmination of two years of planning and preparation by a special team.

Figure 9.4 A column being 'dressed' in the 'cathedral'
The main fractionation tower being prepared for erection. (Photograph by courtesy of Esso Chemical Ltd)

The fractionator column was ordered in sections, which finally arrived at Rosyth Docks for onward transportation to the site. On site the several sections had to be welded up. Then, prior to its lifting into position it was housed in a special tent on the ground. This tent can be seen in Figure 9.4. Under this cover all the relevant equipment, pipework, ladders and platforms were fitted or welded into position, thus minimising the work necessary after erection. We have seen this carried so far as to also complete the insulation before erection, but in our judgement this is not an economy. It would only 'pay off' if it were not necessary to scaffold the column after erection.

As a matter of interest, the enormous tent used to provide weather protection for the men working on the column on the ground was known locally as the 'cathedral'. It was previously used for the Pope's visit to Glasgow in 1982.

The prime objective

We have just spoken of the merits of letting those working on a project know its objectives and purpose. So perhaps it is not out of place for us to advise our readers of the reason for building the Fife Ethylene Plant. It begins with the Brent oilfield, the largest in the UK sector of the North Sea. There is a high gas-to-oil ratio in the Brent field and to ensure uninterrupted production of crude oil, the associated gases have to be transported and processed. There was a very similar situation with respect to the Statfjord field, which we describe in Chapter 17, except that for a number of years the gas was being re-injected into the field. But that was something that could not go on for ever: hence the Statpipe Project.

Here, the associated gases are brought ashore at St Fergus, where a gas separation plant extracts natural gas for the national grid system. The gas liquids, which include ethane, propane, butane and natural gasoline are then piped another 138 miles to Mossmorran to a natural gas liquids fractionation plant. It is the ethane from this installation that is passed over the fence as feedstock for the Essochem Olefins Inc. Fife Ethylene Plant.

The plant can produce about 500,000 tonnes of ethylene a year, thus upgrading the initial national asset. It is hoped that the world's most modern ethylene plant will enable Essochem to take advantage of economic recovery in Europe when it comes. Crude oil and natural gas liquids are normally regarded as an 'energy' source. But the ethylene from Mossmorran will be the precursor to a wide range of household items, such as polythene bags, washing-up liquid, paints, antifreeze and car components: making a highly economic use of an increasingly valuable resource.

References

1 Brochure: *Wimpey Worldwide*, published by George Wimpey PLC, Hammersmith Grove, London W6 7EN.
2 Brochure: *Fluor in Europe*, published by Fluor Europe Inc., Fluor House, Euston Square, London NW1 2DJ.
3 Laverton, A.B.E., 'The modular concept in plant design and construction', paper presented at a symposium on 'Modular Construction' organised by The Institution of Chemical Engineers at the University of Surrey in Guildford, UK, on 22 March 1984.
4 Brochure: *Building a global workforce*, published by the Fluor Corporation, 3333 Michelson Drive, Irvine, Cal.92730, USA.
5 Kharbanda, O.P. and Stallworthy, E.A., *How to learn from project disasters*, 1983, Gower, Aldershot, Hants, UK. 274 pp. See Chapter 11, 'People, Politics and a Pipeline', dealing with the Trans-Alaska-Pipeline (TAP).
6 Stallworthy, E.A., and Kharbanda, O.P., *Total Project Management,* Gower, Aldershot, Hants., UK, 1983, 329pp. See Chapter 16, 'A case study', dealing with the SASOL project in South Africa.
7 Halmos, E.E., *Construction – a way of life – a romance,* Westminster Communications & Publications, Washington DC, USA, 1979, 195 pp. Now only available from the author, PO Box 259, Poolesville, MD 20837, USA.
8 Brochure: *Fife Ethylene Plant*, published by Essochem Olefins Inc., Mossmorran, Cowdenbeath, Fife, Scotland.
9 Report: *Review 1982*, published by Esso Chemical Limited, Arundel Towers, Portland Terrace, Southampton, SO9 2GW.

10 The construction 'jungle'

Over thousands of years man has built, and built, and built – for various reasons. The construction industry has always been and is still one of the largest in the world and the results of its efforts are certainly the most visible and permanent. In the United States alone there are several organisations devoted to the industry, of which but one, Associated General Contractors, has some 10,000 member firms. Indeed, according to the 1970 Census of Business in that country, there were at that time more than 800,000 construction companies, ranging from the family business to mammoth organisations operating worldwide.(1) On this basis, the construction industry may well employ directly more than 4 million people worldwide, and indirectly must keep many more millions in work.

As we have seen already (Chapter 9), the construction industry is a labour-intensive industry and always has been, a fact that has spurred on the development of much of the machinery now used in the industry. Over the centuries it has left behind many noble monuments to the ingenuity, the skill, the inspiration of the men who have worked in the industry. Nor are we restricted to the past. We have not only the breathtaking beauty of the Taj Mahal in India, but also the vast Vertical Assembly Building at Cape Canaveral in the US, a structure so huge that it has had to have internal weather controls to prevent 'indoor rain'.(1)

The building at Cape Canaveral is there to provide a base for men to go into space. Looked at from such a vantage point, the hand of the constructor can be seen at work in the jungle and across the deserts. The challenge is there. That is how many of those engaged in the industry see their work, as we saw in Chapter 9. But the challenge isn't confined to the transformation of raw materials into a reality. We are dealing with people: people who are self-seeking, ambitious, jealous, envious … it is a long list. So, in the construction industry, management has to face up to and cope with theft and corruption, bribery and rivalry.

This is an aspect which we felt could not be overlooked. Certainly those who work in the industry cannot overlook it, whether they be in management or among its humblest employees. All are affected one way or another. Everyone who goes on site has to pass through the 'gate' and is liable to be subjected to search. If we are to make a true survey of 'construction' we have to review the indirect consequences, as well as the direct consequences, of the fact that it is indeed men who are at work and not only machines. Those who work in the industry and for the industry are no better – or worse – than the rest of the world.

The 'lump'

Let us now look at the UK construction industry. In the conditions of the early 1970s, the housing market in particular was, to use a headline in an article 'Constructing the web of illegality',(2) an 'asphalt jungle of misconduct', which was typified by the 'lump' system. To quote:

> The lump serviced a web of misconduct which would have disintegrated without the adhesive of enormous sums of unrecorded and unaccounted-for tax-free cash.

To explain, whilst employees had income tax deducted from wages and salaries before payment, under the PAYE (Pay as you earn) system, the self-employed were paid in full. Their tax should have been paid by them personally later – but very often it was never recovered. Construction companies accepted that a person was self-employed if he said so and many such companies employed no other kind of labour. There were advantages both to the 'skins', as they were called, and for the companies. The men so employed thought they were getting a very high wage, forgetting that they were not entitled to many benefits, such as holiday and sickness pay, which the regular employee received as of right. The company had the benefit that it could 'hire and fire' with impunity, and administration costs were very low. The big loser was the Government, deprived of hundreds of millions of pounds every year in unpaid tax – through the default of the 'skins'.

What is not realised is that business fraud can be far more

debilitating to society in the long term than the more violent acts
that make the headlines. The wider social and business implications range far beyond the immediate events themselves. Nowhere
is this more vividly demonstrated than in the construction
industry, where fraud and corruption have inflicted much havoc on
the economic and social fabric of society.

For instance, the 'lump' system we have just described, with the
associated corruption, did enormous damage to housing programmes in the UK. Inland Revenue estimates placed tax evasion alone
over the years in billions of pounds. For the same public
investment, more honestly applied, post-war Britain would now be
hundreds of thousands of new houses better off. Who can say what
impact *that* would have had on Britain's prosperity?

The disappearing letter

Much of the misuse of funds that occurs in the construction
industry is dependent upon collusion between officials of the
company requesting tenders and the 'favoured' construction
company. To illustrate, the work is to be let out on a Schedule of
Rates, set against a Bill of Quantities sent to all contractors invited
to tender. The Bill is priced using the tendered rates, and the
lowest total should get the contract. But a door is left open. One
section of the Bill calls for 'labour only' rates. When the tenders
come in, the 'favoured' construction company has been underbid.
He learns of this through his corrupt source, and by the time the
tenders are finally assessed, a covering letter has been attached to
his offer, stating that the 'labour only' rates have been priced
inclusive of materials. If the materials were not required, then the
rates could be reduced. Those assessing the several offers adjust
his bid accordingly, and he gets the contract.

But the twist does not stop there. By the time the Schedule of
Rates gets into the hands of the Quantity Surveyors, who have to
price the works done, and authorise payment, that covering letter
has disappeared. So the rate quoted quite clearly in the Schedule
gets paid. Of course, such corruption was far from being general,
but it did exist – and still does exist – on a significant scale. And
not only in the UK: it is worldwide. We have given here just one
example of the corrupt practices that are to be found in the
construction industry. Our breadth of experience across several
continents shows us that such practices and others like them are
fairly widespread all over the world. We doubt whether any
country is immune. After all, construction is, in the ultimate

analysis, carried out by human beings, and they all have very similar attributes wherever in the world we meet them, both good and bad. The only differences are those of detail and degree.

The tricks of the trade

One of the greatest problems in business, to which the construction industry is no exception, is to ensure a sound cash flow, so that the company has cash in hand for its various purposes. There are many ways of doing this quite legitimately: the best way of all is for the owner to recognise the problem and ensure that his arrangements for payment to the contractor are equitable. But the contractor can also have his own 'tricks' to get cash in hand ahead of his outgoings. One is what is called unbalanced bidding, where a higher rate is applied to items in the Bill that can be completed early and hence paid for quickly. Of course, to ensure that the overall offer remains reasonable, certain other items in the Bill will have to be priced at a lower than economic rate. The owner protects himself against this by comparing not only the total cost of the Bill, but also the individual rates of the various firms submitting tenders. But the contractor also runs a risk. If the work covered by those rates he has 'lowed' increases, he will lose out.

On the other hand, the contractor may seek to use potential change in the quantities stated in the Bill to his advantage. It must be remembered that at the tender stage the quantities shown in the Bill are pre-design estimates only. If the contractor thinks that certain elements of the work are likely to grow, he can make the rates for that work high, once again lowering other rates so that the overall total looks good when compared with the other tenders. But if the volume of work where he has relatively high rates does indeed grow, then his profit will also grow.

There is yet another practice, described by the term 'bid shopping', where the main contractor presses for ever lower bids from his subcontractors in order to increase his own profit margin. Sadly, many of the smaller subcontractors, fearful of losing work, are prone to retreat under such pressure, and reduce their prices. Whilst there is nothing wrong as such in attempting to secure the lowest possible prices for work, the contractor who is pressurised to such an extent that he accepts work at a loss will not perform well. To quote:(1)

> To most reputable Constructors, this result isn't worth the prospective extra profit. Over all, no contract is worth more

than the ability and integrity of the people who sign it. If
Constructors working together do not trust and respect each
other's ability and integrity, trouble is a certainty.

Let us be blunt. The main objective of any business is to make a
profit. Without it, the business will cease to exist. It is therefore
very much in the interest not only of the owner, but also his two
arms (consultant and contractor) not to grudge a reasonable profit
to one another. Indeed, they should take steps to ensure that all
those with whom they work are in a position to make a profit. A
contractor facing a loss on a contract is bound to 'cut corners' both
in quality and performance, which in the long run hurts the project
and works to the detriment of the owner far more than any other
of the parties involved.

The legal 'jungle'

We made a brief reference to the existence and need for
'conditions of contract' in a section under that heading in Chapter
6. Every time a construction contractor takes on a new project he
enters into a contract, usually formally. There have been many
attempts to standardise the form of contract used on such
occasions, especially when the contracting parties are in two
different countries, because of the differences in law between
countries, but these attempts have not been too successful in the
construction field. Unfortunately, terms and conditions of contract
can be entered into unwittingly that can end in a disaster that has
nothing to do with the quality of the work done. Once again, the
contractor can be under pressure, in that he is anxious to secure
the contract. He is therefore liable to act unwisely, accepting terms
and conditions that he should have rejected.

Another aspect is the need to comply with a bewildering array of
local, area and governmental laws: laws relating to the inspection
and approval of works, the acceptance of plans, the use of certain
materials, the conditions under which labour may be employed,
health and safety regulations ... the list is endless. Equipment that
comes on site, especially cranage, has to be certified safe for use
under the conditions of use. If equipment is hired, or is being
purchased other than for cash, the construction contractor may
become involved in usury and credit laws, liens and other similar
matters.

To help them find their way through this legal 'undergrowth', most large contractors have their own legal department, usually employing lawyers (attorneys in the US) well versed in construction law. Without such guidance, the construction contractor is venturing into uncharted ground which can result in his ruin.

Contractor versus contractor

There was once a conference convened in London that had as its title 'The construction jungle'. The conference was organised, to quote the brochure, 'to examine the complex interface between the main contractors and the subcontractors involved in international engineering projects'. We live in a cut-throat world, we are told. Main (or managing) contractors and their subcontractors are inherently competing for the same business. Yet at the same time they have to work with one another. There should be, as we have said already, an atmosphere of trust and goodwill if projects are to be successfully completed. Yet there are problems and misunderstandings. The main/sub-contractor relationship rarely runs smoothly. Dissension and strife are rife: companies are even forced into bankruptcy because monies are withheld. What a world!

The conference discussed many things: forms of contract, bonds, guarantees, insurance, penalties, the 'eternal triangle' (owner, managing contractor and subcontractor). All these things are designed to define with precision the relationships between the various parties, to provide financial inducements for good and efficient work, to protect against bad workmanship: they are designed to *minimise* potential areas of conflict. Yet, more often than not they seem to exacerbate them. The whole atmosphere behind the conference was one of strife and turmoil, yet the objective in getting together was to understand, appreciate and accept one another's problems. There was talk of 'claim negotiation', the exploitation of one party by another.

Yet another conference, this time with the title 'Indemnity and insurance aspects of engineering construction contracts' was said to have been convened to discuss 'current trends, problems and developments'. We just cannot get away from 'problems', can we?

For the owner, seeking to have his project completed economically and on time, this is a veritable 'minefield' through which he has to walk. Usually, he finds that his task – or more specifically, the task of his project manager – is to unify the various efforts so that they all work to the same end. He becomes a 'trouble shooter', having to pour oil on trouble waters.

People, politics and a pipeline

Let us turn from the general to the particular as a final illustration of the point we wish to make in this chapter. The heading to this section is taken from a chapter in an earlier work of ours, a case study of the Trans-Alaska-Pipeline – TAP for short.(3) To quote:

> Everything on this project was on the grand scale, even the mistakes and the crimes. The X-rays of the welds were falsified, resulting in repairs costing $55 million. The project manager for the X-ray contract company died in his flat after taking cyanide. Theft and fraudulent billing was estimated at between $40 and $70 million.

All this was on a project costing in total some US$8 billion, and employing over 8,000 people on the various sites at the peak of the effort.

There is no doubt that the construction industry suffers losses amounting to many millions of dollars a year from theft and vandalism, most of it from within its own ranks. It is indeed surprising what employees will do out of mistaken loyalty for their own company. Short of a valve, they will enter the compound of another contractor, cutting through the security fence, to steal and use one – not for themselves, but for the job. Indeed, that highlights the principal problem occasioned by theft: shortages can be created that are not discovered until late in the day. This results in delays in completion, because it is usually the most valuable items, with long delivery times, that disappear. The loss of tools can have a similar impact. One of the greatest types of loss is in this area: hammers, chisels, small power drills, saws and the like. Much of this equipment simply 'walks off' the site in the hands of the workmen. Education can help. If only those working on the project can be brought to appreciate the value and the importance of these tools *to the project*, such losses can be trimmed, because the average worker still has a deal of pride in 'the job'.

So we are back to motivation. Nothing can substitute for, or contribute more, to the success of a project than the sound motivation of all engaged upon it. Motivation may be self-generated or it can be acquired by training. Indeed, it should be an integral part of the training everyone coming on to the project should receive, as we discussed in Chapter 9, in the section on 'Impact on the region'. We have dwelt at length and in detail on the various aspects of training for project work elsewhere.(4)

References

1 Halmos, E.E. Jnr., *Construction – a way of life – a romance,* Westminster Communications & Publications, Washington DC, 1979, 193 pp. Currently obtainable from the author at PO Box 259, Poolesville, MD.20837, USA.
2 Article: 'Constructing the web of illegality', *Management Today,* July 1983.
3 Kharbanda, O.P. and Stallworthy, E.A., *How to learn from project disasters,* Gower, Aldershot, Hants., UK, 1983, 273 pp.
4 Stallworthy, E.A. and Kharbanda, O.P., *Total project management,* Gower, Aldershot, Hants., UK, 1983, 329 pp. (See pages 85–90.)

11 The 'sky hook'

In a sense there is nothing new in the construction industry, but there is continual growth, development, enlargement and adaptation. This is especially true when it comes to the handling of materials on site and putting them into place. The Romans, the Greeks and the Egyptians before them for that matter, inherited the know-how to develop and use such things as the block and tackle. But there has always been a driving need to find better, faster ways of doing things, to make better use of the available resources and manpower. Great impetus has been given to this over the last twenty years or so by the ever-increasing cost of labour and the continuing fact that that labour is much more efficiently employed in the factory than on the construction site. Thus there has been a very powerful cost incentive to reduce the labour employed in the field. This has led to the prefabrication of items off site, to be erected in their entirety on site. The size of such prefabricated items has grown and grown, until now we have what are called 'modules' and even a complete 'plant unit' fabricated and erected in the workshop and then transported from there to the site for final installation.

Such changes in construction practice make new and onerous demands on the transport system, to move such large items from the point of fabrication to the site. But that is a saga in itself, which we have decided to leave over to Chapter 21, where we discuss 'Transport across the world'. For now, we would like to consider the problems that have to be met and overcome on the site itself.

The historical development

The main tool for placing equipment is the crane or derrick. These were probably first developed for the early sailing ships and are a combination of two mechanical devices: the 'lever', and the 'block', which multiplies the power applied by using a series of pulleys. The advent of power other than human or animal – first steam, then the petrol and diesel engine and the electric motor – multiplied the available power many thousandfold. But, above all, it made the equipment mobile, so that in addition to the derrick and the tower crane we have the wheeled and track cranes that move under their own power within the worksite and from worksite to worksite, thus speeding up erection tremendously.

Just to introduce the subject, look at Figure 11.1, where we have a normal construction site, with the 'heavy lift' phase in full swing. A total of 8 cranes of various types are visible, all busy. The column on the extreme right is being site welded, so the crane has to place and then hold each section with precision to allow the welders to make the seam joint. The derrick occupying the centre of the stage is secured with a total of nine guy ropes. The location of both the derrick pillar and the guys, for which foundations have to be provided, has to be planned in great detail, both to ensure maximum use of the derrick and to prevent the guy ropes fouling equipment as it is installed. This is a real 'three-dimensional' study. This photograph is now some twenty years old and we are sure that, if the same plant were to be built today, the construction site would look vastly different. For instance, that column to the far right would have been completely welded up either in the fabrication shop or on the ground at the site before lifting, then fitted out on site with ladders, platforms, piping and perhaps even insulation before lifting into place. We gave an example of this, the latest approach to coordinated construction, in Chapter 9, when we discussed 'the largest lift ever in the UK'.

The handling of heavy loads calls for considerable pre-planning in relation to both their transport and then their lifting into place. This should relate not only to the choice of construction site but also to the siting of heavy engineering workshops. We know one such in Bombay, India, which has neither a railway siding nor a water front. As the capability of the shop grew and the size and weight of the equipment being fabricated increased, special steps had to be taken to ensure that the equipment could be moved out of the workshop. But it would have been better and cheaper to have thought of the problem of 'access' from the start.

The hydrajack

The art of the 'heavy lift' is under continuous development. Now

Figure 11.1 A typical construction site
Here we see the 'heavy-lift' phase in full swing. This photograph is some 20 years old, and we have chosen it to illustrate the differences in heavy-lift construction practice that have developed over the years, as lifting techniques have grown in dimension.

114

we have the hydrajack, a hydraulic lifting system developed by the Engineering Department of Mammoet Transport BV of Amsterdam, which appears to fill a definite need, if the list of users is anything to go by. Leading oil companies and their managing contractors have found a variety of uses for it, but it seems to be a real cost saver when a very heavy item of equipment has to be manoeuvred into a confined space. A feature of the hydrajack is its ability to lift the heaviest loads very high with the minimum of risk.(1)

In recent years, hydrajacks have primarily been used for work on nuclear power stations, the construction of refineries and heavy engine building. It is in these sectors of the construction industry that very heavy objects, such as reactor vessels, tanks, columns or engines, need placing with precision. The lifts are often so complicated that the hydrajack is found to be the only system capable of lifting and placing such items at a reasonable cost.

The hydrajack itself, as designed by Mammoet, has a capacity of some 650 tonnes, so four hydrajacks would have a total lifting strength of 2,600 tonnes. Thus the system is highly flexible. The lifting system can be transported and set up on site very quickly – even transported by air! Whilst the load is suspended, it can be rotated through 360°, its hydraulic and electronic controls being extremely accurate. Every case where the use of the hydrajack is proposed is different, so a good deal of preliminary engineering work is required. The gantry determines the height to which a load can be raised: the present maximum is 120 metres.

A good example of the application of the hydrajack is in the lifting and placing of the reactor vessel at a nuclear power station inside the concrete reactor shell. We illustrate such an operation in progress in Figure 11.2. The site is at Valdacabaleros in Spain. Tasmi-Ibema, of Bilbao, were responsible for erection, and they contracted Mammoet to ship the reactor, which weighed some 600 tonnes, from Santander to Seville, the nearest port, from where it went by road to the site. Everything on site was in readiness for its arrival and the vessel, which was 30 metres high, with a diameter of 6.5 metres, was placed on its foundations in about two days. Figure 11.3 shows the reactor in place. Now you get a much better idea of the 'drop' – some 40 metres.

Pie in the sky

Back in 1976 the skyline at Moerdijk, in The Netherlands, was drastically altered. No longer did a naphtha cracker dominate the

Figure 11.2 The hydrajack in operation
A 600-tonne reactor vessel is ready for lifting, on site at Valdacabeleros, Spain. (Photograph by courtesy of Mammoet Transport B.V., Amsterdam, The Netherlands)

Figure 11.3 The reactor in place
This is the same operation as depicted in Figure 11.2, but now the reactor is set on its foundation within the concrete shield. Notice the confined area into which the reactor has been placed. (Photograph by courtesy of Mammoet Transport B.V., Amsterdam, The Netherlands)

coast by the Hollands Diep. A very special plant had been built, special both in outline and in product. The product was 'needle coke', destined for use in the manufacture of the graphite electrodes that are used in the electric arc furnace for the manufacture of steel.(2) Feedstock for the plant comes mainly from Shell Nederland Chemie's Moerdijk gasoil/naphtha cracker, which Shell state has the high aromaticity and low sulphur content that make it most suitable for the manufacture of premium quality coke.

The process requires that the various stages be built one on the top of the other. The coke is formed in a reactor, of which there are two, one in the reaction phase whilst the other is being emptied. This is done using high pressure water jets that cut the coke away from the drum. These jets are lowered down the depth of the reactor, so immediately we have to have a tower for them, called the 'bore tower', at least the height of the reactor. Indeed, these structural steel towers over each reactor look just like the drilling rigs one sees at an oilfield.

Following the process downhill further, the coke, once cut loose, tumbles down into crushers, and then on down to what are called 'dewatering bunkers', where the water from the cutting process is allowed to drain away. This means that the top of the reactor is some 70 metres above ground. This is where the plant operators have their control room. We are told that from here they have a magnificent view, looking to the north towards Rotterdam and its famous Euromast, and south across Brabant as far as the Belgian border.(2) But what concerns us is that those reactors had to be placed on the concrete structure that carried the crushers and the dewatering bins below. It had to be a rigid concrete structure because the crushers, mounted high in the structure, impart a lot of vibration.

Figure 11.4 shows one of the reactors on the way up.(3) You see a load of 165 tonnes in the tackles. But a lot of long-term planning had to take place to get it there. The reactors arrived at the dockside at Moerdijk on one of the specialised vessels we describe in Chapter 21 ('Transport across the world'). It was unloaded in the normal way and transferred by a multiple-wheel low loader to the construction site. But then!

In order to lift these 165-tonne vessels onto the concrete structure it was necessary to call for the help of Paul Rosenkranz GmbH, of Witten, West Germany, the owner, designer and builder of the largest mobile crane in the world, with a capacity of 1,000 tonnes. This crane had to be specially booked more than a year ahead, and the construction programme at Moerdijk had to

Figure 11.4 The largest 'mobile' crane in the world
The 1000-tonne mobile crane, designed, built and operated by Paul Rosenkranz GmbH of Witten, West Germany, lifting a 165-tonne reactor into place
on a structure itself some 60 metres above ground. (Photograph by courtesy
of Shell Nederland B.V., Rotterdam, The Netherlands)

be coordinated with the utilisation programme for the crane, which was in demand worldwide.

The crane arrived at the construction site in a total of 40 trailers. Once on site, the crane was erected on its truck, which weighed 120 tonnes and had 12 axles and 35 wheels. Sixteen piles had been driven to support four foundation blocks, placed to take the four supports, which stayed out from the truck in the usual way to take the load off the wheels. The lift itself took all of 40 minutes! Needless to say a fantastically expensive operation, if measured in terms of $/tonne/minute of lifting time.

Live site working

The nature of construction work falls, from the point of view of the owner, into two distinct groups, both very different from his point of view. From the point of view of the construction contractor, however, the difference is not *so* significant. The first type of construction work is the building of a separate and distinct facility, which can be pursued without interfering with the existing production facilities, even if the work is going on within the same boundary fence. The second type of construction is where a large-scale integration of a new facility is required with the existing production units.

This second type of construction effort is called 'live site working'. If the contractor is going to modify a working plant, incorporating new equipment, the plants with and in which he is working will have to be shut down in whole or in part from time to time. Obviously, the shorter such shutdown periods the better. It is also almost invariably the case that the contractor will have to work in areas where his access is restricted. It is this aspect of 'live site working' that we want to look at now. The various alternative approaches to 'live site working' and their potential impact on cost have been discussed elsewhere.(4)

A practical example

A practical example is to be seen in the modifications made to the Richmond Refinery of Chevron, one of the oil majors, in the USA. This was a sizeable revamp, introducing a new hydrocracking process developed by Chevron to produce high quality lubricating oils. Four main processing units were required to produce the lube oil and a further three units to furnish feedstock and process byproducts, with the associated utility requirements.

The project cost some US$530 million and the main work was given to Bechtel Petroleum, Inc.'s San Francisco Office.(5) They were responsible for engineering, procurement and construction work. Whilst the sheer size of the project presented a challenge, we are more interested at this time in the physical problems associated with what we call 'live site working'. So let us quote Bechtel's Project Manager, a 30-year veteran of Bechtel refinery and chemical construction projects:

> The part of the site where most of the work is taking place is very small for the number of process units to be installed on it. This calls for compact design. The existing facilities limit access and increase congestion so that working around them to install, say, a 200-foot-high distillation column or a 600-ton reactor, is no easy task.

The site is at the water edge and the plant has been built on land fill over bay mud. So everything has to be supported on piles and special concrete pads had to be built to support the weight of the giant crane used to install many of the vessels.

The heavy-lift crane

An important factor in the successful completion of this project has been, we are sure, the crane that was used for the installation of those '200-foot high columns' and '600-ton reactors' to which the Project Manager referred above. Figure 11.5 shows the crane in operation on the site. Two of the columns are in the left foreground.

Whilst we have not been told, we suspect that this crane was specially purchased for this project, bringing with it the means of overcoming the very special problems of live site working at this particular site. It is a Demag CC4000 Crawler Liftcrane, one of the largest of its class in the world and one of only 13 of this model manufactured. It weighs more than 500 tons, has a maximum lifting capacity of 880 tons and can be fitted with boom lengths of up to 504 feet. As you can see quite clearly from Figure 11.5, the crane is crawler-mounted; it is the only crawler version of this model in the United States at the time of writing. The crane is also unique in its class since it is hydraulically, rather than mechanically, actuated.

Figure 11.5   Bechtel's heavy-lift crane in action
This crane weighs more than 500 tons, has a maximum lifting capacity of 880
tons and can be fitted with boom lengths up to 504 feet. It is crawler mounted
and so self-propelled. (Photograph by courtesy of The Bechtel Power
Corporation, San Francisco, US)

Planning the heavy lifts

We thought we would go into some detail with respect to this crane, both to show you the present state of development in lifting facilities and also to demonstrate that the choice of crane was specific to the requirements of the project. The crawler facility gives the crane the necessary mobility in a confined working area, whilst the ability to boom out to over 500 feet (of course, the weight that can be lifted falls) allows facile placement of smaller items of equipment. The 600-ton reactors were placed using a 156 ft boom at 70-ft radius. Each reactor was picked up, swung into position and placed in a single shift. The vacuum distillation column, weighing 350 tons and over 200-ft long, seen to the far left in our photograph and the very first lift for this crane, was picked up and placed in 75 minutes, using a 256-ft boom at 70-ft radius.

Once the crane had finished its work at Richmond, it had to continue to be gainfully employed. This is one of the problems in the construction industry: the fact that plant can lie idle for months and sometimes years. Yet when it is needed it is indispensable. Bechtel are meeting that problem – indeed, had started to meet it before the project was finished – by offering this crane for rental to others. A leaflet has been printed outlining its capabilities.

We have devoted some time to this particular example because we believe that 'live site working' is going to become ever more important in the construction industry. Thus it behoves the project manager to be aware of the resources available to him to facilitate his work, especially in the 'heavy lift' area. He will find scope for the exercise of much ingenuity.

Once again, that is what construction is all about!

References

1 Article: 'Nothing is too heavy for the Hydrajack', *Mammoet Mail*, December 1982, No. 5, pp.20–2, (*Mammoet Mail* is the house magazine of Mammoet Transport BV, Amsterdam)
2 From various issues in 1976 of *Onder de Vlam*, a fortnightly newssheet published for their employees by Shell Nederland BV, Rotterdam.
3 From 'Shell Allerlei', a regular feature in *Shell Venster*. See Issue 3/77, March 1977. (*Shell Venster* is the monthly house magazine of Shell Nederland BV, Rotterdam)
4 Stallworthy, E.A.and Kharbanda, O.P., *Total project manage-*

ment – from concept to completion, 1983, Gower, Aldershot, Hants., UK, 329 pp.

5   Article:'Presto: Quality', *Bechtel Briefs,* May 1983. *Bechtel Briefs* is the house magazine of the Bechtel Corporation, San Francisco, US.

12   Cost effectiveness

Let us begin with a quotation:

> Project cost control is a vital part of project management. Without effective cost control there cannot be effective management. Too often, in paying lip service to cost *control*, all that is actually being achieved is cost *monitoring*. It is the difference between an active, forward looking dynamic approach and a passive backward looking one.

Thus Professor D.H. Allen, Head of the Department of Management Science, University of Stirling, Scotland, in his foreword to our book *Project Cost Control in Action*. The construction industry worldwide has grown up out of, and built itself upon, the experience of the US industry. Yet after more than thirty years of experience and the vast development in computerised data processing that has taken place, especially over the last ten years or so, it seems as though things are none too happy. We receive brochures from US computer software companies advertising their wares. They speak of 'shoddy project planning, slipped schedules, overrun budgets, sloppy coordination ...'. It seems that they still see tremendous scope in the construction industry for their systems.

We believe that the real problem lies in the fact that, whilst a remarkable advancement has been achieved in the area of networking techniques and sophisticated cost reporting, the rate of *successful utilisation* of these systems has not attained a comparable growth. Hence the situation described by Professor Allen – there is plenty of *monitoring* but little *control*. Let us look at the American scene a little more closely, since if we can see what is going on there, where they should be fully experienced, we may discern the pitfalls that exist for the rest of us, and so avoid them.

The 'cost effectiveness' project

The Construction Industry Cost Effectiveness Project (CICEP) developed by the Business Round Table of New York is a long-range, four-phase effort to develop a comprehensive definition of the fundamental problems in the US construction industry.(1) Problems! After more than thirty years on the 'learning curve'! A Construction Industry Institute (CII) has been formally established as an Institute of the University of Texas at Austin in October 1983, to, and we quote, 'provide an *impartial* organisation which can disseminate meaningful knowledge to enhance the management of construction projects'. Notice that they do not trust one another for a moment. They have to create an organisation under the aegis of a university to ensure impartiality in the distribution of data. There are a total of six research areas. The one that is of particular interest to us at the moment is the fifth, which they say 'will review project control systems with a view towards developing appropriate contract specifications and recommending the most effective techniques for scheduling and controlling projects'.

Of course, the construction industry has its clients – the 'owners' as we prefer to call them. A paper giving the owner's perspective on project management at this point in its development in the US points out that one of the most serious problems facing the US construction industry is how to regain its own cost effectiveness.(2) A banner headline issues a clarion call:

> Let us plan for the day when we can insert intelligence into our systems.

Intelligence! What a commentary on the blind use of computer programs. That same paper went on to say, with respect to project cost control, that there are inherent problems in any system which deals with forecasts and unknowns. It was further said, almost as if they had made a significant discovery, that corrective action must be taken at each step in these systems. What surprises us is the time it has taken for them to get that far.

Cost reporting is *not* cost control

It is very evident from all this that it is all too easy to establish a system of project organisation and administration, with a regular flow of voluminous reports, and be completely misled, believing that costs are under control. The greater the detail in the reports, it seems, the stronger that impression. Process the data through a computer and none dare challenge it! There is a fundamental difference between cost monitoring and cost control, demonstrated graphically in Figure 12.1. Notice that those appraising the problems in the US said that 'corrective action must be taken at each step'. But what they did *not* say was that that corrective action has to be taken *early*. Looking at Figure 12.1 and Case 'A',

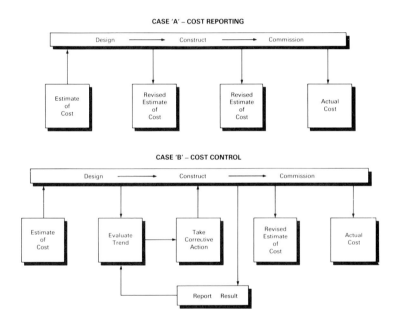

Figure 12.1 Cost reporting *vs* cost control
Reporting is the comment on the activity which is proceeding or has been completed. Control must influence as well as comment.

corrective action might well be taken after each review estimate, but that would be far too late. What we endeavour to inculcate, as outlined in Case 'B', is a process of forecasting, evaluating the trend, and *then* the taking of the appropriate corrective action – *before* the worst happens. Thus a project control cycle is set up:

1   Evaluate
2   Correct
3   Report

This cycle of events, constantly repeated, is fundamental to effective project cost control.

The key to success within the cycle will be a quick effective forecasting procedure, which in its turn demands the establishment of proper targets in terms of both cost and time. We do not propose at this time to enter into the details of project cost control, as a part of the construction activity, even although its successful implementation is vital to the ultimate success of any and every project. Many, many books have been written about that, including one of our own.(3) These books are designed to be studied and their principles and practices applied by cost engineers in the course of their work. We would rather highlight some of the problems and pitfalls that can beset the unwary.

The location effect

We have just said that the key to success in project cost control is the establishment of proper targets for both cost and time. These two targets are of course interrelated. The more a project costs, the longer, broadly speaking, it will take to complete. But of these two targets it is undoubtedly the establishment of the target cost that is the more critical and also the more difficult. That target is first created well away from the construction site, when the project is being approved. It is as well, however, that we give some consideration to the way in which such figures are developed, so that we can see where they are most vulnerable in terms of their accuracy. Their validity is all-important once we come on site. Poor targets not only mislead but they result in increased costs.

The biggest problem confronting the estimator in assessing cost is undoubtedly the impact of inflation. Inflation is a well-understood phenomenon which causes costs to increase with time. What it means for the estimator, however, is that his collected, historical costs become out-of-date as fast as they are accumulated. So he tries to measure the impact of inflation on costs. There are a variety of cost indexes available in different countries which can be used to measure the way in which costs are changing as time passes. Whilst their accuracy is uncertain they have to be accepted, since they are the only guide available. If that were all, that would be enough. But unfortunately there are many other factors that also cause costs to change as time passes, such as technology advancement, changing legislation, changing environmental standards, changing investment incentives, changing labour productivity, and changes in design concepts, such as have been triggered by the succession of energy crises over the past decade. In addition, our construction contractor is anxious to work not only in his own locality, where he has the maximum amount of data on all these things, but also abroad, and overseas, where the data are far more difficult for him to acquire, assimilate and assess. This leads him to the location factor.

To demonstrate the basic problem by taking an extreme case, let us consider the Ok Tedi Project. To quote:(4)

> The Ok Tedi project, among the largest engineering and construction challenges ever undertaken by the mining industry, is catapulting one of the world's last frontiers into the 20th century almost overnight. The lure is 20 million tonnes of gold ore, capping a mountain in the Star Mountains of Papua, New Guinea, which forms the eastern half of the world's second largest island. This ore cap will produce 100 tonnes of gold. Beneath the gold, there is an estimated 400 million tonnes of copper ore, targeted for future expansion by the mining venture. The challenge is getting to it.

We see the completed plant in Figure 12.2. Ok Tedi Mining gave the Bechtel/Morrison-Knudsen joint venture, set up for the project, notice to proceed in August 1981, with a project startup of May 1984. That date has been achieved and the gold plant is now approaching full production. But the problems that arose because of the location!

The ore is in the middle of a rain forest near the Equator. The humidity is high and oppressive. It's one of the wettest places on earth – an average of eight metres (311 inches) of rain falls annually. The ground is geologically young and unstable. Landslides are commonplace. The forests are nearly impenetrable. A pioneer road had to be built between Kiunga and Tabulil, a distance of 139 km, to transport heavy equipment, fuel and supplies. One of the biggest challenges was the ground conditions and, in particular, the mud. The road was to climb steep, unmapped slopes from an elevation of less than 50 metres at Kiunga, on the coast, to 650 metres at Tabubil and 1,500 metres at the process plant. It would traverse some of the wettest, muddiest ground known. At the mine site, rain falls an average of 339 days a year and the clouds cling to the damp landscape.

Figure 12.2 Ok Tedi Gold Mine
An aerial photograph of the gold mine built on a remote site in New Guinea, in the middle of a rain forest near the equator.
(Photograph by courtesy of Bechtel Power Corporation, San Francisco, USA)

So, never forget the location factor! Whilst the very complexities which we have just outlined mean that there is no simple answer to the development of a location factor and none could ever have been developed for Papua, attempts have been made to calculate location factors to compare costs between one country and another. Unfortunately, however, it is not possible to say that a facility in location 'A' will, for instance, cost 20 per cent more than a facility at location 'B', so that the location factor, A/B, is therefore 1.2. On the contrary, detailed studies have shown that the location factor for buildings can be, and often is, different to the location factor for plant. Thus the location factor for one type of installation can be quite different to the location factor for another type of installation.

Let us illustrate that. Figure 12.3 shows a typical textile plant. Practically all the operations are conducted under cover, in airconditioned buildings. So you see great expanses of roof. Single-storey buildings, multi-storey buildings: the only visible plant is a few storage tanks. Now look at Figure 12.4. Buildings are hardly to be seen. We have what we call an 'outdoor' plant. So the overall 'location factor' for these two plants can well be quite different. Even within those two sharply distinct cost areas of 'plant' and 'buildings' there can be still further variation. One of us once had to learn how to estimate costs in The Netherlands, bringing with us the experience on costs that we had acquired in the UK and found that, even in so relatively straightforward an area as the construction of buildings, no simple solution was available. Look, for instance, at this series of cost comparisons which we developed at the time:

	The Netherlands	United Kingdom
Open structures	100	90
Warehouses	125	130
Manufacturing	215	250
Laboratories	310	400

The comparison is made on the basis of the cost of each type of building per cubic metre of building space. Whilst the cost increases as the complexity of the building increases, the 'curve' was not so steep in The Netherlands as it was in the UK at that time. Thus whilst the location factor for open structures was 100/90, or about 1.1, that for laboratories was very different, 310/400, or about 0.75. Just another illustration of the complexities inevitably associated with the location factor! So be warned.

Figure 12.3 A typical textile plant
Great Coates Works, Grimsby, in the United Kindom. (Photograph published by courtesy of Courtaulds Engineering Limited, Coventry, UK)

Figure 12.4 A typical 'outdoor' plant installation
The Sasol Two Synfuels Plant at Secunda, Eastern Transvaal, in the Republic of South Africa. (Photograph by courtesy of Fluor Corporation, Irvine, California, USA)

The small construction company

The Associated General Contractors of America keeps its members in touch with one another through the *Constructor* magazine, which has a circulation of some 40,000. Using this as a yardstick, there is every likelihood that the number of construction companies States-wide large enough to contemplate some form of cost control administration could well exceed 100,000, and worldwide there must be more than a million such companies. In this assessment we are trying to exclude what we might term the 'one-man business', where the planning, the costing and the control never will be formalised. Amongst this vast number of firms needing technical expertise we hear of just a few. Yet the many have the same problems as the few. In particular, they have to set up administrative procedures in order to control costs and complete projects on time. To quote:(5)

> Sometimes we get confused with the notion that the Bechtels, Fluors and the MWK's etc., are the only people in the construction industry. Attention should be drawn to the fact that cost engineering is also a concern to the nonentity fledglings who also compete in the marketplace.

The paper that starts with that reminder goes on to point out that the cyclical nature of the construction business means that with the smaller firms only a minimum of staff survive the valleys of such cycles. This has the result that such firms do not have the staff or the experience immediately available, when work builds up, to accumulate costs in an orderly fashion and predict trends. It appears that two schools of thought seem always to emerge in cost reporting systems. Some managers want a system to be extremely comprehensive and define every detail. Others prefer a skeletal framework. We ourselves would emphasise the need for simplicity. Our watchword is KISS – Keep It Stupid Simple. We would insist, what's more, that this should be so not only with the smaller construction companies but with them all, large or small.

More men, less work

For each project, for each site large or small, there is an optimum number of workmen beyond which the productivity per worker begins to drop. The larger the project, the greater the danger of

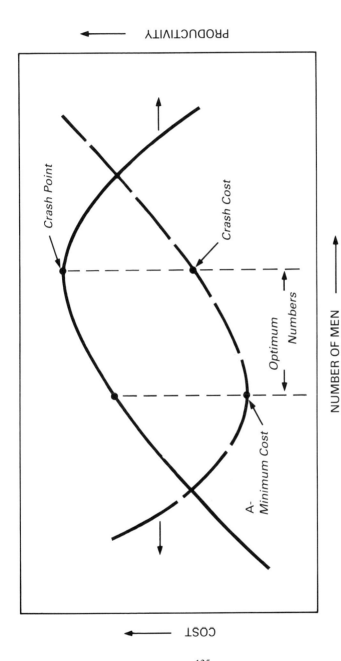

Figure 12.5   The relationship between productivity and cost
It is not necessarily advantageous to organise a workforce so as to achieve minimum cost in the field. The immediate cost saving could well be outweighed by the cost of delay in completion. Yet the pressure towards early completion can also go too far, being ultimately counter-productive.

this happening without the site management being aware of what is going on. The multiplication of activities will normally lead to waste and a fall in productivity unless the construction site is well organised and closely supervised. In Figure 12.5, depicting a concept first developed by Starr,(6) we have a very interesting representation of the actual state of affairs at the worksite. The two vital factors, productivity and cost, have been plotted against the numbers of men on site. The key fact, so clearly demonstrated by the graphs, is that the minima of the cost curve do *not* coincide with the maxima of the productivity curve.

Consider the implications carefully. The site manager, naturally enough, seeks to complete the project at minimum cost in terms of the labour that he employs. That will be achieved if he works at point 'A' on the cost curve. But he is not then working with as many men as he could and so the project will take longer to complete. There is always pressure to complete a project as quickly as possible, and so he is driven to increase the number of men on site. As we see, that is effective up to a point. Productivity improves, but his total cost is also rising. There is a point – we call it the 'crash point' on the graph – when all of a sudden productivity collapses. They are now all falling over one another's feet and stagnation develops.

Thus we end with a paradox. Beyond the 'crash point' even massive increases in manpower achieve nothing. Indeed, they achieve *less* than nothing, since not only do costs continue to climb but completion is *delayed*. Having more and more men on site only pushes that completion date ever further away. It may sound paradoxical, but it *is* a fact of life, borne out by experience on site.

If, however, our site manager, or the project manager, is not wise to this particular paradox, then when he gets into a situation where he has lost time and wishes to make it up, he may well seek to redeem the situation by bringing more and more men on site. But as he does that, he moves steadily to the right on our graph, Figure 12.5, and finally reaches the 'crash point'. From then on he gets nowhere. A chain reaction builds up: low productivity delays completion and costs mount rapidly. Despite all his efforts, he is moving ever further away from his cost and time targets.

The Owner *must* be involved

We have emphasised earlier, in Part 2, that the owner has the largest stake in any project, even if at times the bulk of the funds that he uses has been borrowed. Earlier in this chapter, when discussing 'cost effectiveness', we made mention of the activities of CICEP and the CII. We are told (7) that the Business Round Table that encouraged these organisations consists of the chief officers of some 200 leading US corporations and that the main thrust of their project is for the *owners*, as well as the contractors, to do a better job in the management of their personnel. Further, the CII has been sponsored by *owners* as well as contractors. Leading contractors, such as Brown & Root, Fluor, Lummus and Stearns-Roger have been joined by leading producers such as DuPont, Proctor & Gamble and Texaco. Emphasis is to be placed on the development of management tools and the techniques that will improve the execution of engineering and construction projects. All this revolves around cost control and cost effectiveness, as is very apparent from the work published to date. So please give cost control its proper place in your project.

References

1 Neil, James M., 'Construction Industry Cost Effectiveness Update given; implementation phase described', *Cost Engineering*, 26, pp.14–17, April 1984. (*Cost Engineering* is the journal of the American Association of Cost Engineers.)

2 Beaton, H., 'The Owner's Perspective on Project Management'. *Cost Engineering,* 26, pp.18–21. April 1984.

3 Kharbanda, O.P., Stallworthy, E.A. and Williams, L.F., *Project Cost Control in Action*, Gower, Aldershot, 1980, 273 pp.

4 Brochure: *Ok Tedi – Ready for the production of gold*, published by the Mining and Metals Division, Bechtel Civil & Minerals, Inc., San Francisco.

5 Thomas, K.O., 'Cost Control and the Small Construction Company', *Cost Engineering 25/6-a*, November 1983.

6 Starr, M.K., *Operations Management*, Prentice-Hall, 1978, 618 pp.

7 House journal: *Construction Update*, Spring 1984, p.6. Published by Lummas Crest, Broomfield, NJ, USA.

Part Four

DISASTER STRIKES

13   The nuclear power station

Nuclear power arrived on the scene some thirty years ago now: an awe-inspiring development full of promise for the future. It was anticipated that its use would immeasurably enhance our daily life by providing energy in abundance at minimum cost. To quote the chairman of the Atomic Energy Commission, as it was called in those early days:

> Nuclear energy ... would deliver electrical power too cheap to meter.

The basic source of electricity in most countries has been the coal-fired power station. It had been thought that even in countries rich in coal resources, such as the US and Britain, nuclear power would eventually take over as the prime energy source, but this has not happened.

It is apparent that there is a great deal of prejudice against nuclear power plants. For instance, as early as 1973 consumer advocate Ralph Nader admitted that he could *never* support nuclear power, no matter how safe it proved to be. A few years later anti-nuclear critic Amory Lovins admitted that even if he were convinced that nuclear power had *no* safety, proliferation or economic drawbacks, he would still oppose it for political reasons. Thus, whilst nuclear power still offers electrical power at competitive rates, as illustrated in Figure 13.1, it fails to make headway in the US.(1)

The disposal problem

Part of the problem, now coming more and more to the fore, is the

fact that the impact of the nuclear power station does not stay with
the station. We have an associated activity – the processing of
nuclear fuel – a work that *must* go on if the nuclear power station is
to remain in operation. Much of this fuel processing takes place at
British Nuclear Fuels Ltd in the UK. Maloperation of that plant
has resulted in 'radioactive' beaches in Cumbria, thus providing
the environmentalists with yet another stick with which to be-
labour the nuclear lobby.

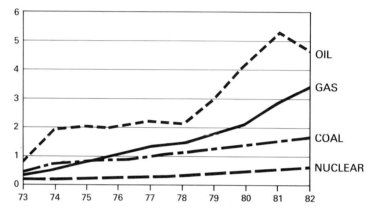

Figure 13.1   The cost of primary energy sources
This graph illustrates that, for the US, nuclear power stations still provide the
cheapest source of electrical energy. (Figures in current dollars)

The impact of safety regulations

Whilst the atomic energy industry in the US may well be the most
advanced in the world, it is now getting into very serious difficulties both from spiralling construction costs and ever more severe
safety requirements. The two are, of course, interrelated, as we
have demonstrated elsewhere.(2) To illustrate the trend, we can
cite the unprecedented refusal by the Federal Nuclear Regulatory
Commission in the US to license a new US$5,000 million nuclear
power project in Illinois because it had 'no confidence in its
safety'. The reason was said to be 'inadequate quality controls'
during its construction.(3) But the Byron Station in Illinois is only
one of at least a dozen new plants now approaching completion in
the US, and thus going to apply for operating licences in the near
future. The threat to their future is very real, because this refusal
was completely unexpected. No one can assess how many other
plants will be in similar trouble.

But many stations in the US, either planned or under construction, are not even being brought to completion. Not a single nuclear facility has been put on order since 1978. One of the most momentous cancellations came at the beginning of 1984. A half-finished nuclear power station at Marble Hill, Indiana, was abandoned after US\$ 2,500 million had been spent. The Marble Hill Plant is thought to be the most expensive nuclear project ever to be abandoned. One unit at the plant was said to be about 60 per cent ready, the other was about a third of the way along, but the electric supply company, the Indiana Public Service Company, said that they did not have the cash resources to finish the project. They have since rejected a joint proposal from Westinghouse, Bechtel Power Corp. and Sargent & Lundy for a management package designed to bring the project to completion.(4)

Of course, the reasons for all this are obvious enough to project engineers – and especially the cost engineers – involved in such projects. Estimates of the total erected cost of the installation had more than trebled in the ten years since the project was first approved. The first estimate, in 1973, was some US\$1,400 million. Now, ten years later, US\$2,500 million having been spent, the final estimated cost was being put at US\$7,000 million. Plans for more than a hundred nuclear power plants have been scrapped since Three Mile Island, but most of them, of course, at a much earlier stage in their development than Marble Hill.

All this presents an ever-increasing threat to an industry that at one time was said to be going to provide more than half of the electric power requirements of the US within the next twenty years. The present status is, roughly, that some 80 reactors have been put into successful operation and are producing about 15 per cent of the country's electricity. There are a further 60 stations under construction, of which perhaps 40 are more than half-completed, but as you can see from the examples just quoted above, this number is steadily dwindling as the cost of completion rises and the demands of the safety regulations increase, helped along by disillusioned shareholders and much public mistrust. Some estimates of cost are now more than ten times the estimate which had been the basis for approving the project in the first place.

Whoops!

But we are not out of trouble even when the plant is built and running. Apart from the potential threat of another 'Three Mile Island' incident, the plant has to pay its way. Not only has it to meet the cost of depreciation on the much increased capital investment, but the new stringency in operating conditions also increases running costs. So we meet the headline – 'Whoops, we cannot pay £1,433 million'.(5)

The name 'Whoops' has been given to the Washington Public Power Supply System by both consumers and investors. Since the early 1970s, 'Whoops' have been busy with a most ambitious nuclear power plant construction programme. Five plants, which were to have supplied a total of more than 80 public utility companies, were originally budgeted at about four billion dollars. By early 1982, that had soared to US$24 billion – six times! Now two of the plants have been cancelled and work has stopped on two others – that leaves them with one.

The acres of rusting steelwork at the construction sites present us with a grim picture of the present crisis facing the nuclear power industry, not only in the US but worldwide. But all that rusting plant and equipment has still to be paid for. It is that that led to the headline that caught our eye. The money had been borrowed, and the news was that the consortium of public utilities involved were expected to default on about US$2,250 million in bonds. 'Whoops' had indicated that they would be unable to meet the monthly interest payment on the bonds, which are widely held by large and small investors throughout the Pacific Northwest.

Years behind schedule

We have been looking, so far, at the American scene, but the situation in the UK is no better, even although it was in the UK, at Calder Hall, that the first nuclear power plant ever went on stream back in 1956. The Central Electricity Generating Board in the UK – there they have just the one, not the multiplicity of utility companies that there are in the States – placed their order for Dungeness 'B' nuclear power station back in 1965, for an estimated cost of some £90 million (US$ 150 million). Commissioning was planned for 1971. By 1982, with plant completion now more than *ten years* late, the final cost was said to be in the region of £550 million – costs had escalated more than six times.

Dungeness 'B' is just one of three advanced gas-cooled reactor power stations being commissioned at about the same time. The others are Hartlepool, ordered in 1967, also at an estimated cost of about £90 million, and *also* now going to cost more than £500 million, and Heysham 'A', ordered in 1969, at an estimated cost of £140 million. Of course, we do not need to tell you what *that* will cost on completion. You know already: more than £500 million! All three have been subject to much the same problems and much the same delay in completion. Of course, in comparing the first and last estimates for these plants, we must not forget the impact of inflation, which has been quite severe over the period of construction. Without doing any complicated calculations, it is probably fair to say that the true cost of these plants has about doubled and that factor of 2.0 is average for development projects, such as these undoubtedly were.

Nuclear power still in the development phase

If we take the story behind Dungeness 'B' as an illustration, it becomes very clear that all such plants are still 'development projects'. How foolish to begin three development projects all at about the same time, so that there was no possibility at all for the 'learning factor' to come into play and so reduce costs. Had they but delayed the second plant by three years, and begun the third plant some two years after that, they might well have halved the total cost.

But look at the explanation from one of the officials of the CEGB.(6) His use of the word 'prototype' makes it very, very clear that these were indeed development projects. He explained:

> Part of the problems have been due to prototype design troubles, but certainly the deterioration in equipment which has been standing doing nothing for many years has been a contributory factor. But we are now satisfied that the equipment is now up to the necessary standards and there are no safety risks.

The fact is that the time taken to move from the initial research through all the phases that eventually result in a commercial plant just is not appreciated. This has been very well illustrated in diagrammatic form in a paper on the 'energy outlook'.(7) The writer says that in general it takes 30 to 40 years for generation technology to work its way from early development to significant commercial penetration. This is illustrated graphically in Figure 13.2.

The PWR – case not proven

The pressurised water reactor (PWR) is one of several different

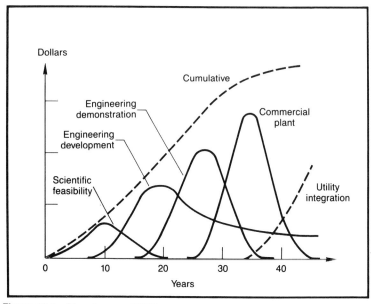

Figure 13.2   The phases of R&D
Here we see it can take up to 30 years to get from the first concept to
commercial availability where power generation technology is concerned.
(With acknowledgements to Mr Blair G. Swezey—see Ref. 7)

technical approaches to the production of the heat required for
making electric power from nuclear energy. We have just mentioned Dungeness 'B' and the other new stations in the UK that
will be using the advanced gas-cooled reactor, but in the US all the
stations built so far have utilised the PWR. The PWR system uses
enriched uranium with water as coolant and moderator. Due to
the activities of the US construction companies in this field, the
PWR has been largely used elsewhere in the world, notably in
France and Spain, despite the fact that the first public nuclear
power station to go on stream, in the UK, used natural uranium,
with gas as coolant and graphite as the moderator, this leading on
to the advanced gas-cooled reactors now coming into use in the
UK.

All this would lead one to believe that the 'development' phase
in nuclear engineering for electric power plants was well behind
us, especially with respect to the PWR. Some 200 plants are
running or nearing completion in the US, and 30 operating in
France. Worldwide there could now be more than 500 reactors in
operation or close to it. The profile against the skyline of such

plants has indeed become standard. They are almost invariably
built with two reactors and we present a completely typical view of
one such nuclear power station as Figure 13.3. The CEGB in the
UK certainly seemed to be of this opinion. For their next round of
nuclear power plants they decided to abandon their own 'gas
cooled' system and go for a proven design – the PWR. What
happens then?

Figure 13.3   A typical nuclear power plant
The TVA Sequoyah Nuclear Power Plant, substantially completed in 1979.
(Photograph by courtesy of the Tennessee Valley Authority, US)

That brings us to the heading of this section: 'A case not
proven', since that was the headline to a paper on the subject of
the public inquiry into the plans of the CEGB to build a PWR at
Sizewell in Suffolk, England.(8) It was anticipated that the results
of that particular inquiry would determine the future of nuclear
power in Britain. It was also expected to influence similar programmes in other countries, since the UK was pretty well the last of

the industrialised nations to adopt this particular reactor technology.

There are a number of very different factors involved in this
particular debate. There is the economics of production: what will
electricity from such a plant actually cost? There is the question of
capacity need: is such a plant required at all, with anticipated total
energy consumption estimated to fall, rather than grow, up to the
year 2000? Then there is the issue of 'fuel diversity'. With the
CEGB currently using coal for some 80 per cent of its supplies, it
could well be argued that it is desirable to diversify, but how much
and with what? Surely diversification should not be exclusively
towards nuclear power. What about 'renewables', such as wind,
tides and geothermal energy?

Yes, what about them? Unfortunately they are all largely
impractical in terms of coping with major power demands. For
instance, the Rance Power Station, driven by the tides, to which
we refer in some detail in Chapter 24, the largest such station in
the world, only delivers some 160MW out of a total installed
capacity of 240MW. This is but one sixth of the output of a single
nuclear power station. Geothermal plants are equally ineffective.
The total output of electricity from all the geothermal sites in the
world in 1975 was only 1175MW, just a little more than the output
of one single nuclear power station. So power from such sources is
not going to cope with the ever-growing demands of an industrialised society.

The estimates of cost and time

Of all these issues, the one that concerns us is the economic
argument, since that brings in the capital cost of the installation. It
is interesting to follow the arguments that have developed over
this issue. The initial cost appraisals made by the CEGB used
'targets' rather than expected values for construction cost and
project duration. They were compelled by the criticism to revise
their figures and to use estimates reflecting the 'most likely
outcome' rather than their earlier, highly optimistic 'targets'. In
passing, this debate throws an interesting light on those capital
cost estimates that get approved and later are so much overrun.
Here we see a bias, not only with those immediately involved in
the project but also with senior management, to present the
project in the most favourable light. Of what value, then, is later
comparison of those first estimates with the actual cost? Very
little, we fear.

But let us consider this subject a little further, and see what the Board had to say about 'sensitivity'. This is an assessment of the risk involved. What likelihood is there of the estimates used being met and what are the consequences if they are overrun? Can those consequences be borne? The evidence from the US, a little of which we have quoted above, would lead one to think that there was every likelihood of both cost and time being doubled. Would the plant still remain profitable if that happened? The Board were not prepared to consider that eventuality: for them, that could never happen. Yet consider their own record. The average real cost overrun on any kind of fossil-fired project had been some 25 per cent, and the *minimum* overrun on any of their nuclear installations had been more like 40 per cent. By 'real' overrun, we mean to imply costs with the impact of escalation excluded, since escalation is a separate factor in all such cost assessments. But the Board had, politically, to assert their ability to control nuclear construction costs and project durations. So their assessments did not really cover the credible range of possible outcomes, let alone what was still possible, if not probable.

The world's largest PWR construction programme

It is said that France builds nuclear reactors like other people build cars – on a production line. When France foresaw, in 1970, the coming significant increase in oil prices, oil being the fuel providing energy for some two-thirds of their needs at that time, it was decided to go ahead with a nuclear programme, standardising on 900-MW PWRs built under Westinghouse licence.(9) In 1976, Electricité de France (EDF) moved on to a second stage, using 1300-MW reactors. There are now some 60 units either commissioned or under construction which, when complete, will provide about 50 per cent of the total energy requirement of that country.

What interests us is the way in which these projects were handled. Whilst there was a high degree of standardisation, each unit had to be different, in that it had to be adapted to the specific conditions of each site, such as the method used for cooling, or the earthquake risk. The French nuclear power industry was reorganised to cope with the construction in series of the principal components, ensuring at the same time its technological independence.

The ecological problems also seem to have been overcome. Whilst there is still a 'hard core' of resistance to nuclear power, the public at large seem to accept the development. This is no doubt due to a great effort on the part of EDF. For instance, over a million leaflets have been distributed in response to requests, on subjects as diverse as geothermal power, biomass and heat pumps, as well as the French nuclear programme. Every day more than 500 letters seeking information are received and dealt with, and more than 20,000 people visit one or other of the nuclear power stations every year.

This demonstrates the degree to which success in project construction these days is dependent upon public relations. The project manager must indeed recognise the need for keeping the public, and especially the local people, fully aware of what is happening on their doorstep, and its relevance to *them*. The project managers for EDF make every attempt to weave the plant into the local economic fabric by helping local firms to share in its construction and by training local people so that they can be employed to work on the project. Yet another lesson for the project manager.

References

1   Walske, C. and Dobkin, R.A., 'The nuclear controversy', *Nuclear Active*, No. 30, January 1984. This is the house journal of the Atomic Energy Corporation of South Africa Ltd.

2   Kharbanda, O.P. and Stallworthy, E.A., *How to learn from project disasters*, 1983, Gower, Aldershot, Hants, UK, 274 pp. See particularly Chapter 2, 'Killed by kindness' and the section 'Nuclear regulations beat them all'.

3   News item: 'Safety curbs put U.S. atom industry in jeopardy', *Daily Telegraph*, London, 18 January 1984.

4   News Item: 'Marble Hill Owner rejects industry joint venture bid to complete unit'. *Nucleonics Week*, vol.25, no.25, 21 June 1984.

5   News item: 'Whoops, we cannot pay £1,433 million', *Daily Telegraph*, London, 17 May 1983.

6   News item: 'Nuclear plant equipment had to be replaced', *Daily Telegraph,* London, 4 August 1982.

7   Swezey, Blair G., 'Energy outlook: How much at what price?', *Cost Engineering,* 26, No.3-A, May 1984, pp.6–13.
8   Mackerron, G., 'A case not proven', *New Scientist,* vol.97, no. 1340, 13 January 1983, pp.76–9.
9   Carle, Remy, 'How France went nuclear', *New Scientist,* vol.97, no. 1340, 13 Jan. 1983, pp.84–6.

14   A desert dream becomes a disaster!

Back in 1975 a 50:50 joint venture company was formed between the National Iranian Oil Company and the Iran Chemical Company, a Japanese investment company formed by five companies in the Mitsui Group. They planned a petrochemical complex. Construction began in 1976, and it was all due for completion some three years later, in 1979. Now, another five years on, there is still no certainty: the project may be completed or it may be abandoned. Meanwhile the cost has escalated from an original estimate of some US$600 million to US$5.6 billion.

A desert dream ...

Our story goes back to 1968, when Sueyuki Wakasugi, then a top official in the Mitsui Group, unique in that it was established in the seventeenth century and is perhaps the oldest trading company in the world, was driving through the hot barren wasteland near Abadan, some 700 km south of Tehran. He saw something quite picturesque – the gas flaring at the distant oilfields. To give you some small idea of what he saw, we show you a flarestack with two flares in Figure 14.1. But he must have seen a forest of them. This sight led Wakasugi to dream of converting Iran's wasting resource, natural gas, into profitable petrochemicals through the use of Mitsui technology. There were a few years of gestation, then the dream led to the birth of the most expensive and the most embarrassing investment ever undertaken by a Japanese company.(1)

Figure 14.1 A typical flare stack
This photograph is typical only, and shows two flare stacks with the gas flaring to the sky. (Photograph by courtesy of Escher BV, The Hague, The Netherlands, manufacturers of specially designed plant for the oil, chemical, natural gas and process industries.)

... turned a nightmare

Now, two oil crises (1973 and 1979), one revolution (in Iran, 1978) and one war (between Iraq and Iran, 1980–) later, Wakasugi's dream has turned into a nightmare. After three years spent in feasibility studies, construction started on site in Iran in 1976. The project was reported to be 85 per cent complete and within six months of completion in March 1979, when work on site had to be stopped due to the Iranian revolution. The cost of the project had by then nearly doubled to US$1 billion, but there is much conjecture associated with that estimate and we suspect that it was on the low side.

The project as finally agreed consisted of a world-scale ethylene cracker, with a capacity of 330,000 tonnes per annum of ethylene, together with other derivatives and liquefied petroleum gas. The project made technical, commercial and even political sense. A waste resource was being converted into valuable products for which there was not only a direct need within Iran itself, but also an increasing world demand. Mitsui not only provided the necessary initiative but also the technology and the finance. In addition they underwrote the marketing of a substantial proportion of the finished products, since the Iranian domestic market was not all that large. It was a project patently in the best interests of both the main parties involved and, if it had been brought to a successful conclusion, both would have been well satisfied. But ...

The revolution as such over, construction of the complex was resumed in the summer of 1980 after protracted negotiations, but was halted again in October of that same year because of the outbreak of the Iraq–Iran War and the aerial bombing of the worksite. After several false starts and some further tough negotiation, the Iran government finally agreed to provide *all* the further finance required to complete the project.(2) But then Iraq threatened to bomb the site again (it had already suffered bomb damage) if work was resumed. This was what is known as a 'Catch 22' situation. The most recent news is that Mitsui have ordered their 135 Japanese engineers to stay away from the project site following a further attack by Iraqi warplanes.(3) It also appears that the Mitsui Manufacturing Bank is now in serious difficulty because of a high proportion of 'troubled loans' in its portfolio.(4) We ask ourselves: is the Iran project a significant contributor to these financial problems?

Petrochemicals and politics are 'oil and water'

Petrochemicals and politics just do not mix! This is to be seen worldwide, but the Bandur Shahapur Project, renamed the Bandur Khomeini Project after the Iranian revolution, must surely rank as a classic example. Those 'in the know' have ventured to term it 'the most expensive white elephant' in the history of the petrochemicals industry. This was said back in 1979 and it now seems that the most sensible, if sadly traumatic, decision even then would have been to abandon the project then and there. This because, had there been no further problems and the plant had been completed, it could not have made a profit till the late 1990s.

The project illustrates very clearly the problems of risk analysis when it comes to political judgements. Just two years prior to the revolution Iran was considered to be politically stable: one of the most stable countries in the Middle East and a prime area for industrial development. This must also have been the considered opinion of those shrewd Japanese businessmen who put their money into the venture, or they would never have begun. Of course, there was strong motivation for the project in that the Japanese were thereby making sure of a crude oil entitlement. This was undoubtedly the main factor and a fundamental prerequisite to Mitsui investing in this billion-dollar project. But that too was very dependent upon political stability.

A prime lesson to be learnt from this project is that risk analysis is valueless in the face of political uncertainty. The only way to assess the political prospects is by 'intuition', a 'gut feeling' or a 'sixth sense': what you will. If you are prepared to put your trust in such an emotional assessment, then do so, but recognise that you can still be wrong. Without the political problems, and given the normal measure of goodwill from both sides, this project could have been completed very satisfactorily, to the mutual profit of both partners. Once 'politics' took over, far and away the best thing for the Japanese to have done would have been to get out and cut their losses. But that is easier said than done. Mitsui did indeed try, but Japan has so few options. Japanese investment in Iran and elsewhere in the Middle East has been dictated mainly by the desire to ensure an uninterrupted supply of crude oil and related products.(5) This is the object of 'entitlements', as they are called, an integral part of the contract entered into for this project. This basic motivation behind such Japanese investment has been confirmed by independent Western observers.(6)

A private project becomes a national problem

So far as the Japanese were concerned, this particular joint venture started out as a 'private sector' project, involving some companies in the Mitsui Group of Japan. The government were not consulted. Presumably there was no legal requirement to do so and perhaps Mitsui thought that they had negotiated such a good deal with Iran that they had better keep it all to themselves. This approach was in sharp contrast to that adopted by the joint ventures for petrochemical complexes entered into by Mitsubishi in Saudi Arabia and Sumitomo at Singapore. Both of these were declared 'national projects' from the very start. They were approved by the government beforehand and as government-sponsored projects they enjoyed financial and other support from the Japanese government.

When the Iranian project ran into trouble it was burdened with interest payments then running as high as US$450,000 *per day*. Apart from loss of 'face', Mitsui stood to lose some US$68 million in hard cash, this representing the uninsured portion of the project. This came at a time when the overall prospects for the Group were none too good. So – this was in December 1978 – the then Chairman of Mitsui, Yoshido Ikeda, suggested that real political determination was now needed to deal with a very serious situation. He therefore requested the Japanese Prime Minister to declare the project a 'national project'. The reaction of the government was that, whilst they were prepared to 'pitch in', they were not willing to bail Mitsui out. As for declaring the project a 'national project', why should they? The Government had not been consulted as had been the case with the other two projects termed 'national projects'.(1)

One of the prerequisites to declaring a project a 'national project' was that a number of different Japanese companies were to be involved, but here there was only one – Mitsui. To overcome this particular hurdle, Mitsui persuaded some 70 other Japanese companies and 20 banks to invest a total of US$23 million in the project. This was designed to secure Government support. At the same time, representatives from MITI and the Ministry of Finance, who had underwritten the project, visited Iran. They concluded that, whilst the project did not have a very bright economic future the Japanese Government would be the biggest loser, since they had insured the project.

As a result of all this 'wheeling and dealing' the project was finally declared a 'national project', the Japanese government together with the Export-Import Bank agreeing to help to salvage the project by investing in it.(7) This was in October 1979. The total new investment at that time was some US$440 million, of which US$88 million had been found by the Japanese government and the rest by the Import-Export Bank and some other commercial banks. At this same time the estimated cost of the project had risen to US$3.2 billion.

A political football

Just to see how politics now played a key role in the further progress – or lack of progress – of this project, let us follow its history from October 1979 onwards, when the Japanese Government finally took a hand.

January 1980	In order to safeguard its venture, Japan will not join with the US in imposing sanctions against Iran.
May 1980	Mitsui allowed to resume work following tense bargaining in Tokyo, Tehran and Washington.
June 1980	Work will only resume after resolution of the dispute over the American 'hostages'.
October 1980	The Bandur Khomeini complex bombed several times by Iraq. All 750 Japanese workers transferred from site to Tehran. The Iranian Government want them to stay. Were they, too, hostages?
November 1980	Japan must decide whether to pull out with a potential loss of US$1.4 billion or come up with a further US$80 million or more to keep the project afloat.

It is at this point that a Mitsui executive declares: 'If we continue we will fall into hell. If we withdraw we fall into hell.' Iran was pressing Japan to pay half the construction costs incurred before suspension, some US$120 million, together with the costs of repatriating the Japanese workers and the interest payments on loans and salaries for 1,400 Iranians. Don't forget that Mitsui had a 50 per cent stake in the project and should therefore have borne 50 per cent of the cost. The Vice-Minister for International Affairs back in Japan, Naohiri Amaya, declared:

> Japan must not give up the project ... it will decide the destiny of relations between Japan and the Middle East.

But despite all the pressures, the Japanese companies flatly refused to send any more workers to Iran until the war was over.

Just in passing, the total estimated cost had now risen to US$4.8 billion.(8)

The sorry tale continues. Let us bring the story more or less up to date now that we have come so far. The emphasis now moves from the 'political' as such to the 'financial'. Thus:

April 1981	Pending further negotiation Mitsui will not invest further funds.
July 1981	Mitsui will spend no more money, but remain ready to sell equipment and offer technological aid.
January 1982	Mitsui seek one-year delay in the repayment of US$22.7 million in loans from Japanese banks.
May 1983	Japan reaches agreement with Iran to resume work on the complex, stalled since October 1980. Iran has agreed to meet *all* additional finance required. But Iraq threatens to bomb the installation again if work is resumed.
February 1984	Mitsui have ordered their 135 Japanese engineers to stay away from the site once again, following attacks by Iraqi warplanes.

Well, that is as far as we can take the history of this project at the moment. As you will see, it is effectively 'stalemate'.

Enough is enough

We are looking at Japan's biggest single foreign investment. The Japanese consortium decided in April 1983 that they would not make any further investment, despite Iran's insistence that Mitsui should increase their investment to cover their share of the enormous cost overrun, both present and future.(9) A Japanese official working at the site had sought to take stock at this time, when some US$3.6 billion had already been spent and estimated that a further US$2 billion would be needed to complete the project and get it working. This further expenditure has to be viewed against falling oil production and a large reduction in the oil revenues accruing to Iran. Also, as a result of the Iraq–Iran War and the destruction that had occurred at the Abadan Refinery, that cheap gas feedstock had also largely disappeared.

All these factors brought Mitsui to the conclusion that 'enough was enough'. The 'last straw' apparently was an Iranian veto on a plan to pay off the Iranian workers for the duration of the war.

The Japanese Government had also backed out, refusing to pay the US$94 million that they had agreed to provide earlier. Mitsui, to protect their own interest in the project, continue to express their determination to complete the project, but they at the same time resolutely refused to commit any more funds.

A peep into the future

By 1981 the complex had already been bombed five times. The immediate future, whilst the war continues, seems to hold only the threat of further bombing if work is resumed. In addition, due to the passage of time, much of the equipment on site has deteriorated due to lack of protective maintenance.(10)

Meanwhile the international scene had changed quite drastically. In view of the limited domestic market, the bulk of the products from the complex were to have been exported, but now two other world-scale petrochemical complexes have been completed, one in Saudi Arabia and the other in Singapore, and are taking up the market long before Bandur Khomeini is finished. In addition, looking only at the Near and Far East, further projects in China, India, Indonesia, Malaysia and Thailand are in advanced stages of planning. Except for those in India and China, these plants will all be making the bulk of their products for export. Since there is still general overcapacity in petrochemicals worldwide, the gravity of this in relation to Bandur Khomeini is apparent. There is no longer a market. They are going to be far too late. This is a continuing dilemma for both parties.

The motivation appears to remain political, rather than economic. Iran, as a matter of national pride, will want to see the project completed and producing. Perhaps, if it provides adequate protection against imports, the home market could be large enough to keep the plant operating at an economic level, even if it works well below capacity for many years to come. Iran, despite the fact that the original approach was on a 50:50 basis, is now likely to insist on complete management control.

Mitsui have even greater problems, in that having lost so much they just cannot afford to lose any more. They are willing to complete the project, but only if they are adequately paid for the work that remains to be done. It is very evident that there will have to be a large measure of goodwill and a real spirit of 'give and take' if the two parties are ever to agree to cooperate once again.

Overshadowing it all is the fact that the economics of operation have come into question. There are many who argue that it is still cheaper to scrap the entire project, sell off what can be sold off, and so 'cut the losses'. So the debate goes on ... and on.

Could it have been foreseen?

We have taken a look at this particular project to see what lessons there are for the construction industry. It is very clear that disaster came primarily because the political situation changed drastically overnight. Could that have been foreseen? The answer to that is simple and direct: it is *no*. The future *cannot* be predicted, however much economists would like us to believe that it can. This is therefore a 'fact of life' that the construction industry has to reckon with, but cannot avoid.

For example, only a few months before the oil crisis of 1973, the pundits were full of predictions, but they were all rosy ones. They saw no change coming. But, once the change came, they pointed out that their predictions had been qualified. So they still professed to be right. It is somewhat like the weather-man telling us that there is a 10 per cent chance of it raining today. Whether it rains or not he is right! However, having heard his forecast and seeing that the possibility of rain was less than 50 per cent, we made our judgements, went out without an umbrella – and got wet!

So did Mitsui.

References

1   Wiegner, K.K., 'Saving Skin but Losing Face' *Forbes*, 124, 74ff., 15 Oct. 1979.
2   *New York Times*, 19 May 1983, IV, 6:1.
3   *Wall Street Journal*, 17 Feb. 1984, 34:2.
4   *Wall Street Journal*, 19 March 1984, 1:6.
5   El-Zaim, I., 'Japanese Corporate Strategy and Orientations', *Arab Economist*, 2, 5–32, December 1978.
6   Report: '*Middle East Industrialisation*', published by the Royal Institute of International Affairs, 1980, 220 pp.
7   *Wall Street Journal*, 15 Oct. 1979, 12:3.
8   *Wall Street Journal*, 25 Nov. 1980, 30:2.
9   Editorial: 'Mitsui moves to a showdown', *Economist*, 279, pp.79-80, 2 May 1981.
10 Hyde, M., *Chemical Insight*, no. 200, 1980. (*Chemical Insight*, published twice monthly, presents Mike Hyde's perspective on the international chemical industry.)

15   A Vienna waltz

We are now going to review a project in Austria, the home of the waltz. We are going to take a look at the Vienna General Hospital. Contracts for this 2,100-bed hospital complex were awarded in 1960, for completion in 1968, at an estimated total cost of some US$320 million. The decision to build such a hospital, a joint venture between the Austrian Federal Government and the Vienna City Administration, was first taken in 1955. Planned for completion some fifteen years ago, it is not yet complete, nor is it expected to be before about 1990 – and then at a cost of some US$4 billion. In other words, by then the cost will have escalated roughly thirteen times. In this it parallels the construction of the Sydney Opera House, which we shall review in the following chapter (Chapter 16), but without the same excuse. Here there is no question of technical development: we are talking about a standard hospital complex – up-to-date, for sure, but no more than that. No, as we shall see, the causes of the devastating delay and enormous increase in cost have nothing to do with design development or the complexities of construction.

We have here a classic case of bribery and corruption, leading to one of the greatest political scandals of our times, that finally resulted in the resignation of Austria's Foreign Minister. In Chapter 10 we discussed some of the things that go on in the construction industry which those who have to work in it and with it have to be aware of and cope with. We thought it appropriate, therefore, that one of our case studies should highlight this particular aspect of construction work.

A tale of delay and bribery

A typical headline in 1980, when the scandal first broke loose, ran

'Vienna Waltz – A tale of delay and bribery'.(1) It all started innocently enough, with a routine progress report in 1979 which expressed concern at the lack of progress and suspected mismanagement. This suspicion was leaked to the press, but it only confirmed what was already common knowledge: that there was a huge cost overrun and a twelve-year delay in completion (1968 to 1979). No one was particularly interested.

However, the Austrian weekly news magazine *Profil* took up this issue and its reporter interviewed Adolf Winter, director of Vienna's *Allgemeine Krankenhaus* (General Hospital). The resulting investigative report indicated that the project involved the biggest bribery scandal in Austria since World War II. Winter immediately denied it, but since the interview had been taped by the reporter, he had no way out. On further investigation the magazine discovered a 'web of payoffs, fraud, corruption and secret bank accounts', its story rocking the Socialist government of Chancellor Bruno Kreisky to its foundations. Apart from damaging the ruling party's reputation, the disclosures led to sweeping investigations into tax fraud not only with respect to the construction of the hospital, but also in relation to other large construction projects such as the Zwentendorf Nuclear Power Station, the headquarters of the International Atomic Energy Commission and UNIDO (United Nations Industrial and Development Organisation). Norbert Steger, head of the investigating parliamentary committee, warned: 'huge amounts of money have been illegally handled ... the taxpayers have been defrauded beyond belief'.

A bribe the norm

Such investigations have now become big business in Austria. The evidence from public polls is that three out of four Austrians believe that bribes are the 'norm' with public construction projects. Newspapers give prominence to such news almost every day and the TV news broadcasts go so far as to use charts to explain the link between the federal and city officials and the 700 or so contractors and subcontractors involved with the hospital project.(1)

To get down to detail, Siegfried Wilfling, at 41 the Director of the city's Hospital Department and Adolf Winter, at 40 the Technical Director of the hospital project, were accused of having millions of dollars held in secret bank accounts in Liechtenstein, Switzerland and the Cayman Islands. To pay for such services the contractors would 'overbill'. Then the accused would pass those bills, a fee being deposited in their secret accounts. Apart from these two officials, another seven top executives of ITT Austria, Siemens Austria and Knoblich-Licht, all contractors working on the project, were taken into investigative arrest, under which they can be held for investigation for a period of up to three months. The Chancellor's own reputation did not suffer, since he was not personally linked with the scandal, but the disclosures did hurt the political standing of his ambitious Finance Minister and possible successor, Hannes Androsch, who ultimately had to resign. A Socialist Party official commented: 'It's an unholy mess'. The charges were ultimately proved and the guilty were sentenced to several years' imprisonment. But the project has still to be completed. As we said earlier, it is now likely to take up to 30 years in all to bring to final completion, at a total cost perhaps 15 times the original estimate.

A sorry story

The hospital consists of a massive complex topped by two 13-storey towers that have become infamous landmarks in Vienna city. A construction period of some 30 years and a cost of about US$2 million per bed (2,100 beds at a total cost of US$4 billion) must remain an all-time 'high' for any hospital anywhere ever. It is certainly far higher than the cost of another hospital that achieved notoriety in somewhat similar fashion – the King Feisal Specialist Hospital at Riyadh in Saudi Arabia, to which we shall return later.

The story of the disclosures goes roughly as follows:

February 1980   Following the disclosures in *Profil* five officials are arrested pending investigation. Adolf Winter is charged with having accepted US$8.3 million, paid by Siemens into his bank account in Liechtenstein. Four executives of Siemens and its associated companies are arrested with him.

July 1980   Nine officials now under arrest. This could become the biggest corruption scandal ever. The Mayor and the Finance Minister, both strong contenders to succeed the Chancellor, must assume ultimate responsibility for the huge 'kickbacks' that have been paid.

August 1980   Since four of the nine accused are Freemasons,
                     that society is accused of misusing its connec-
                     tions. Judge Helene Partik-Pable is under
                     police guard after receiving an anonymous
                     death threat.

An all-party Parliamentary Committee had been set up to investigate the matter, with the result that public attention was now
focused on the 'business among friends' system apparently ram-
pant throughout Austrian society. Mention was made in the press
of the powerful 'Club of 45', also known as the 'Red barons', a
group of bankers with leanings towards the 'left' in politics. Three
of those detained were members of this 'club'.

By September of 1980 the scandal was surging towards a climax.
The press, not only in Austria, but abroad and especially in New
York, were full of items on various aspects of the case. These 'tales
from the Vienna Woods' seemed but echoes of the stories one
once used to hear about Tammany Hall in New York. The
investigators had obtained access to the accounts of Plantech and
Geproma, letterbox companies set up by Adolf Winter, and found
a total of US$4 million. About US$1 million had come from ITT
and US$3 million from Siemens in payment for 'consulting ser-
vices'. An ITT aide, Fritz Mayer, testified that US$1.6 million was
the 'normal' commission on a US$32 million contract, and that the
payment of such commissions was a common practice.

Another year passed, and by November of 1981 the Austrian
Courts had convicted and sentenced a total of 12 defendants for
bribery in connection with the construction of the hospital. They
were mostly business executives of various companies who had
contracted for work on the hospital. The sentences ranged from
one year on probation to 5–9 years in jail. It was estimated that the
total paid out in this way was some US$2.7 million. Perhaps it is
invidious to mention names, but one of those sentenced was the
Chairman of ITT Austria and also Chairman of the Austrian
Industries Association. At the age of 74 he received a three-year
sentence.

Is that the end of the story?

Not really! How could it be? It is but the end of a phase – a gloomy
and dark one, at that. This story shows very clearly that human
greed knows no bounds. Not only is it unlimited in extent, but the
highest in the land can succumb. Truly international construction

is 'big business', but unfortunately that can only mean that the corruption is on an even bigger scale.

Do not think for a moment that this story is exceptional. It is perhaps noteworthy chiefly because we are able to 'read all about it'. You will have noticed that the defence was that what was being done was 'customary' and 'common practice'. We are looking at a project in Austria, so we observe that in that country this was not the only 'scandal' of its type. A headline in April 1983 attracted our attention. It told us that nine Austrians had been convicted of siphoning off millions of dollars in relation to a housing complex in Bergenland province. It is happening all the time – and not only in Austria.

Dark deals – a crown slips

This was the headline to a detailed account of the Vienna Hospital scandal in one of the weeklies.(2) We are told that the daily revelation of corruption in relation to this project and elsewhere had two indirect and unexpected results. Firstly, there was press-ure on the Government to introduce new legislation, providing stiffer penalties for cases of corruption. The second was that it brought welcome publicity to an opposition party, the Freedom Party, its new and then unknown leader, Norbert Steger, being catapulted into the headlines. Back in 1980 this weekly magazine, an impartial onlooker, published from the UK, predicted that the scandal could well lose the ruling Socialist Party the majority in the next General Election. It did.

Hannes Androsch, the Finance Minister and chief architect of Austria's economic success for a decade, had the unique distinc-tion of support not only from the trade unions but also from the business community. The youngest Finance Minister ever (thirty-two) when appointed to the post in 1970, and also the longest serving, he was considered to be the logical successor to the then Chancellor, Bruno Kreisky, coming up to 70 and due to retire. But a promising future collapsed overnight. He had an interest in a tax consulting firm, Consultatio, which was a beneficiary of the project. Although not directly implicated in the scandal, Hannes Androsch could not evade responsibility. Even though he agreed to sell his consultancy firm and reorganise the Finance Ministry so that he had less power, these moves came too late. The intensive investigations disclosed damaging circumstances that had nothing to do with the hospital scandal as such. For instance, it appeared that he helped his father-in-law obtain a very favourable loan for the purchase of a luxurious villa, and had put close friends in charge of banks and nationalised industries.

Finally, he fell out with the Chancellor himself. There was only one piece of evidence linking Hannes Androsch with the scandal, a document held by a former manager of his consultancy firm Consultatio that hinted at his indirect involvement. This Hannes Androsch strenuously denied. However, when the Chancellor, Bruno Kreisky, was asked whether he believed in this denial, he replied: 'When the Vice-Chancellor says something, I must believe him'. This was less than the full backing that Hannes Androsch had desired and as a result the relations between the two worsened, climaxing in the resignation of Hannes Androsch in disgust. When the elections came in 1983 the Socialist Party lost their absolute majority, and true to his promise the Chancellor, Kreisky, resigned. He was succeeded by Fred Sinowatz, a Socialist, who now leads a Coalition Government with the Liberal Party. Incidentally, Kreisky remains unscathed and his record of effort for peace and amity among the nations remains outstanding. He has received the 1984 Nehru Award for International Understanding.(3)

Another white elephant

The King Feisal Specialist Hospital at Riyadh in Saudi Arabia is a wonderful example of the latest technology. It is claimed to be the world's most advanced and it has certainly been a showpiece for visitors to Saudi Arabia. It was intended to translate into practice a dream of King Feisal. He wished to provide the latest that medicine, engineering and modern technology could offer for the health care of the people of his country. The King did not live to see his dream fulfilled. Indeed, we dare to say that although the hospital has now been completed and is in full operation, his dream has still not been fulfilled.

The King died a few weeks before the hospital was finally opened in 1975. Perhaps that was just as well since the hospital has since been described as a 'white elephant', a classic example of 'everything that has gone wrong with modern technology'. These are the words of Dr Kenneth Williams, the British physician who planned the hospital and helped to create it. He now laments: 'It was a fascinating study in the uncontrolled use of money'. First estimated to cost some US$10 million, the final price tag is believed to be of the order of US$250 million.(4) That gives us a final cost of roughly US$1 million per bed, roughly half that for the hospital in Vienna that we have just been looking at, but still an exorbitant price to pay. It may be thought of as a 'showpiece', but what does it actually show? It shows the way in which the latest technology, together with the greed displayed by the contractors and medical hardware suppliers of the various countries involved, can escalate health care costs to dazzling heights.

This 250-bed hospital is the very first to be built in a developing country with an integrated, computerised control system. There are 18 computers and the system processes all sorts of data, from a patient's case history to his menu for the day, and finally prints his bill. Cardiac patients are each 'hooked' into their own individual computer terminal, whereby all the vital data are recorded, such as body temperature, blood pressure and pulse rate. Intensive care patients are televised on a closed circuit system so that doctors and others can maintain a close watch whilst sitting in their offices. Operations are filmed and recorded on videotape in full colour. With such comprehensive automation one would surmise that far fewer staff would be required as compared with the average hospital and that the doctors would have 'all the time in the world' to devote to their patients. Far from it! The total staff numbers 1,200 and is still growing. The patients have become but numbers, lost within the complexity of the system. The personal touch, so essential for confidence in the staff and the cure of the patient, is completely missing.

Although this hospital was British in concept, it was built by a Lebanese contractor, using technology and hardware from Britain, Europe and Japan. It is now managed by the Hospital Corporation of America. This health care project became a political football, the hospital a stadium and the patients merely spectators! For the person who first planned the project, Dr Williams, the dream now only exemplifies an escalation of health care costs that brings no reward, with the transformation of a noble cause through greed and corruption, whilst at the same time the patient, for whom it was all being done, has been completely dehumanised.

Construction or corruption

Throughout this chapter we have reviewed, not the technical aspects of the construction of the projects under review, but the 'human factors'. Back in Chapter 10 ('The construction "jungle"') we dwelt at length on the 'ugly' side of the construction industry. Here, in the building of what should have been a noble project, a hospital for the benefit and wellbeing of the sick, we see the end result of such practices. We see that where greed and corruption dominate, the project will inevitably overrun in terms of cost and time. With our first case study, the corruption was uncovered and some of those involved were punished. With the second case study, there were no such disclosures, but the end result is equally unhappy.

Let those involved in construction at whatever level recognise that the 'human factor' can either make or mar any project. Success or failure depends, ultimately, on the sincerity, the honesty and the integrity of the majority of those involved. We say 'majority' because there will *always* be a minority who cheat, and steal, and deceive. Among the majority we have identified some of the people involved in the 'dark deals' associated with the construction of the Vienna General Hospital. Among the minority is Chancellor Kreisky, who continues to 'shine' in the 'darkness'.

References

1 'A Vienna Waltz', *Time*, 25 August 1980, p.28.
2 'Dark deals – A crown slips', *Economist,* 276, issue of 9 August 1984, p.41. See also issue of 27 Sept. 1980.
3 *Times of India*, 13 July 1984.
4 O'Brien, R.B., article in the London *Daily Telegraph* of 30 October 1979 with the headline 'Saudi's space age hospital "inhuman" says doctor'.

16   The Sydney Opera House

So much has been written about the Sydney Opera House, built on Bennelong Point and overlooking Sydney Harbour, that our readers may well wonder why we have chosen to return to the subject once again. This wonderful building has been written about from so very many different points of view. As long ago as 1973 a book appeared with the title, *The Other Taj Mahal: What happened to the Sydney Opera House*.(1) The title of this book tells us well enough its theme. This is also true of another book *Great Planning Disasters*,(2) which has a chapter entitled 'Sydney's Opera House'. The writer declares plainly:

> Even if the Sydney Opera House is a great architectural triumph, it is without doubt a planning disaster.

Our attention was first drawn to the building because of its cost: the cost escalated some 14 times from the date of the first estimate (1957) to completion of the building in 1973. It is true, of course, that the very first estimate was only prepared to obtain 'a price comparison between the three winning schemes' that were then under consideration and was never intended to be an accurate estimate of the cost of construction. Indeed, it never could be, because the sketches available gave far too little information. Nevertheless, it is the figure that is always quoted when comparisons are made. For this reason it was featured as a frontispiece in our book *How to learn from project disasters*.(3) So what else is there to say about this building?

Those sailing roofs

Whether seen by day or night, the unusual sailing-ship form of this building is a sight that no one forgets. Its design may still be the subject of debate, but many, not only the visitors but also professional architects, declare it to be one of the twentieth century's great buildings. People become lyrical when describing what they see. To quote:(4)

> A splendid craft about to set sail on a mythical voyage. A flight of gulls, wings spread, motionless, fishing. The Sydney Opera House seems to belong for all time to the water. A lyric symbol anchored at the heart of the city, this city that looks out to ocean's horizon, with houses and gardens flowing down slopes to the inlets, its life always in some way bound up with the sea and ships. The Opera House seems to rise up out of the waves: the entire structure rests on a Tarpeian rock bed of sandstone outcropping at water level. It is crowned by three articulated roof systems, which from some angles resemble gigantic shells, or sails billowing in a wind forever captive.

To see what our writer is getting at, look at Figure 16.1, where we see the building in the context of the city of Sydney.

Seeing that the theme of this present book is 'construction', we thought we could well take a look at and learn from the construction of those 'shells' that form the roof of the building and give it its characteristic appearance.

Design development

When the building was first conceived the architects of the day had great faith in the omnipotence of the shell, or curved dome design for roofs. The chief design problem in those early days was the design of the shell roofs themselves, in order that they might be structurally viable. Their very shape did not let them act as true shells, as their form produced very high stress concentrations at the base. The firm of Ove Arup & Partners (now the Ove Arup Partnership) had been appointed as structural and civil engineering consultants directly after the competition result was known in 1957, and the design of these shells became a considerable task for them from then onwards. By 1965 they had spent nearly 400,000 hours on the project, the root of the problem being the difficulty in determining a satisfactory solution to the shell design.

Work on construction in the field began early in 1959, on the foundations. The roof design was finally ready in 1962, after five

Figure 16.1 Sydney from the air
This view illustrates the contrast between the Sydney Opera House and its immediate environment. (Photograph by courtesy of the New South Wales Government Offices, London)

Figure 16.2   The Sydney Opera House
This view, where the roofs show up stark against the sky, demonstrates very
clearly the final form that the shells took. (Photograph by courtesy of Ove
Arup Partnership, London)

years' work by the Ove Arup Partnership. There was a continual progression in design development, as various forms were investigated which were structurally feasible and might also satisfy the rigorous aesthetic demands of the architect. Once an approved design was available, the contract for the roofs was negotiated, but the work was not completed until 1967.(1) But although the roof had presented so many problems from a design point of view, it was not really a significant factor so far as cost was concerned. By 1967 the frame was there, but what was to go inside ? It is here that so many, many changes were made and it is here that the costs escalated.

The shell

Well, what have we got? The shell or sail-like form of the roofs is at its most impressive when seen silhouetted against the sky as one stands in the shadow of Sydney Harbour Bridge and looks across the harbour at the building, as in Figure 16.2. Here we are some 700 metres distant. We can see the shell roof to the main hall, with to the right a second roof, where the Harbour Restaurant is located. Behind the roof to the main hall, but hardly to be seen in this view, is the roof to the smaller hall designed for the presentation of opera.

The original concept was by Utzon, an architect from Denmark, whose design was chosen in open competition from some 200 entries from more than 30 countries. It has been said of him that he was a man of immense imaginative gifts, that his concept was of a building 'not of this age'. To quote from the report of the assessors (all architects) who awarded Utzon's design the first prize in the competition:

> The drawings submitted for the scheme were simple to the point of being diagrammatic. Nevertheless we have returned again and again to the study of these drawings and we are convinced that they present a concept of an opera house which is capable of becoming one of the great buildings of the world. We consider this scheme to be the most creative and original submission. Because of its very originality it is clearly a controversial design. We are, however, absolutely convinced about its merits.

Of course, Utzon's submission comprised a number of drawings, plans and elevations. We present a simplified version of his competition entry, longitudinal section, as Figure 16.3.

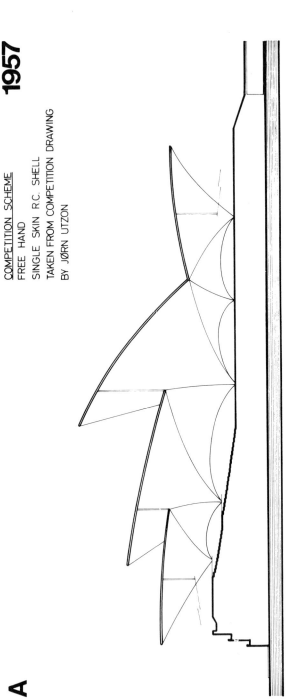

A

1957

COMPETITION SCHEME
FREE HAND
SINGLE SKIN R.C. SHELL
TAKEN FROM COMPETITION DRAWING
BY JØRN UTZON

Figure 16.3   Utzon's competition entry
A longitudinal section, showing the initial concept of the sailing roofs very clearly. This was the basic design in 1957.
(Reproduced by permission of Ove Arup Partnership, London)

He had been considerably influenced by Mayan and Aztec architecture which he had seen in Central America. There the temples were built on platforms and this design is to be seen in the Opera House. The platform is approached by steps, and it is possible to walk round the stage areas on this elevated platform, the harbour being in view at all times through the extensive glass walls in the side and end foyers. It would appear that Utzon conceived his scheme unaided by any structural engineering advice. Once the design had been accepted, his outline had to be converted into concrete reality. This was a saga in itself, as we have seen. Whilst Utzon had conceived the roof as thin shells, it was said that this was not technically feasible, since the very shape of the roof introduced high bending moments.

Development and finalisation of the design of the roofs alone, as we said earlier, was not achieved until 1962. You will notice that Utzon's initial design, Figure 16.3, is labelled 'A'. The final spherical scheme for the roofs, labelled 'M', is presented here as Figure 16.4.

To reach this point demanded intensive research, not only into the design of the roofs themselves, but also into the geology of the chosen location on Bennelong Point, the design of the foundations and base of the building that would have to support the roof structure. The roof structure itself had to be proved stable under all possible loads, without undue distortion and the wind load on a structure of this type of curved surface was completely unknown. So wind tunnel tests had to be carried out. These were conducted at the National Physical Laboratory at Teddington on a mahogany wood model. The technical aspects of the developing design have been presented in great detail in a paper first published in the *Structural Engineer* in 1969.(5)

The problems involved in project management, where experiments were being conducted on the other side of the world, whilst at the same time construction was proceeding on site, need only to be mentioned to be appreciated. This type of problem, typical of what we call a 'development project', always adds substantially to the final cost.

The glass walls

Another outstanding feature of the building are the glass walls that enclose what we might call the 'open end' of each shell, thus enclosing the openings betweeen the roof shells and the podium structure. These walls were all part of the original concept by

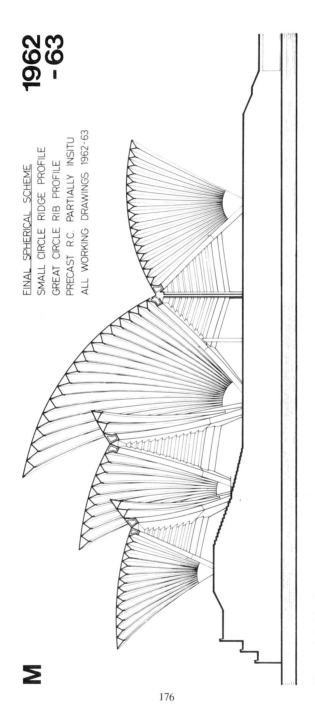

FINAL SPHERICAL SCHEME
SMALL CIRCLE RIDGE PROFILE
GREAT CIRCLE RIB PROFILE
PRECAST R.C. PARTIALLY INSITU
ALL WORKING DRAWINGS 1962-63

1962
-63

M

Figure 16.4   The final spherical scheme
The scheme as finally adopted and built. Each shell is made up of two half-shells, mirrored about the vertical plane of the hall axis. Each half main shell is formed of concrete ribs, as indicated on the diagram, and the smooth outer surface is covered with ceramic tiles, off-white in colour. (Reproduced by permission of Ove Arup Partnership, London)

Utzon. At the time when he resigned from the project, in 1966, the foundations, podium and roofs were almost complete, but the building an empty shell. The architectural practice of Hall, Todd and Littlemore was specially created for the project and appointed to complete Stage III, the halls themselves. Hall was responsible for the design whilst Todd and Littlemore were responsible for contract drawings and documents, project progress, etc. They were immediately confronted with the problem of the design of the glass walls. Numerous alternative geometrical forms and materials had been investigated, but no satisfactory solution had, up to then, been found.

The scheme finally selected, consisting of a continuous glass surface enclosing a steel structure, was adopted in 1967. To achieve a successful detailed design there had to be extensive research into both construction materials and construction techniques. Construction of the glass walls was finally begun in 1970 and completed in 1972. Despite three years of preparatory work, the design of the glass walls was in fact carried out in parallel with their construction, since time was running out: the building had to be clad if only to keep the weather out and so allow all the other interior works to proceed.

The choice of glass (laminated safety glass) was determined by the need to cut the glass to shape on site, so complicated was the final design. In Figure 16.5 we see all the various shapes required for just one wall – and almost every sheet had to be a different shape. There were in all some 20 such walls to be constructed. As will be realised, there was an enormous amount of glass to be sawn on site: so much that it was feared that the work of sawing would not keep up with the rate of construction. To overcome the problem, two purpose-built sawing machines were designed and built by specialist subcontractors and what amounted to a factory was set up on site to deal solely with the processing and handling of the glass prior to erection. The glass was cut by the saw on a single pass, and on its return the cut edge was arrised by abrasive wheels. For those who like numbers, the average cutting speed was 0.5 metres per minute. Of course, in introducing you to the complications of the glass walls, we have skipped all the technical details: the design and erection of the ribs, mullions and glazing bars, the sealing and water-proofing techniques. But those whose interest goes that far can read it all up in the technical journals.(5)(6)(7)

Once again we have seen design running parallel with construction, but bringing the glass cutting operation to the site was undoubtedly a very astute move. What we hope we have demonstrated by our study, first of the shells and now of the glass walls, is

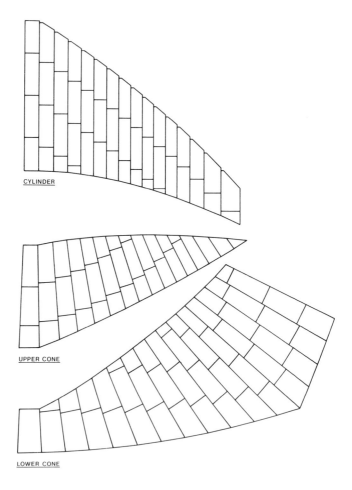

CYLINDER

UPPER CONE

LOWER CONE

Figure 16.5   Glass wall at entrance to Opera Hall
This is known as Wall A4. The drawing shows the developed glass surface.
The wall is to the Concert Hall, at the northern end of the larger of the two
main halls. (Reproduced by permission of Ove Arup Partnership, London)

that in the Sydney Opera House we have a development project where the concept demanded that those developing the design entered new fields and found solutions to the problems they then encountered. To quote Jack Zunz of the Ove Arup Partnership:

> We were stretched to the limit of our skills. In extending ourselves and making that extra effort we developed our know-how just that little bit more. We use this knowledge in other fields. When we have been extended as much as we have, it makes our ordinary jobs easier and we hope to do them better.

That is what construction is all about. And our example certainly shows construction operating internationally, spanning the world. The concept was born in Denmark, designed primarily in the UK and constructed in Australia.

A thing of beauty

Let the General Manager of the Sydney Opera House, Mr Lloyd Martin, sum the matter up for us, and bring our study to a conclusion:(4)

> The design and furnishing of the inside of the building are the result of years of calculations, expert opinion and research. Glass walls and ceilings, timber panelling radiate out to merge in the sculptured shell of the concrete, seeking to reconcile the notions of acoustics, elegance and comfort. The different auditoria are full of light and warmth thanks to the universal presence of wood, radiating a beauty both powerful and sober.

The solutions found for the host of problems of construction and equipment of the Sydney Opera House have benefited architects, engineers and technicians all over the world. The Australians are the fortunate owners and beneficiaries of this extraordinary cultural centre. Like all masterpieces, the Opera House will remain a universal source of creative inspiration.

Figure 16.6, presented at the end of this chapter, lets us see all that has been so graphically described for us above in action. This, after all, is why they built it. The original brief, back in the mid-1950s, to those who entered the competition that Utzon won, was to design a complex of buildings to provide facilities for the musical and dramatic arts. This has indeed been done and they can be enjoyed in a building that is a delight to see.

References

1 Yeomans, J., *The other Taj Mahal: What happened to the Sydney Opera House*, Camberwell, Vic., 1973.
2 Hall, Peter, *Great Planning Disasters*, Weidenfeld and Nicolson, London, 1980.
3 Kharbanda, O.P. and Stallworthy, E.A., *How to learn from project disasters*, Gower, Aldershot, UK, 1983.
4 Martin, Lloyd, 'The Opera House', *Total Information*, 1980, no. 84, pp.29–31. (*Total Information* is a quarterly magazine published by Compagnie Française des Pétroles, Paris.)
5 Arup, O.N. and Zunz, G.J., 'Sydney Opera House', *The Structural Engineer*, 47(3), pp.99–132, 1969. (Republished in the *Arup Journal*, October 1973.)
6 Hooper, J.A., 'On the bending of architectural laminated glass', *International Journal of Mechanical Sciences*, 15(4), pp.309–23, 1973.
7 Nutt, John, 'Influence of corrosion on some aspects of design of the Sydney Opera House', paper presented at the Seventh Annual Conference of the Australian Corrosion Association, held at Manly, New South Wales on 7–11 November 1966.

Figure 16.6 Sydney Opera House interior
The Concert Hall, the largest hall in the Sydney Opera House, seats 2,700 people. It is used for symphony concerts, recitals, jazz concerts, light entertainments and is an excellent venue for conventions. The ceiling and upper walls are panelled with white birch plywood, and the lower walls, floors, stairs, boxes, stalls, terraces and the orchestral platform are panelled with reddish brown box timber. The organ was designed and being built by the Australian, Ronald Sharp. It is due for completion late in 1987, and will be the largest mechanical action organ in the world, with 127 stops, comprising 10,500 pipes.

Part Five

ON THE ROAD TO SUCCESS

17　The Statpipe Project

It is our continuing theme that the construction industry is continually working up against the frontiers of knowledge and nowhere is this truer than in the North Sea. It has been said that the North Sea is the world's 'most demanding commercial test bed'.(1) The work being carried out there, whilst of prime importance to the countries bordering that sea, Britain and Norway in particular, is also of worldwide concern. At the moment the works being carried out in the North Sea account for between a third and a half of the world's total offshore spending. All this work, some calling for very high technology, has to be carried out in a hostile environment.

Indeed, the North Sea is generally acknowledged to be one of the toughest areas in which the construction industry has ever had to operate. When exploration began, back in the 1960s, seasoned offshore personnel described it as 'the world's worst marine environment' and it has hung on to that reputation ever since. The North Sea is rarely calm. Storms can blow up with little warning. Gales gust up to 150 knots, whipping waves to heights of more than 30 metres.

The depth of the water is a further complicating factor. Most of the discoveries have been made at depths of up to 200 metres. Till now, the largest discoveries of both gas and oil have been located in that area of the continental shelf assigned to the United Kingdom, but both oil and gas have also been found in the areas assigned to Norway and The Netherlands.

Norway has had especial problems, in that whilst important discoveries have been made in its areas – the Frigg Field (gas) and the Ekofisk Field (oil) are cases in point – it was not technically feasible at the time the fields were developed to bring the oil and gas to Norway. The Frigg Field, for instance, is only some 200 km from the Norwegian coast, but the gas is piped all the way to the British mainland, a distance of nearly 400 km, twice as far. The reason for this was what is known as the Norwegian Trench, a sort of 'ditch' in the seabed that runs down Norway's western shoreline, some 300 metres deep. Only a few years ago pipelaying operations at this depth were not considered practicable. Now such depths have become almost routine, if the project we shall now review is taken as an example.

It is the Statpipe gas-gathering system, some 850 km in all, now being built in the Norwegian sector of the North Sea, that we want to look at in some detail. The system calls for two crossings of the Norwegian Trench and, however 'routine' those currently involved in this project may consider their work to be, there is no doubt that once again the construction industry is being 'stretched', as we shall see. At all events, this project has been declared to be 'the biggest offshore pipeline operation ever', with a total cost in the region of US$3 billion.(2)

The compelling necessity

Projects should be entered into because they are needed. Perhaps the need for the Statpipe Project might be considered obvious enough, but we think its history is of real interest. A very difficult engineering operation is being undertaken: the crossing of the Norwegian Trench and the provision of a related onshore installation. Why ?

It is of course true that without Statfjord, the North Sea's biggest oilfield, there would not be a Statpipe project. Norway had been debating the merits of crossing the trench for a long time. Whilst oil from the field could be brought to Norway by tanker, the only way to bring gas from the field would be by pipeline. It was almost literally true that the pressure of the associated gas produced with Statfjord's oil made a decision about the 'pipelining' of the associated gas urgent. As oil was taken up from the field, the associated gas was being re-injected into the field, but by the mid-1980s, it was estimated, this continuing re-injection would begin to damage the oil reservoir.

So a decision was urgent. At the same time feasibility studies demonstrated that both oil and gas should be 'pipelined' direct to Norway if that were technically practicable. The technical feasibility was assured by the growing size of and experience of the construction industry in what are known as 'laybarge' operations, making the laying of pipelines across the trench a practical possibility.

Figure 17.1   Gas Separation and Storage Plant at Kårstø
An aerial view, taken in April 1983. This terminal at Kårstø covers some 180 hectares and is initially designed for a handling capacity of five billion cubic metres of gas/year. (Reproduced by permission of Den Norske Stats Oljeselskap AS (Statoil)).

Despite the attention given to the trench crossing, we do not think that that is the most innovative area of work on the project. The technology selected for crossing the shore/surf zone on the west side of Karmøy is most interesting. The area is rocky and bouldered. Figure 17.1, showing the terminal at Kårstø, gives some impression of the terrain. Blasting a trench or driving a tunnel were first considered, these being conventional methods of bringing the pipeline ashore. However, the Norwegian contractors F. Selmer suggested an immersed concrete tunnel for the guidance and protection of the two gas lines as they came ashore. Statoil found this proposal competitive in terms of both efficiency and time and it has been adopted. This immersed tube concept has never been tried out before, but following model tests and the development of high-quality concrete mixes Selmer have been able to complete the work successfully and well within the contract deadline.

In praise of Statpipe

In the course of our review of the Sydney Opera House (Chapter 16) we saw how lyrical those engaged on the project and those who later were managing the building could become over the beauties of that building. Natural enough, you might say. But this almost fanatical fervour is not limited to 'things of beauty'. Similar emotions are displayed in relation to the construction of something that will largely be hidden on the seabed: the Statpipe Gas Gathering Pipeline System we are now looking at. Just consider this description of that pipeline:(2)

> It snakes along the ocean floor like a mammoth sea animal, with tentacles of pipe and concrete. The man-made arms and legs of it rise out of Statfjord, in the North Sea, and make their way onshore and off, as if caught in a metamorphosis between land and ocean. This sea creature brings with it energy – natural gas – the lifeblood of an industrial world. It is the US$3 billion Statpipe System, and it will transport 200 billion cubic feet of gas a year to Western European nations.

Well! That is certainly one way of looking at our subject. Let us now look at it on the map. Figure 17.2 shows the proposed run of the pipelines, designed to bring wet gas from the Statfjord Field ashore at Kårstø. Here, after processing, the dry gas is pipelined out to sea again, southward to the Ekofisk complex, picking up dry

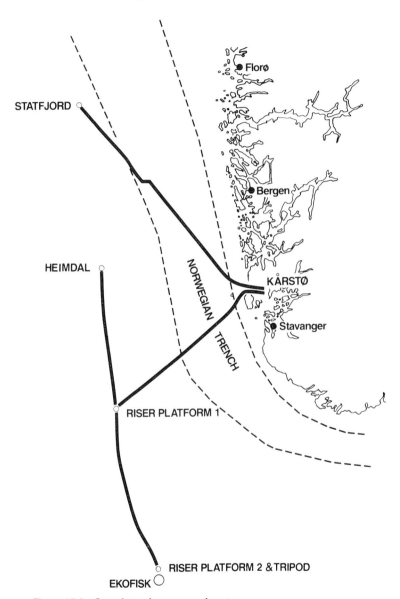

Figure 17.2   Statpipe – the proposed route
Statpipe makes two crossings of the Norwegian Trench, with its flat
bottom at around 300m depth (map shows 200m depth contours).
The western slope of the trench is relatively gentle, but the eastern
slope rises steeply, close in to the shore. (Drawing by courtesy of
Fluor Europe Limited, London)

gas along the way from Norway's Heimdal Field. At Ekofisk it will go into an existing Norpipe line to Emden in West Germany. With Norway's convoluted coastline, the pipeline landfall at Kårstø is actually on an island nearly 20 km from the terminal itself and separated from it by three fjords. To reach the terminal the pipelines will run overland and through three tunnels, totalling in all some 12 km, running about 50 metres below the fjord bottoms and more than 150 metres below the surface of the sea.(3)

In all some 400,000 tonnes of steel pipe will be incorporated into the project, with the 710-mm-dia. pipe coming from five mills in Japan and the 915-mm-dia. pipe coming from Mannesmann of West Germany. The line pipe is concrete coated. A joint venture has been set up to do the work using both an existing yard in Denmark and a new yard in Norway set up specially for the project, where highly sophisticated handling facilities and concrete batching equipment have been installed.

In order to determine the route of the pipelines in detail, a full range of surveys were carried out, from sub-bottom profiling to submersibles. A route had to be selected that avoided the 'pockmarks' which occur in the seabed, particularly on the western slope of the trench. Such 'pockmarks' can be quite large: several hundred metres in diameter and five metres or more deep. Another hazard is seafloor gullies. In general they are avoided, although occasionally it has been necessary to provide supports over large scour marks, or to infill.

Let us remember, as we describe in this casual way laying a line to avoid holes, bridge gaps and infill, that we are not talking about a landscape that one can see with the eye. It is all more than 200 metres below a rough sea.

The project management

Earlier in this book we have stressed the need for the owner to play a serious role in the management of the project, even when he is employing a major managing contractor. In this case Statoil, the Norwegian state-owned oil company, have set up a separate company, Statpipe, to supervise the construction and operation of the pipelines and related facilities. Whilst Statoil have the controlling interest (60 per cent) in this company, a number of oil majors also have an interest – Elf, Norsk Hydro, Mobil, Esso, Shell, Total and Saga. Of these, Total, Shell and Esso have appointed personnel specifically experienced in pipeline operations, who have been seconded from each of these three companies in various managerial positions. Here we have a solid demonstration of the transfer of experience. For instance, the engineering manager, appointed from Total, was for four years manager for the then world's biggest recent pipeline scheme, at Upper Zakum. This involved some 700 km of line with more than 300 pipeline crossings.

One of the engineering and construction company majors, Fluor, has been appointed as 'project services' contractor, and they are handling the project through their London-based company, Fluor Ocean Services. The relationship between such a managing contractor and the owner is all-important. We have stressed this elsewhere.(4) To quote:

> For both the sake of the project and their own sake, they [the project managers representing both owner and managing contractor] must work together to ensure the ultimate success of the project. This will only happen if both owner and contractor approach the subject in the right spirit, working with one another rather than against each other. The true concept, with a managing contractor, is that he acts as the owner's 'right arm' and both partners should see it that way, and rely upon one another accordingly. The project managers are the 'catalysts' that bring about this happy result. (Chapter 8, 'The total project manager')

No pun was intended in relation to the French oil major (Total) participating in this particular project.

This principle is exemplified in the project before us. One of the project managers for the managing contractor – he is called the 'executive project director' – puts it thus:(3)

> We have as broad a scope as our client – we are here partly to supplement their staff, and with some things to do of our own.

Once again, previous experience is brought to bear, since he was earlier project manager for Alyeska on the trans-Alaska oil line, which we have dealt with elsewhere (5) under the heading 'Dare we tell the story? Whilst this was a great project, it was also the private sector's most costly venture at that time and probably still is. The project manager sums up the value of that experience for himself personally in these words:

> Going through a pioneering project like that, so much in the public eye, shows the things that need to be done.

Fluor's 'project services' contract, which was let to them in two parts, first the offshore and then the onshore portion, is estimated to total some US$ 100 million, and is likely to employ around 250 personnel directly. Of course, indirectly they are responsible as managing contractors for the work of the many thousands of people employed by the multitude of subcontractors involved, from the suppliers of materials to the construction companies on location. The sophistication of the control exercised is well illustrated if we consider the course of the pipe material itself through the project.

Piping material control

We begin, obviously enough, with pipe procurement. This involves, as we said earlier, the purchase of roughly 400,000 tonnes of pipe from seven mills, five in Japan and two in Germany. To coordinate, control and document this intricate operation, Fluor adapted its PROMPT materials tracking computer system. The updated program is capable of following every pipe from raw steel to seabed. To quote the logistics supervisor (3):

> I don't think there is anything they can ask us that we can't answer about every single piece of pipe ...

The materials engineer asserts:

> We can locate the pipe at any stage from mill to seabed. The system is multipurpose. It gives us a basic metallurgical history of each pipe, monitors its progress from manufacture onwards, provides verification for invoicing (for example to pay for precise lengths of corrosion coating), records anode and buckle arrestor positions, retains technical information such as pipe heat, and fulfils the Norwegian Petroleum Directorate requirements for records.

The coating yard set up by Bredero Norwegian contractors at Åndalsnes is so sophisticated that the cranes feed pipe weights directly into the yard's computer as they are lifted. Then each day the stored information is dumped into Fluor's London computer. The computer is still active when we board the pipe-laying barge, not only in controlling the location of the barge for pipe-laying purposes, a subject to which we wish to come later, but also in selecting what the barge needs 48 hours in advance so that the pipe can be shipped out. Once it is received, the lay barge records the joint welding information, laying sequence and seabed location of each pipe, which once again is passed on to London to complete the file.

We realise that our readers may not necessarily be familiar with terms such as 'anodes' and 'buckle arrestors', but we do think you will appreciate from these brief quotations the complexity of pipelaying operations these days and the high degree of sophistication in terms of supervision and control that has been reached. Just to explain, the anodes and buckle arrestors are installed to prevent catalytic corrosion of the pipe underwater.

Seaborne 'tools'

Both in this project and another we shall review later, in Chapter 19, the 'floating tools' play a leading role. Whilst the two projects are utterly different, yet we are sure the technical demands of the Delta Works in this area are reflected in the operations called for during the laying of the pipelines on this project.

The prime need is for very precise surveying. Two survey vessels, the *Labrador* and the *Lador*, have been carrying out both pre- and post-lay surveys as well as touch down monitoring and the provision of 'as laid' information. That last is similar to the 'as built drawings' always called for as any project on land is completed. The vessels employ what are called 'ROVs', which run continuously about a metre above the pipe, fitted with two TV cameras and recorders, providing profile and plan measurements.

Whilst deepwater pipelaying does not normally require the use of divers on the seabed, the pipe being laid down completely mechanically, nevertheless diving support vessels are on standby. During the 1983 season this was provided from the *Seaway Condor*, which however was largely engaged on surveying work. Other vessels are brought in as required for the hyperbaric welding test, carrying out the tie-ins, seabed trenching and the like. But the most fundamental area for the use of vessels is in the laying of the pipe itself. These vessels are called lay barges.

The lay barge operation

The selection of the vessels for the laying of the pipelines was

Figure 17.3   Pipelaying vessel ETPM 1601
This photograph shows the Pipelaying Vessel ETPM 1601 commencing the
laying of the 36–inch Statpipe leg from the Ekofisk Field northwards to
Heimdal. (Reproduced by permission of Den Norke Stats Oljeselskap AS
(Statoil)).

governed by the commercial considerations of price and time. Despite the record water depths involved for such large diameter pipelines, there seemed to be no question as to practicability. In fact, the operation was regarded as 'routine'.(6)

The 36-inch pipelines in the Statpipe System have been laid by the ETPM 1601 Lay Vessel. These lines do not cross the Norwegian Trench, but run from Heimdal, via Riser Platform 1, to Ekofisk. If you will refer back to Figure 17.1 you will see these lines running from north to south. The total run was some 350 km of 36-in. diameter line and the contract, let to ETPM/Borge Enterprises, was said to be worth about NKr. 550 million (say US\$ 75 million). Figure 17.3 shows the barge in operation. The sections of line crossing the Trench were a somewhat different matter. Here was a total run of some 550 km, from Statfjord to the shore and then back from the shore across the Trench once again to the first riser platform. Here it was considered that McDermott's LB 200 could be best suited to cope with the enormous strains that would be encountered. The overriding concern is to prevent a buckle in the pipe as it hangs between the barge and the seabed. In the event of what is called a 'wet buckle' divers would have to be called in. This demands a further support vessel, in this case the *Seaway Condor*, which is equipped to take care of such potential tasks as cutting the line and installing a pull head.

Crossing the slopes is the most difficult part of the operation, since, as the pipe goes down (or up), the laying parameters are constantly changing. A typical rate of lay is somewhere between 2 and 4 km per day. Progress was planned in order to complete one crossing of the trench during each 'weather window': the period, roughly from April to September, when work is possible. The first crossing was made in 1983, the second in 1984.

In Figure 17.4 we present an outline drawing of Lay Barge 200, to illustrate the complexities of the work that goes on on board. The vessel itself is, if we are to be precise, 179.6 × 58.5 × 33.2 metres, of some 20,000 gross registered tons. The barge has airconditioned living quarters for roughly 400 people, together with hospital, laundry and recreational facilities. Not only does the barge carry about 350,000 gallons of fresh water on board, but it is fitted with three water distillation units.

The mooring system, not indicated on the drawing, consists of fourteen 50,000-lb flipper anchors, with hoists, each driven by a

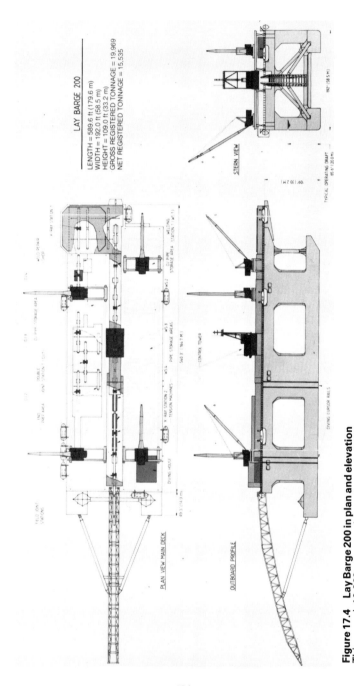

LAY BARGE 200

LENGTH = 589.6 ft (179.6 m)
WIDTH = 192.0 ft (58.5 m)
HEIGHT = 109.0 ft (33.2 m)
GROSS REGISTERED TONNAGE = 19,969
NET REGISTERED TONNAGE = 15,535

STERN VIEW

PLAN VIEW MAIN DECK

OUTBOARD PROFILE

Figure 17.4   Lay Barge 200 in plan and elevation
This vessel, 10,969 gross registered tonnage, is a semi-submersible pipelaying barge for offshore service. Six columns on two large submerged hulls support the barge superstructure. Draft is typically 20 metres under operating conditions and 8 metres in transit.

196

2,000 HP motor. It will be appreciated that proper anchorage is vital to the success of the pipelaying operation, so that cable tension, cable footage and cable speed are all monitored from the control tower. Closed circuit television provides a visual check to ensure the cable is spooling correctly.

Coming to the welding of the pipejoints, the pipe assembly area can be seen along the centreline of the barge. There are four double joint welding stations as indicated (WS1–WS4), together with two X-ray stations and two field joint coating stations. Remember that the steel pipe is coated, and once the pipe ends have been welded together the weld has to be coated. As it is welded, the pipe has to be laid on the sea bed, using the lay-down hoist, the pipe going over the stern ramp into the sea. The laying operation is fully instrumented and controlled from the control tower, with TV cameras mounted at the ramp stern for inspection purposes. There is a retraction system for the ramp to raise it clear of wave action when the vessel is not operating in the pipelay mode.

In theory, as the pipe goes overboard and is laid on the seabed, that is that. But of course, troubles can come. So there is a diving house, completely fitted out to handle a three-man diving bell, and provisions to go down to a depth of more than 450 metres (1,500 feet).

Well, perhaps we have said enough to give some idea as to the complexities of pipelaying for what has been described as the biggest offshore pipeline operation ever. In total it is said to be a 3 billion dollar project, due for completion early in 1986. But notice that despite the fact that the project approaches the boundaries of technical achievement in many areas of operation, it is being handled in a completely routine manner, with due weight being given to commercial factors, such as cost and time, as we can see if we turn to consider the manner in which the contracts for the work are being let.

Conditions of contract

Despite the evidently hazardous nature of the work, the main pipelaying contracts themselves were let as 'lump sums'. Only the higher-risk sections in the Norwegian Trench and its side slopes were let at what are known as 'day-work' rates, where the time actually taken is paid for at agreed rates. To quote Ed Wictor of Esso, (3) one of the project managers seconded to Statpipe –

> this would allow sharing the risk with the contractor so that he can give a better price and is not penalised if we want to be cautious.

The contracts that have been let are unusual in terms of North Sea operations because of the degree to which associated services have been hived off. Diving services, pipe survey and pipe carrying are all cases where the owner, Statpipe, have let contracts directly to the appropriate companies. The reason is of interest to every project manager. It is said to give a better grip on costs. To quote Ed Wictor once again:

> We've tried to work the interfaces so that there is no overlap, and provide a clearly identifiable work scope.

We endorse wholeheartedly the concept that one of the best ways to both limit and control costs is to have a 'clearly identifiable work scope'. This should be a basic objective with *every* project manager.

The objective in view

We have been looking at the technical details of this project in order to learn something more of project management and the skills called for. We see that this project rests upon the construction of a series of earlier projects, where the conditions have been progressively more arduous. So experience has been built up over the years, across not only the North Sea but also many similar locations. It is said that the offshore construction industry began all of thirty years ago in the Gulf of Mexico, where pipelaying began in shallow water. When construction began in the North Sea, techniques were developed so that pipes could be laid in depths of 100 metres or more. Crossing the Norwegian Trench, some 300 metres deep, has been technically feasible for some six years now, so that this operation was not regarded with any particular awe. As McDermott, the pipelaying contractor, put it, it was 'just deeper and longer'.

That's all!

References

1 'The North Sea: a springboard for British industry', a report commissioned by Shell UK Limited and available from Shell-Mex House, Strand, London WC2.
2 Moore, S., 'Up from the deep', *Fluor Magazine*, vol. XL, no. 2, 1983.
3 'The Statpipe Project', *Offshore Engineer*, July 1982, pp.25–9.
4 Stallworthy, E.A. and Kharbanda, O.P., *Total Project Management*, Gower, Aldershot, UK, 1983, 329pp.
5 Kharbanda, O.P. and Stallworthy, E.A., *How to learn from project disasters – true-life stories with a moral for management*, Gower, Aldershot, UK, 1983, 274pp.
6 Article: 'Statpipe', in the house journal *Noroil*, May 1983.

18 India's pride – Bombay High

The whole world has heard the saga of the discovery and development of the oilfields in the North Sea because of their dramatic impact on the economy of the United Kingdom, the very specialised technology and even the high drama that has been associated with the recovery of oil and gas under such difficult conditions. The development of the oilfields of the far north, in Alaska, reviewed by us elsewhere, (1) also reached the headlines of the world's press because of the difficulties associated with the construction of pipelines across the frozen wastes. But Bombay High – who has heard of that?

Bombay High is in fact India's 'North Sea'. It was discovered just at the right time, for the projections with respect to India's bill for imported oil looked extremely threatening, as can be seen from Figure 18.1. The value of oil imports escalated rapidly from 1950 onwards. Expressed as a percentage of export earnings, which was the only way India could pay for its imported oil, they rose from 9 per cent in 1950 to some 30 per cent by 1971, then to nearly 80 per cent by 1981. This was partly due to the increased oil requirement, but the sharp increase in the price of crude oil in the 1970s was also a very significant factor.

An oil crisis averted

A simple projection in 1980 would have shown that within perhaps three years the entire export earnings of India would not have been sufficient to pay for the growing requirement for oil and petroleum products. This could have been a catastrophe, crippling an economy that was already suffering from other causes. But fortunately by that time the Bombay High offshore gas and oil

	Domestic (million tonnes)	Crude oil Imports* (million tonnes)	% of entire exports
1950	0.3	3.0	9
1960/1	0.5	7.9	12
1970/1	6.8	12.8	29
1975/6	8.4	15.8	31
1977/8	10.8	17.7	29
1979/80	11.6	20.8	50
1980/1	10.5	23.5	79
1981/1†	16.9 (16.2)	23.0 (20.2)	90 (67)
1982/3†	20.5 (21.1)	23.0 (22.2)	101 (63)
1983/4†	21.3 (26.6)	23.0 (22.3)	115 (55)
1984/5†	21.6 (30.2)	23.0 (20.0)	131 (50)
1985/6†	22.1 (34.0)	23.0 (20.0)	149 (45)

Source: Centre for Monitoring Indian Economy, Bombay, India, various documents and Databank.

* includes petroleum products
† Projections as of December 1980. Assumptions then made:
   Implementation of oil conservation measures
   Price increase imported products 5% per year
   Exports growth 10% per year

Figures in brackets (): Actual, or as projected early 1984.

Figure 18.1   India averts oil crisis
This table allows one to see the relationship between the cost of imports and exports, thus demonstrating the crucial impact of the domestic production of crude oil.

field had already been proven. Thanks to the foresight of the Government, who decided on massive investment in this new oilfield, together with the firm commitment of the Oil and Natural Gas Commission (ONGC), the looming crisis was averted.(2) The extent of the crisis can be seen by reference to Figure 18.1, the projections for 1985/86 indicating that by then the oil import bill would have been about one and a half times the entire foreign exchange earnings of the country from its exports. Thanks to Bombay High and the fine performance by ONGC these projections were proved totally incorrect. We present alongside the original predictions the actual figures to date, together with the current projection. There has been a radical improvement, not only in the figures to date but also in the potential for the future.

Present indications are that the prospects associated with Bombay High and the other offshore areas are such that India could not only be self-sufficient with respect to oil and petroleum products during the next decade, but also a net exporter. These forecasts are to some extent dependent upon the international price for crude oil and India's need to earn additional foreign exchange. It could well be a prudent decision to limit production to immediate internal needs, so conserving a most valuable resource. Factors such as the extent of the proven reserves and the balance of trade will no doubt determine the decision in due course.

The Oil and Natural Gas Commission

In 1947, on attaining independence, the Indian Government took the vital policy decision to develop the country's oil resources, both onshore and offshore, even although at that time the total requirement of oil and petroleum products was less than 3 million tonnes, met almost entirely by imports. This was a momentous decision in the circumstances. The international crude oil price in those days was very low, at around US$2 per barrel, cheaper than home-produced coal on an equivalent energy basis and of course much easier and cleaner to handle. The Indian Government were aware that with their ambitious development plans the requirement would escalate rapidly and in addition they wished to be self-sufficient in this key commodity.

To implement the decision then made, the first practical step was taken in 1955 by the creation of a Petroleum Division within the existing Geological Survey of India for countrywide oil exploration. This Division soon grew into a separate Directorate of Oil & Natural Gas, leading on to the formation of an autonomous commission, the ONGC, by an Act of Parliament in 1959. ONGC was charged to:

> plan, promote and implement programmes for the development of petroleum resources and the production and sale of petroleum products produced by it.

Within 25 years (1959 to 1984) ONGC has brought India's hopes of attaining a measure of self-sufficiency in oil close to reality.(3) Naturally enough, the initial effort was onshore, and reserves were

Figure 18.2 *Sagar Samrat*
Here we see India's first offshore drilling rig, the *Sagar Samrat*, in operation. (Photograph by courtesy of the Oil & Natural Gas Commission, Bombay)

discovered at Ankleshwar, Kalol and Sanand in the State of Gujarat and Rudrasagar in Assam.

Encouraged by these discoveries and having the 'feeling' that the coastline of India should have hydrocarbon-rich basins, ONGC ventured into offshore exploration, employing the SS *Mahindra* in 1963 for an experimental seismic survey of the Gulf of Bombay, one of the areas considered promising. This survey helped to identify several potentially rich structures, including the Aliabet structure, where the first offshore discovery was finally made. Subsequently ONGC chartered a Soviet seismic survey ship, the *Akademic Arkhangeliskey,* and the exploration exercise was extended to other areas along the coast, such as the Gulf of Cambay, Kerala coast, Gulf of Manar, Palk Strait, Coromandel coast and the Bay of Bengal.

The particularly promising offshore structure in the Aliabet region was christened 'Bombay High' by the Soviet geologist Kalinin. Whilst surveys continued elsewhere, ONGC now concentrated their attention on 'Bombay High', ordering a sophisticated jack-up type rig from Japan in 1971. This drilling rig, *Sagar Samrat* (which means 'Emperor of the Sea'), docked in Bombay two years later and started drilling at Bombay High on 31 January 1974. Three weeks later, on 19 February 1974, oil was discovered in a limestone reservoir. We see the *Sagar Samrat* at work in Figure 18.2.

From this point onwards there was no looking back. ONGC, backed by the Government with full financial and other support and the determination of their personnel, made rapid progress in the development of this new resource. Within the short span of six years from that first discovery in Bombay High by the *Sagar Samrat*, production had reached 150,000 barrels a day. The year was 1981. Since then, in as many years, production has more than tripled! With the discovery of several other commercially attractive structures in the area, the future looks bright indeed.

The saga of exploration and production

How is an oilfield developed? Let us highlight the significant events in the growth of Bombay High as a graphic illustration.

1963	Experimental seismic survey by SS *Mahindra*, leading to the discovery of 'Aliabet'.
1964–67	Regional surveys by the Soviet seismic survey ship

Akademic Arkhangeliskey, culminating in the confirmation of Bombay High as a promising area.

1970–71   A 'Mercury' class self-propelled rig ordered at a cost of Rs. 12.7 Crore, or US$13 million.

1973–74   *Sagar Samrat* commenced drilling operations, discovering oil on the L-II horizon three weeks later. There was also a hint of gas-bearing sand at about 1,160 metres and another oil-bearing reservoir was discovered at 1,300 metres about a year later.

1975   ONGC purchased their own seismic vessel, the *Anweshak*, at a cost of Rs. 3 Crore (US$ 3 million). This had sophisticated geophysical equipment, a proton magnetometer for simultaneous collection of geophysical data, two digital computers and a satellite navigation system enabling the positioning of the ship anywhere in the world in any kind of weather with no assistance from shore-based stations. To cover the entire Indian continental shelf, ONGC supplemented their own efforts by hiring in contractors with the necessary equipment.

1976   Following the successful find of oil in Bombay High, twelve assessment holes were drilled and steps taken to procure and install platforms. The very first barrel of oil was up within six months, and an output of 40,000 barrels per day had been reached by the end of the year. Surely a world record!

1977   Production now doubled. The oil was being loaded into the tanker *Jawaharlal Nehru*, moored by the SBM (Single Buoy Mooring) System and then brought ashore by a shuttle tanker. The associated gas was being flared.

1978   An oil and gas submarine trunk pipeline 204 km long laid from Bombay High to Uran and then on to users such as refineries, fertiliser plants and power plants in the Trombay area. Gas pretreatment and pumping facilities in operation.

1979–81   Production soared to 100,000 barrels per day by the end of 1978. By March 1981 production had reached 180,000 barrels per day. Several associated facilities, both offshore and onshore, were now complete, such as a crude stabilisation unit and a 180,000 tonnes per year LPG plant with a pipeline to the refinery for bottling.

1981–83   30 platforms, including BHS and Ratna-A installed at the average rate of one a month.

Figure 18.3　The BHS Platform Complex
This complex, in the southern part of Bombay High, is the largest offshore complex in India, installed in a water depth of 76.8 metres. The basic design for the Complex was carried out by Engineers India Ltd. (Photograph by courtesy of the Oil & Natural Gas Commission, Bombay)

BHS is the largest platform complex offshore in India and has a capacity of 360,000 barrels per day. Figure 18.3 shows us this complex in full operation. The ten-well Ratna-A platform is the first in a satellite field outside Bombay High. A production target of 400,000 barrels per day was reached in March 1983, two years ahead of schedule.

Another 20 platforms are now in course of completion, bringing production to over 20 million tonnes of crude oil a year, together with some 20 million cubic metres of free gas a day. These platforms will also tap other satellite fields outside Bombay High, such as Heera (pearl) and Panna (diamond) in the South Bassein Field.

This eventful story of ONGC's offshore efforts has its roots in India's growing energy needs and the end is nowhere in sight. The exploration effort continues unabated and up to the end of 1983 138 offshore exploratory and assessment wells had been drilled, leading to a string of successes not only in Bombay High but in satellite structures. Elsewhere offshore oil has been discovered in the Godavri region and Palk Bay. Of the total of 138 wells drilled, only 60 have proved to be dry, giving ONGC a success ratio of 1:1.8.

Self-reliance with international cooperation

The overall objective of India's oil exploration and production pragramme is to make that country self-sufficient with respect to oil and petroleum products. This is being achieved largely through India's own efforts, but help and assistance is required from abroad, both in terms of 'know-how' and equipment. There are no hard and fast rules, ONGC pursuing a policy of part ownership and part charter hire. Thus ONGC now own five jack-up rigs and one drillship, but their own efforts are still supplemented by chartered vessels, not only for drilling but also for supply to the rigs. The main aerial transport between the offshore platforms and the shore is provided by helicopters, either owned by ONGC or chartered, and maintained by the Indian Airforce. The Coast-guard Service provide a security system for the various platforms offshore and also keep a close watch for pollution.

India's policy of self-reliance in the development of self-sufficiency involves a three-pronged stategy:

1 To master the core technology relating to exploration and production.

Figure 18.4 The LPG Plant at Uran
This is India's first cyrogenic LPG Plant. Built at Uran, it uses Bombay High gas. (Photograph by courtesy of the Oil & Natural Gas Commission, Bombay)

2 To increase oil production, even if that requires the hire or purchase of services and equipment abroad.
3 To build up total Indian capability with only marginal input from outside.

The first of these three objectives has been substantially achieved, with the second well on the way. Even when hiring in equipment or services, ONGC have retained complete control of the management of the operations. The third element depends for its success on the way in which organisations and companies outside India respond to the calls made upon them. Considerable success has been achieved in this area, judging by the fact that more than half of the platforms now in use have been designed and built in India. Their first cyrogenic LPG plant was also designed, fabricated and commissioned using wholly local resources. We present a view of that plant as Figure 18.4. Specialist services firms such as Schlumberger have been willing, contrary to their normal policy, to lease equipment to ONGC and transfer their latest technology in well-logging.

The organisation behind Bombay High

The basic organisation chart of ONGC is presented as Figure 18.5. We have only detailed the offshore section of that organisation, since it is that that interests us at the moment. The efforts of that one department have made a notable contribution towards India's objective of self-sufficiency, as is clearly evident from the data we presented earlier in Figure 18.1, but this fact is further highlighted when production for the year 1984/5 is analysed as follows:(4)

	Tonnes per year
ONGC offshore, almost entirely from Bombay High:	20.7
ONGC onshore:	6.9
Total production via ONGC:	27.6
Other agencies, all onshore:	2.6
Total:	30.2

The Bombay Offshore Project is the executive arm of ONGC and manages the offshore effort, drawing timely help and backup from

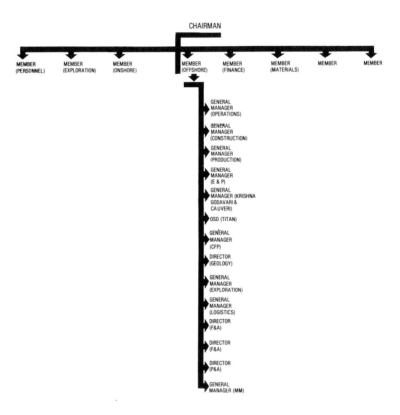

Figure 18.5.   Outline organogram for ONGC
This organogram only presents the departments of the Offshore Section in any detail.

other divisions of ONGC and also other companies and organisations in India. These are employed as and when required for specific tasks. For instance, the Institute of Petroleum Exploration at Dehradun provides geological and geophysical expertise, although ONGC operate an R&D activity with their own personnel that has provided excellent support. The Institute of Drilling Technology, also at Dehradun, provides solutions to any drilling and cementation problems encountered and the Institute of Reservoir Studies, located at Ahmedabad, helps carry out secondary recovery as well as reservoir studies for Bombay High, closely cooperating with the various branches of ONGC. Thus we have integrated endeavour, all within India.

When we turn to consider the manufacture of the specialised equipment, we find large-scale involvement by Engineers India Ltd, of New Delhi, a large public sector consulting and engineering company, whom we mentioned earlier in Chapter 4, 'The changing scene', in the section 'New entrants'. This company has been closely associated with ONGC in the design and engineering of the offshore platforms. The basic engineering for the SA Process Platform was carried out without any foreign collaboration whatever. Engineers India Ltd went on to undertake the design and construction of the Uran LPG Plant on a 'turnkey' basis with complete success. Mazagaon Docks Limited, a public sector shipyard, have undertaken the fabrication of several well platforms and, with ONGC assistance, are now developing the know-how and hardware required for the transportation and installation of such platforms. Numerous other companies in both the public and private sectors have assisted to develop the supply of related hardware and consumables, such as oilwell chemicals. This is a continuous development that has yielded good results in terms of import substitution.

In citing all this, we ask you to remember that the technology only began to take shape in India in the 1970s. Considerable planning expertise has been called for. Apart from developing their own in-house capability, ONGC have played an important role in helping other Indian organisations and manufacturers to acquire offshore technology. This team effort has already paid rich dividends in helping India towards its goal of self-sufficiency, but we wish to emphasise the management aspect – the forethought and the ability to appreciate both the weaknesses and the needs of others, together with the realisation that unselfish cooperation is for the good of the project. This is part of the art of project

management. The good project manager, as we have demonstrated earlier, thinks more of the project than of himself.

In their preoccupation with exploration and production, ONGC
have not lost sight of the long-range R&D and related effort that
will be required to sustain their ambitious programme of expansion in the long term. To take one example, ONGC have decided
to set up two new institutes, an Institute of Engineering and Ocean
Technology and an Institute of Production Technology. These are
to be established at Panvel, New Bombay, not far from the current
major operations in the offshore area. These Institutes will serve
ONGC in relation to their research and development needs in
both ocean and production technology, thus helping to sustain
their plans in the years to come.

The figures speak for themselves

The data presented earlier, in Figure 18.1, show the overall results
achieved by ONGC in the production of oil in India. Let us now
look at the relevant figures, starting from the general energy
scene.

India consumes energy in a variety of forms, derived from a
wide range of sources, such as nuclear power, animal dung and
manual and animal power, apart from the main conventional
sources, oil and coal. Between 1953 and 1978 the proportion of
energy provided commercially has risen from about one third to
one half, and is expected to reach 90 per cent by the year 2000.
Oil's contribution to this commercial sector has doubled in the last
twenty-five years and is now about 25 per cent. Its share of the
commercial sector is expected to rise to 35 per cent by the year
2000.(4)

If we now translate these projections into the expected demand
for crude oil, we get the following figures:

	Million tonnes per year
1982 (actual):	35
1990:	70
2000:	93

These projections include gas recovery, which has been translated
into the equivalent tonnage of crude oil (20 million tonnes in

1990). This tremendous projected increase in the consumption of oil is unlikely to be met from known reserves and these estimates highlight the urgent need to curtail demand, conserve output and accelerate the oil exploration and production effort.

In 1982 the prognosticated reserves were set at some 15 billion tonnes, of which 60 per cent was anticipated offshore. If the anticipated demand for oil by 1990 is to be met entirely from local production, then a massive effort is called for, with the drilling of about 2,000 wells over the next five years! This could call for a further 200 production platforms. To see what this means in relation to the efforts made so far to expand exploration and production, consider the data in the following table. We have given the value in US$billion, rather than rupees.

	Total budget US$b.	Construction budget US$b.	Platforms installed No.	Wells drilled No.
1980–81:	0.5	0.23	11	18
1981–82:	1.1	0.47	14	34
1982–83:	1.4	0.64	16	47
1983–84:	2.2	0.62	6	69
1984–85:	1.6		15	111

It would appear that present efforts will have to be more than doubled if self-sufficiency is to be achieved and sustained.

Time is money

This is by no means the first project we have reviewed built in India. On other projects we have had to comment that the fact that 'time is money' was a lesson still to be learnt in India (1). We even went so far as to quote the words of Omar Khayyam in this context:

> The Moving Finger writes; and having writ,
> Moves on; nor all your Piety nor Wit
> Shall lure it back to cancel half a Line

In our judgement much of the delay, and hence cost overrun, with projects in India was occasioned by divided responsibility. We feel that ONGC demonstrate the truth of this assessment. The delays had nothing to do with India or the Indians as such, because once we have a single authority, such as the ONGC, purposeful and positive action *has* been taken. Targets can not only be met: they can be beaten.

Yes, this is the silver lining. *Even in India* (an Indian wrote those words!) – even in India projects *can* be completed on time. We see quite clearly what is necessary: the appropriate power and authority to *get on with the job!* ONGC have shown us this very clearly. Have others in India – or the rest of the developing world for that matter – learnt this lesson yet?

References

1 Kharbanda, O.P. and Stallworthy, E.A., '*How to learn from project disasters*', Gower, Aldershot, UK, 1983, 273 pp. See Chapter 11, 'People, Politics and a Pipeline' with respect to the project in Alaska and Chapter 3, 'Developing countries are difficult' for an analysis of the failure of 'departmental execution'.

2 Kharbanda, O.P., 'Oil crisis looms large in India', *Energy Policy*, December 1981, p.329 (published in UK).

3 Report: 'Samundra Manthan – the Bombay High Story', published by ONGC, March 1981. 'Samundra Manthan' means 'Churning of the sea'.

4 Malhotra, A.K., 'Energy and Oil', paper presented at the World Energy Conference, New Delhi, September 1983. Also Annual Report for 1982–3, published by ONGC. Dr Malhotra is Member Offshore for ONGC.

19   The drama of the Delta Works

The history of The Netherlands and the Dutch is a story of a long, long fight against the sea, punctuated by floods. Slowly, over the centuries, dikes have been raised and areas that were once sea enclosed and pumped dry. The windmill, which one might well call the trademark of Holland, has played a great role in the winning back of land from the sea. At one time, more than 17,000 windmills were busy pumping and keeping The Netherlands dry. Over the centuries the map was continually changing, as storm and flood engulfed one area, whilst others were drained and recovered.

One of the greatest Dutchmen in the battle against the sea was one Jan Adriaanszoon Leeghwater, who designed a windmill which had a much greater pumping capacity than any windmill then known. This was way back in the seventeenth century, nearly 400 years ago now. His great ambition was to reclaim an area called the Haarlemmermeer, an area of some 18,000 hectares of lakes and swamps, which during storms threatened both the cities of Leiden and Amsterdam, for it lay between the two. According to his calculations, 160 windmills would have been required to pump out and keep that area dry, but his dream had to wait for more than 200 years, for the Haarlemmermeer was not reclaimed till 1852. When its turn came, the windmill had already been superceded as a source of power for pumping: steam-driven pumps, the invention of a certain James Watt, an Englishman, were then in vogue. Today, of course, it is the electrically-driven pump that keeps The Netherlands dry.

Schiphol – the International Airport

As we have just said, Haarlemmermeer was drained dry some 130 years ago now. Today giant jets land where in earlier days the winds drove sailing ships to the safe harbour of Schiphol – that name, literally translated, means 'a hole (shelter) for ships'. For many years all who landed by plane at Schiphol were reminded of its remarkable history by a sentence blazoned on the control tower for all to see: 'Aerodrome level 13 feet below sea level'. But today

Figure 19.1   The Netherlands today
The area of land below sea level is shaded and is more than half the total area of The Netherlands. The most vulnerable land is that directly behind the sand dunes and dikes which form the 1700 km. (prior to Delta Works) coastline.

they see it no more, since they walk through covered corridors from plane to Passport Control. Not only Schiphol, but nearly half The Netherlands is below sea level, as is illustrated in Figure 19.1.

Looking at the map of The Netherlands, Figure 19.1, you will see in the far north of the country a great dike, enclosing what is today called the Ijsselmeer. This dike, some 30 km long, was built to close off the Zuiderzee. On 28 May 1932, at 1.20 pm precisely, when the tide was on the turn, two boulder clay cranes emptied their loads in the last gap, and the Zuiderzee ceased to exist. Ships' sirens shrieked, the flags were raised, the National Anthem was sung, and the two provinces of North Holland and Friesland were linked. At the spot where the last gap was closed a monument was erected, with at its foot the words 'A nation that is alive builds for its future'. The Dutch continue to 'build for their future' in their fight against the sea. We are going to look in some detail at the next great work of theirs in this continuing saga, the Delta Works. But let us see, first of all, why the Delta Works were ever begun.

The great flood of 1953

It was the time of the full moon, the time when what are called the 'spring tides' occur. Sun and moon combine to drive the sea high against the coasts of Western Europe. On Saturday 31 January 1953, the wind joined forces with the sun amd moon to drive the water with angry force against the coastlands of England and The Netherlands. The seawalls and dikes broke in hundreds of places, with disastrous flooding. For The Netherlands it was a great tragedy. In the provinces of Zeeland and Zuid-Holland more than 150,000 hectares of fertile land were engulfed, 1,800 people died and there was great loss of livestock. The cost was immeasurable, for the land takes many years to recover from the effects of salt water.

Up in the north it was a different story. The great causeway stood firm, though damaged in several places. Catastrophe had been averted. They had indeed 'built for the future'. A previously vulnerable coastline of some 300 km had been reduced to 30 km and was safe. So the Dutch wasted no time. Three weeks after this tragic event the Minister for Transport and Public Works had inaugurated the Delta Committee. In August 1957 the very first quarterly report (*Driemaandelijks bericht – Deltawerken*) was published – a report that was to be issued every quarter for the next 27 years! By May 1958 the Delta Act became law and a new battle against the sea began.

The Delta Plan

Whilst the debate that led to the Delta Act had been going on, the inroads of the sea had been dealt with: dikes had been repaired and the land pumped dry once again. Now the engineers in drawing offices and laboratories began to get busy. It had been calculated that it would take roughly 25 years to complete the plan as drawn up and approved by Parliament, at a total cost of some 2,500 million guilders (US$ 1,600 million in those days – say US$9 billion at 1983 prices).

The heart of the Delta Plan was the closure of four wide, deep sea arms, the Haringvliet, the Brouwershavense Gat, the Oosterschelde and the Veerse Gat. Two other estuaries, the Nieuwe Waterweg and the Westerschelde, were to be left open because they gave access to the ports of Rotterdam and Antwerp. Completion was planned by 1978, as illustrated in Figure 19.2. You will see that the closure of the Oosterschelde, the largest sea-arm in the Delta area, was the last project. This is some 9 km wide at the mouth.

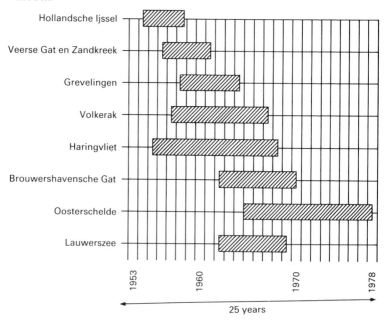

Figure 19.2   The Delta Plan closures
When complete, the coastline of south-western Holland will have been shortened by some 800 km. This means that there is less chance of flooding and so increased safety from the terrors of the sea.

The East Scheldt closure

The original plan left the method of closure for the East Scheldt open, with two main alternatives.(1) These two alternatives were:

1 A system of sluice-gate caissons. It was estimated that 70 caissons would be required to close this last tidal gap, at a cost of some 1 million guilders per caisson.
2 Closing by degrees, using a telpher line.

Both these systems had already been used when closing the other estuaries in the south-west of The Netherlands and either would have resulted in the complete closure of the Eastern Scheldt, with a system of locks for the passage of ships. It is this final closure that we now want to look at in some detail. These plans are now more than 25 years old. What actually happened?

The storm surge barrier

Work was started on the Eastern Scheldt in 1967: the original programme (Figure 19.2) envisaged a start in 1965, so we already have a two-year delay. Various preliminary works were undertaken, including the forming of three artificial construction islands. This brings us to the year 1973. At that time the intention was still to close the estuary completely, and work was started on the closure.(2)

However, heated discussions had been going on for some time as to the wisdom of this particular course. A number of groups were opposed to complete closure. The clamour for the preservation of the valuable tidal environment eventually grew so loud that the Government decided not to seal off the estuary completely. Instead a 'storm surge barrier' would be built, which would allow some 77 per cent of the present tidal movement. When dangerously high tides threatened, the barrier could be closed, thus guaranteeing the safety of the land in the area.

The barrier would be in three sections, connecting the islands that had already been built, as illustrated in Figure 19.3. The new objective was to have the storm surge barrier operational by 1985, so the design process and the study of construction methods were commenced simultaneously. Rijkwaterstaat, the Government Department concerned with roads and waterways, was the client, and the work was coordinated by the contractors Dosbouw, assisted by a wide range of consultants and advisors. In 1981 it became clear that completion could not be achieved before 1986. Hence we have a further plan, as illustrated in Figure 19.4.

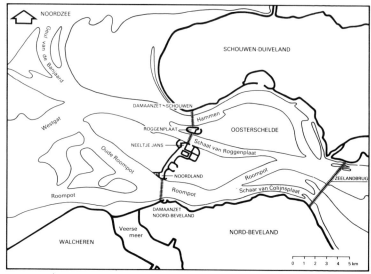

Figure 19.3 The Eastern Scheldt Closure
The three sections of the storm surge barrier cross the channels Hammen, Schaar and Roompot. The island Neeltje Jans is now being used for construction purposes. It is here that the greater part of the prefabricated components are being built.

Construction time table of storm-surge barrier (as per february 1983)

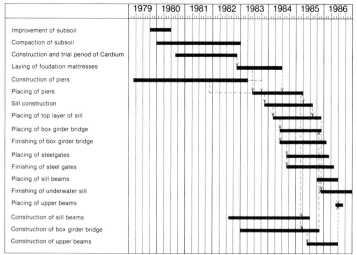

	1979	1980	1981	1982	1983	1984	1985	1986
Improvement of subsoil								
Compaction of subsoil								
Construction and trial period of Cardium								
Laying of foudation mattresses								
Construction of piers								
Placing of piers								
Sill construction								
Placing of top layer of sill								
Placing of box girder bridge								
Finishing of box girder bridge								
Placing of steelgates								
Finishing of steel gates								
Placing of sill beams								
Finishing of underwater sill								
Placing of upper beams								
Construction of sill beams								
Construction of box girder bridge								
Construction of upper beams								

Figure 19.4 The storm surge barrier
This construction timetable (as at February 1983) details the main operations to completion.

In accordance with this plan, born in 1973, but changing and developing over the years as the research and the design progressed, the storm surge barrier would be in all 3,000 metres long, closing the three tidal channels seen in Figure 19.3. The barrier is to consist of a total of 65 prefabricated piers, each weighing some 18,000 tonnes. Between these piers 62 sliding gates are to be installed, which can be raised or lowered as required. These gates, made of steel, will each have a span of more than 42 metres. The precise lengths can only be determined once the piers have been installed and the distances between them measured. The height of the gates will vary between about 6 and 12 metres, since they will follow the contour of the seabed beneath them. This means that the weight of each gate will vary: the weights will range between 300 and 500 tonnes each.

The gates will be raised and lowered hydraulically and operated from a service building to be called 'Ir. J.W. Topshuis'. This building is to be located on the work island Neeltje Jans, giving a splendid view of the entire barrier. Since the work of construction calls for a very heavy power load, a power plant has been built on this work-island with a total capacity of 12 MW, sufficient for a town of some 30,000 inhabitants. Fifteen generators have been installed for this, of which ten will, after completion of the barrier, be installed in the service building.

More than 2,000 men are engaged on the construction work, who go to and fro daily via a temporary bridge, some 3 km long, which is also used for the transport of those materials not brought in by ship. To accommodate those of the workforce who cannot get home each night temporary living quarters, capable of accommodating up to 260 men, have been built in the grounds of Moermond Castle in Renesse. The castle itself is used for meetings. Since a knowledge of the impending weather conditions is vital to the success of many of the construction operations, a special weather station has been set up in cooperation with the KNMI (Royal Netherlands Meteorological Institute), which provides forecasts up to 48 hours ahead. These are but a few of the details of the complexities involved in the construction of the works, just to give you some impression of what is required when building in the sea itself.

Placing the piers

Perhaps the most impressive phase in the construction of the barrier is the casting and the placing of the concrete piers, 65 in all, each one weighing 18,000 tonnes. The piers have been built on the work-island: Figure 19.5 shows the island with the piers in course of construction. Figure 19.6 gives a close-up of one pier, which has a base some 25 by 50 metres and towers almost 40 metres into the sky. Each pier takes about 18 months to build. A new pier was started once a fortnight, so that eventually there were more than 30 piers under construction at any one time. The work, started in March 1979, was completed mid-1983.

You will see that the construction area for the piers is divided into compartments (Figure 19.5). Once all the piers in a compartment had been completed, it was flooded to a depth of some 15 metres. This allowed the lifting vessel *Ostrea*, which had been specially built for the job, to lift the piers one by one and transport them to their location. Since, once in the water, the piers develop their own buoyancy, and so appear to weigh only 9,000 tonnes, a hoisting capacity on the ship of 10,000 tonnes was adequate. The ship can be seen, with a pier in place, in Figure 19.7.

Floating 'tools'

The *Ostrea* is by no means the only 'floating tool' employed in the construction of the Delta Works. Three other such 'tools' have been designed by Bureau voor Scheepsbouw BV.(3) There are the *Mytilus*, used for improvement of the seabed by depth-compaction with vibrating needles: the *Cardium*, used for levelling and then covering the seabed with mattresses: and the *Macoma*, used in conjunction with the *Ostrea* to enable the accurate positioning of that ship when the piers are being placed on the seabed.

There are yet other 'tools'. There is a pontoon with a specially adapted crane, and a stone depositing barge to place the stone used in the sill that will be constructed around the bases of the piers once they have been installed. The stone cannot be dumped from the surface of the sea, since it would damage the piers in its fall. Further pontoons are to be used to compact the dumped layers. To safeguard the piers from being damaged by heavy stones (some weigh up to 10 tonnes each), a protective layer of asphalt will be installed. This calls for an asphalt-laying barge complete with asphalt plant. That reminds us that another asphalt-laying barge, the *Jan Heijmans*, was converted to work in conjunction with the *Cardium* in the laying of the foundation mattresses and filling in the spaces between the mattresses with layers of coarse gravel and small stone.

Talking of stone, perhaps it is of interest to record, as another

Figure 19.5   The work-island Neetje Jans
This aerial view shows two compartments nearly full of piers in the course of construction and before flooding. (Photograph by permission of Rijkswaterstaat)

Figure 19.6 A concrete pier
This monolith, one of 65, weighs some 18,000 tonnes, being 25 × 50 metres at the base and almost 30 metres high. (Photograph courtesy of Rijkswaterstaat)

Figure 19.7   The Ostrea
This ship, designed by Bureau voor Scheepsbouw bv, has a lifting capacity of 10,000 tonnes. Its main features are the U-shaped hull to embrace the concrete construction and the two heavy bridging arches housing 8 lifting tackles. Main characteristics: LBD = abt. 87×47×12.5 m. Loaded draught abt. 10 m. Power prime movers: for propulsion 4×1,350 KV, network, 4,200 KW. Owner: Rijkswaterstaat. (Photograph courtesy of Rijkswaterstaat)

indication of the scale and magnitude of this particular operation, that a total of 4.5 million tonnes of stone will be placed in a period of some two years. The stone used has a high specific mass, so that it is not too easily swept away by the sea currents, and had to be imported, since no such material is available in The Netherlands. Basalt was imported from Germany and granite from Finland. A stockpile was created over a period of four years, since it could not be imported as fast as it was to be used once placing commenced.

The cost

Of course, the change in plan from a dike to a movable barrier brought a tremendous increase in the cost of the Delta Works as compared with those original estimates. In addition the delay in completion, from 1978 (Figure 19.2) to 1986 (Figure 19.4) brought further increases in cost due to continuing escalation.

The actual cost and its causes have been the subject of furious debate in The Netherlands. The building of the storm surge barrier has been called a 'bottomless pit' so far as money is concerned.(4) Much of the debate has arisen due to misunderstandings. The Eastern Scheldt Project includes not only the storm surge barrier but also a number of related works, such as the two dams in the eastern part of the Eastern Scheldt, costing in total some 2.5 billion guilders. In these discussions inflation is also often ignored, resulting in public opinion concluding that the cost is now some three times the original estimate made in 1976.

If, however, we consider the movable barrier alone, the first realistic estimate, made in 1976, totalled some Nfl.3.0 billion (say US$2 billion). Remember that the original estimate for a closed dam way back in 1958 was Nfl.70 million (70 caissons at Nfl.1 million). So the cost has already escalated more than 40 times, but of course the design concept was utterly different then.

By the end of 1983 that estimate had risen to Nfl.5.4 billion, of which roughly Nfl.1.3 billion was occasioned by inflation. This leaves a cost increase, due largely to design development, of about Nfl.1.1 billion, an increase of almost 25 per cent.

If, however, we look at the costs of the Eastern Scheldt Project as a whole, as set out in Figure 19.8, we get a somewhat different picture. The estimated cost today is Nfl.7.8 billion, in which the additional costs are about 14 per cent. This does not surprise us. This is an outstanding development project with continuous change in the design concepts, so that what is being built cannot be compared, in terms of design, with what served as a basis for the estimates prepared in 1976. But people are afraid to confess: 'I did not know what was involved then'. Yet it is true: they *did not know*! And they still do not know what it will finally cost. That will only be known when *all* the works are complete and have been in successful operation for a couple of years. It is also interesting to note that whereas the overall increase is some 14 per cent, the storm surge barrier itself increased in cost by 24 per cent, as also indicated in Figure 19.8. This shows us where the technical problems were the most intense.

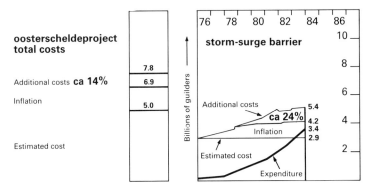

Figure 19.8   The latest estimate
This is the latest estimate for the Eastern Scheldt Project, which includes not only the storm surge barrier, the cost of which is shown separately, but two dams and a dozen or so smaller works.

Much of the extra cost has been occasioned by foundation problems. Even in 1976 the exact composition and bearing capacity of the subsoil was not known, and it took another three years to establish that the foundation and erosion problems were more complicated than had earlier been expected. But not everything is adverse. Just to illustrate yet once more, for the guidance of project managers courageous enough to take on a development project – and there are many more of them about than are recognised as such – and also to show that not everything goes wrong, we would mention that even in the closing stages of this project (February 1984) savings had come to light. The original design of the storm surge barrier provided for a total of 66 piers, but this has now been reduced to 65, with a decrease in costs of some 12 million guilders. The reduction by one pier was possible

because further research had shown that the hydraulic circumstances at the barrier were more favourable than had been foreseen.
This meant that a reduction in the number of barriers could be
achieved whilst still maintaining the final tidal movement at 77 per
cent of the present movement.

Final brave words

A brochure with the title *The Delta Project: defending the Netherlands against the sea*, (5) first issued in 1980, tells us that
construction work on the Delta Project began over a quarter of a
century ago. The last element of the scheme, they say, the storm
surge barrier across the Eastern Scheldt, may be seen as an
enlarged version of the project with which the work began in
January 1954, the storm surge barrier across the river Hollandsc
Yssel. The two steel gates over that river can be let down if high
winds begin to drive up the water level, and this protects the two
million inhabitants of the lowest part of the Netherlands – it is
around six metres below sea level – from the intrusive sea.

   When the Delta Project has been completed, they continue, and
the dikes elsewhere along the Dutch coast have been heightened,
then the fourteen million people now living in the Netherlands will
know that, within the limits of human calculation, they are safe.
We do indeed hope that they will then be safe from the sea. To
achieve that, they will have built a storm surge barrier that will be,
without doubt, one of the wonders of this modern world. In
addition, they will have:

1   Shortened the coastline by some 800 km, by closing the
    sea-arms of the Delta.
2   Increased the safety factor against the sea for millions of
    people. And the old dikes still remain intact as a reserve
    defence.
3   The fresh water management will be much improved. The
    inland waters will suffer much less pollution and the salinity
    will be much reduced.
4   The roads across the new dams will free a large part of the
    Netherlands from its age-old isolation. Travelling time to the
    islands will be halved.

5 The amount of fertile land will be increased by at least 15,000 hectares.
6 More recreational areas will become available for the use of the most densely populated country in the world. The freshwater lakes formed behind the sea dams are sure to attract hundreds of thousands of tourists and lovers of aquatic sports.

All this at a cost, over 30 years, of say, at today's prices, some US$ 20 billion. But, of course, the benefits cannot be quantified. What is certain is that the quality of life for many millions will have been appreciably improved.

References

1 Noordam, B.W., *When the tide turns*, Uitgeverij W. van Hoeve, The Hague, 1965, 56 pp. + 80 photographs.
2 Ministry of Transport & Public Works, The Netherlands, *The storm surge barrier in the Eastern Scheldt*, Informatieblad No. 22E, January 1981.
3 Brochure: *Floating tools for Eastern Scheldt Barrier*, published by Bureau voor Scheepsbouw BV, 12 pp.
4 Dings, M. and Kuin, D, 'Dossier Oosterschelde: reconstructie van een drama', *De Tijd*, 30 July 1982, pp.7–15.
5 Brochure: *The Delta Project: defending the Netherlands against the sea*, issued by the Information Division, Ministry of Transport and Public Works, The Hague, June 1980, 15 pp.

20   Partners in Indonesia

This is the story of an owner courting a contractor – or did the contractor court the owner? We do not really know. The owner is the company P.T. Pupuk Sriwidjaja (PUSRI) of Jakarta, Indonesia. The contractor is the M.W. Kellogg Co., of Houston, Texas, USA. For those who do not know the language of the land of Indonesia (and we don't), 'P.T.' stands for 'Persoaran Terbatas', or 'Public Limited', whilst 'pupuk' means 'fertiliser' and 'Sriwidjaja' is the name of a former prosperous kingdom in Indonesia.

The contractor, the M.W. Kellogg Co., is an American company founded in 1901 by Morris W. Kellogg. The company began with a capital of US$2,750 fabricating pipework and vessels. The philosophy of Mr Kellogg, the founder, was said to be: 'Show me something new.' The company seem to have taken this to heart, since they were one of the first construction companies to set up a Research and Engineering Department and have taken out more than 1,000 patents. They are now one of the world's leading engineering contractors.

Let us look at each of these two parties in turn.

PUSRI

The Indonesian company have abbreviated their name to PUSRI (from PUpuk SRIwidjaja). Founded in 1959, all their production facilities are located at Palembang in Sumatra. PUSRI are the largest fertiliser company operating in Indonesia and manufacture nearly 80 per cent of the country's total production of urea. Recent reports (1) put PUSRI's production from their four urea plants at around 1.62 million tonnes in 1983, some 2 per cent higher than the output achieved in 1982. This is a record, the highest in their twenty years of operation, and has been achieved despite a number of setbacks, such as power failures, leaks in a pipeline, a rotor defect in PUSRI II and damage to a reformer in PUSRI III.

In the old days the entire fertiliser requirements of Indonesia were imported at the cost of scarce foreign exchange, but today no imports at all are required, production being in excess of local requirements. In fact, the surplus is exported to other countries in South East Asia. The fertiliser plants have been constructed by a division of the company called PUSRI Projects that has done so well in terms of completing plants on time and within budget that its efforts have been described as Indonesia's 'biggest industrial success story'.(2) Thanks to this success there is sufficient food grown locally to support an ever-growing population and this despite the limited extent of farming land and the havoc occasionally caused by pests or the weather. PUSRI's production of fertiliser has increased some 16-fold since 1969, and their interests now extend beyond fertilisers to feedstocks and irrigation, thus bringing within their grasp the whole range of operations associated with the production of food grains.

Jane Ram, the writer of the paper referred to above, (2) tells us that PUSRI are professionally managed, with tight management control. The President Director of the company is assisted by three functional directors responsible respectively for production, finance and commerce. The company's operations extend to distribution and marketing for the entire production of the country. To facilitate distribution the company operate 7 bulk carriers, each of 7,500 tonnes, 295 railway cars and 5 fertiliser packing units, which are located at strategic points.(3) PUSRI have about 4,000 employees and are benevolent employers, caring for the needs of their workers and their families in areas such as health, child care, education, housing and training. They sponsor those who deserve it on study and training courses abroad.

In sum, PUSRI compare well with any progressive, well managed industrial enterprise anywhere in the world, and are well aware of their social obligations both to their staff and to the nation. Now let's look at the other partner in the alliance.

M.W. Kellogg Co.

This company were acquired by Pullman Incorporated in 1944, changing their name to Pullman Kellogg in 1964. Then, in 1980, Pullman were merged into Wheelabrator-Frye Inc., and the Pullman Kellogg Division were renamed M.W. Kellogg Co. The

company operate as a subsidiary of Wheelabrator-Frye Inc., with
headquarters at Houston in Texas.

At the time of the merger in 1980 there was quite a battle for
Pullman, the 'jewel in the crown' that made it so desirable being
the Pullman Kellogg Division. The firm of J. Ray McDermott,
another international construction contractor, topped the initial
bid by Wheelabrator-Frye Inc., but finally lost the battle.

The Pullman company are well-known worldwide because of
their Pullman railcars, and it was a railcar contract that created the
conditions that led to the 'takeover' offers. In 1972 Pullman
accepted a fixed-price contract for 745 cars at a time of runaway
inflation. Their selling price was US$282,000 per car, whereas by
1975 the going price was US$730,000. In addition the terms of
payment were such that Pullman had to spend US$50 million
before they received any payment. They thought they had no
choice but to accept such onerous conditions, but Pullman's
Chairman said later that unfortunately they did not have a smart
fellow to say to them: 'If those are the terms they insist upon, we
should walk away ...'. We mention the story only to show you why
the company were ailing.

Wheelabrator-Frye Inc. were after the 'jewel', Pullman-
Kellogg, set in the 'railcar crown'. After the acquisition, however,
they discovered that the jewel had several flaws. Overheads were
excessive and the market was in decline. For perhaps twenty years
Kellogg were probably the largest engineering construction contractor in the world, but by 1979 they had fallen to fifth largest and
only a year later to tenth largest amongst US firms in the industry.
Customers with projects having long lead times were uneasy as to
the fate of their projects in view of the financial problems in the
'railcar' side of the business. Following the takeover by
Wheelabrator-Frye Inc., Kellogg merged with Rust and Swindel,
two companies already in that company's portfolio, thus cutting
their overheads drastically.

M.W. Kellogg, by this time with their headquarters in Houston
– they were originally based in New York – had about 4,000
employees in the US, a further 1,500 at their satellite office in
Wembley, London and another 400 with Kellogg Continental in
Amsterdam. This latter company was formed to take over the
operations of Continental Engineering, a design company developed by the large Dutch machinery and equipment manufacturer VMF-Stork, who still retain a minority interest. This 'takeover'
of an established company is the usual approach to expansion in a
new market.

Among Kellogg's 'firsts' in process engineering and design
development are:

Graphic instrument panel display
Uranium 235 Gaseous Diffusion Plant
Phenol from Cumene
Large-scale, single-stream ammonia plants

Their fabrication and construction 'firsts' include:

Wide-scale welding of alloy steels
Field fabrication of refinery vessels
Integrally-clad steels
Stress relieving of vessels in the field
Automatic welding of cement kilns in place

Frank H. Shipman, when newly named as President of M.W. Kellogg, was very clear as to where the strength of this company lay. He declared:

People, that's what Kellogg is all about. They are the prime resources we have. We are going to get more good people, activate them and keep them ... During the next five years our engineering population probably will at least double. We are already the best engineering and construction company in the world. We just may become the largest. The merger of Pullman into Wheelabrator-Frye is just the shot in the arm we need.

The administrative changes following upon the takeover, with the change back to the 'old-fashioned' but historically significant name of M.W. Kellogg brought a new bumper sticker for display by employees: 'MWK – Great Careers. Great Engineers. Great Constructors'. Paraphrasing the message of this sticker Harold S. Eastman, a Wheelabrator-Frye Senior Vice-President, said:

Many companies are good ... some companies are excellent; but few companies are great ... Kellogg is one.

We bring you these statements to give you some idea both as to the character and quality of this construction company and the spirit pervading their employees: Kellogg did indeed have a very sound reputation in the construction industry. They were a company one could be proud to work for.

Why so much fuss?

What is the point of entering into such detail as to the history and the achievements of these two companies, PUSRI and MWK? Well, we want you to see how they must have viewed one another when they came to form a joint company in August 1980. We are looking at a typical owner and a typical construction contractor who have established an 'ideal' relationship which thus becomes an example to all such. If we can see the principles behind their most successful cooperation, we can learn the relevant lessons for application in other owner–contractor relationships – a relationship all-important to the success of the projects they *jointly* undertake.

Partners in Indonesia

Indonesia is where it all began. Kellogg had been active in Indonesia since 1971, the year in which self-sufficiency in fertiliser production became a national objective. It was then that PUSRI, the first of several state-owned chemical fertiliser companies established in Indonesia, decided to expand their ammonia-urea facility near Palembang in South Sumatra. Three large expansions were carried out by Kellogg over a six-year period. The company increased the total output of drilled urea at the Palembang facilities from 300 tonnes per day to 4,900 tonnes per day. As part of a cooperative effort, Kellogg provided additional knowledge and experience to the management and staff of PUSRI which prepared the ground for the future industrial development of that company in Indonesia.(3)

During those first six years, Kellogg Plant Services supplied training, operating and plant-management services for the projects. For the first expansion, PUSRI engineers received two months of classroom training in Houston. Operating personnel received four months of on-the-job training at a host plant, while maintenance supervisors visited vendor fabricating facilities worldwide for technical training. This was followed by three months of hands-on training at a host plant. Operating and maintenance personnel also received some classroom training. Then, the PUSRI management welcomed an 18-member Kellogg Plant Services team for a one-year assignment to assist them in the operation and management of the plant.

The second and third expansions were similar to the first, but utilised the first PUSRI plant as the training ground for all personnel. Kellogg-trained Indonesian personnel have, in turn, trained other Indonesians at fertiliser projects throughout the country. That brings us to the fourth main development in fertiliser production with which Kellogg were involved in Indonesia.

The Kujang complex

It was in 1978 that Kellogg completed their fourth large-scale ammonia-urea complex in Indonesia. Built for P.T. Pupuk at Kujung near Dauwan in central West Java, the complex raised fertiliser production in Indonesia to more than two million tonnes a year. The ammonia and urea plants are similar in size to those installed in PUSRI III and PUSRI IV. Substantial offsite facilities were also called for, such as electric power generation and water treatment. As at Palembang, the Kujang Ammonia Plant is based on Kellogg technology and utilises natural-gas feedstock provided by Pertamina from various gas fields in Java.

This particular development was different in that the delivery of the main plant items to the site, some 35 km from the island's northern coast, presented a particularly difficult problem. Shipment by rail was not feasible, and no waterways existed for barge transport. The only approach to the site was by narrow roads through the plains. It was rice-growing country, criss-crossed by an elaborate network of irrigation canals. Kellogg's civil engineering expertise was brought to bear upon the problem to ensure delivery of the equipment, which included several large vessels weighing as much as 380 tonnes each. During an 18-month period 28 bridges and culverts were reinforced and modified and entire road sections were upgraded. A receiving wharf was designed and built on an irrigation canal about three kilometres from the coast and from this wharf equipment and materials were moved to the site in time to meet construction schedules.

Completion to schedule

The main features of the four plants we have just mentioned are:

Plant	Capacity		Completion
	Ammonia	Urea	
	Tonnes per day	Tonnes per day	
PUSRI II	650	1,150	Sept. 1974
PUSRI III	1,000	1,725	Dec. 1976

| PUSRI IV | 1,000 | 1,725 | Aug. 1977 |
| Kujang: | 1,000 | 1,725 | Dec. 1978 |

That all the plants were completed well to time and within budget is demonstrated by the following table.

| | Months to completion | | Project Cost | |
	Target	Actual	Target m.US$	Actual m.US$
PUSRI II	30	34	67	77
PUSRI III	32	31	166	165
PUSRI IV	30	26	157	130

All this was a joint effort, with the Indonesian Government and Kellogg working together to enhance the country's management capabilities.

There is no doubt that the success of the PUSRI projects has been due to complete cooperation between owner and contractor. Both were looking after their *own* interests, but they worked alongside one another, and *not* opposite one another: an outstanding example of the type of relationship which we exhorted these two parties to establish in Chapter 6. This is the 'secret of success' in international construction, although really it is no secret.

Another factor which contributed to the success of these several projects was the very clear demarcation of functions between the main contractor, who operated on a 'turnkey' basis, the owner and the subcontractors, who were largely local. Ambiguity in this area always leads to problems and can bring disaster. Indeed, it *has* brought disaster to fertiliser projects in the past.(4) Divided responsibility is always undesirable.

This joint effort not only increased Indonesia's grain production, but prepared a base of engineering and construction skills for a nation hungry for technical knowledge.(5) One most significant outcome of this continuing cooperation over a period of some ten years was the formation of the engineering and construction company P.T. Kellogg Sriwidjaja (KELSRI).

The partners pitch in

KELSRI is a joint venture between Kellogg and PULSRI. Drawing on the blended talents and prior working relationship of the two companies, KELSRI provide engineering, procurement and construction services not only to Indonesia, but to other countries worldwide. Their project experience, as detailed in a brochure advertising the company, already includes a fertiliser complex in Algeria, where Kellogg France SA were the main contractor. KELSRI provided startup operators.(6) Figure 20.1 not only allows us to show you the distribution of their activities in Indonesia but also to present to you an outline of that country.

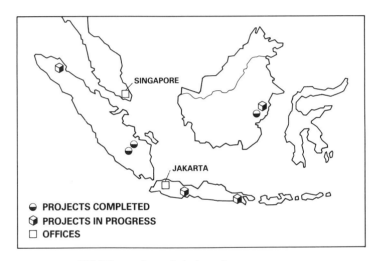

Figure 20.1 KELSRI experience in Indonesia
This map outlines the Indonesian Archipelago and gives the location of the activities of P.T. Kellogg Sriwidjaja (KELSRI) of Jakarta.

It is but an 'outline'. Indonesia, with a population of some 150 million, is the world's largest archipelago. It contains some 13,000 islands, including Java, Sumatra, Bali and most of Borneo, now known as Kalimantan, Celebes (Sulawesi) and western New Guinea (Irian Java). The nation extends from the edge of continental Asia southeastward for 3,000 miles toward northern Australia, almost the width of the American Continent.

KELSRI offer engineering, procurement, consulting, advisory construction and training services, primarily in the fertiliser industry, but their direct experience now includes the design, construction and startup of a water treatment plant, the design of a fertiliser plant water supply system, construction of units in a tyre

expansion project and the supplying of operations and maintenance personnel. Of course KELSRI rely heavily for support on
their two affiliates, PUSRI and MWK. PUSRI have brought to the
organisation a large group of trained Indonesia-based project and
construction engineers, operators and workers, whilst with the full
backing of Kellogg Rust Incorporated of Houston they can
provide engineering and technical assistance, together with construction management. They have already become involved in oil
refinery expansion projects and an LNG complex in Indonesia.

The PUSRI Fertiliser Complex

Perhaps we should take a closer look at the projects which created
the conditions for this most successful working relationship. The
current annual design capacity of the plants at the Palembang site
is 1.6 tonnes of urea. This compares with the very modest 300
tonnes a day, the entire capacity of Indonesia's first fertiliser plant,
PUSRI I, when it was started up at Palembang in 1962.

In 1983 Indonesia set a world record in urea fertiliser output. In
so doing, PUSRI produced 900 thousand tonnes of ammonia and
all but a fraction of this output was converted to urea fertiliser. In
achieving this output, PUSRI operated their ammonia plants at
106 per cent of design capacity and their urea plants in excess of
100 per cent of design – a degree of operational reliability which
normally would only be expected in nations with a long history of
fertiliser production experience and a longstanding technical
labour force familiar with process plant operations. Further,
PUSRI ran one of their ammonia plants continuously for 650 days,
thus shattering a 1979 operating record of 633 days previously
claimed by CF Industries of Donaldsonville, Louisiana, USA.

This story demonstrates that the efforts of Kellogg in the
transfer of their skills and experience to the local personnel have
been highly successful. The rapport and the close working relationship thus established were, of course, the motivating factor in
the eventual creation of the joint company now offering similar
services from their base in Jakarta.

A characteristic feature of all such fertiliser plants is the prilling
tower. Our view of the Palembang plant, Figure 20.2, shows three
such towers, since there have been three major phases of expan-

sion, as mentioned earlier, increasing the production of urea from 300 to 4,900 tonnes per day.

References

1   *Daily News Bulletin*, 2 January 1984, p.4. Published by the Indonesian News Agency Institution.

2   Ram, Jane, 'A key to partner in efforts to boost agricultural output', *Kaleidoscope,* vol.V, no.9. pp.124–7, July 1979.

3   Report: *Helping nations develop their resources*, published by the M.W. Kellogg Company of Houston. See article 'Helping Indonesia grow more rice and produce petrochemicals'.

4   Kharbanda, O.P. and Stallworthy, E.A., *How to learn from project disasters*, Gower, Aldershot, UK, 1983. See Chapter 8, 'The Trombay Fertiliser Plant Project'.

5   Brochure: *Partners in Indonesia*, published by the M.W. Kellogg Company.

6   Brochure: *P.T. Kellogg Sriwidjaja – Engineering and Construction Management*, published by Kellogg Sriwidjaja from Jakarta, Indonesia, November 1983.

Figure 20.2 The PUSRI Fertiliser Complex at Palembang
The three prilling towers are a dominant feature on the skyline. (Photograph by courtesy of P.T. Pupuk Sriwadjaja, Palembang, Indonesia)

Part Six

THE SKY'S THE LIMIT

21 Transport across the world

The Dutch author Jan de Hartog has gained fame in his own country, The Netherlands, with a book entitled *Holland's Glorie*. The title, at least, can be understood by those who know no Dutch. The book describes the activities of seagoing tugs during the first few decades of this century, when Dutch sailors set the pace. Even today the Dutch still have a leading position in this field, but the importance of maritime towing has declined insofar as the transport of large objects is concerned. This has come about because in recent years a large number of very specialised vessels have been built for this purpose: dock vessels, self-propelled pontoons and heavy-lift module carriers are now available for such work. Yet in this relatively new branch of transport Dutch companies are still playing a leading role, their market share of the tonnage in current use being estimated at more than 50 per cent.

The construction industry, as we have said earlier, has been seeking to increase the size of items constructed off site and then transported and erected in place. This desire has led to the design of what is called the 'module', an integrated unit consisting of many separate items of equipment incorporated in structural framing. We have already seen in Chapter 17 that offshore engineering, particularly in the North Sea, has given much impetus to this particular approach to construction, but the economic success of such developments is dependent, at least in part, on the transport facilities that are available. Indeed, it can also be that the transport facilities will affect the design development. We read a paper on the modular concept (1) that made the comment:

> It has been reported recently in the technical press that one of the leading offshore contractors is considering the building of a 9000 tonnes lift capacity semi-submersible crane ship.

Therefore we will have to consider the movement of even larger modules.

It sounds almost as if the 'tail is wagging the dog', and we do believe that there is an element of that in this area. It takes some two years to design and build such a ship, and firms in the transport industry, anxious to develop their business, will be seeking to keep ahead of the competition by ensuring that they have the appropriate facilities available.

The self-propelled pontoon

Before specialist vessels were available, the tug towed the load, but towing is by no means an ideal means of transport. The shapes of the submerged parts of most objects to be towed are far from perfect. This results in slow progress, with the journey taking a long time. There is also the possibility of losing the tow *en route*, if there is a storm. An outstanding historical example of that was when Cleopatra's Needle was towed from Egypt to London, to be later installed on the Embankment, by the Thames. It was lost in the Bay of Biscay, but fortunately later found and taken into tow once again.

The specific disadvantage of a poor shape below the water level can be overcome by putting the tow on a pontoon shaped like a ship. It should, for preference, be possible to sink the pontoon in order to position the item to be towed over it. This development came about, with towage companies building fleets of such pontoons, but the disadvantage of two vessels, two crews and a thin, vulnerable towing hauser remained. So came the next step – self-propelled pontoons. By putting the deckhouse at the extreme end of the foredeck a self-propelled pontoon retains the advantage of a fairly large flat deck, and such pontoons have been largely used for the transport of drilling platforms.

So far as we can ascertain, the self-propelled pontoon did not appear until about 1980. Two such ships, designed by Wijsmuller and commissioned in 1982, are the latest. These have a free deck measuring roughly 32 by 102 metres, can be sunk horizontally to a depth of 6 metres and have a carrying capacity of some 20,000 tonnes. With their spacious decks and large carrying capacity such ships are most suitable for large and heavy objects, such as floating factories and drilling platforms. It does not matter if the cargo is wider than the ship: deck cargoes projecting as much as 20 metres over both sides can still be transported quite safely.(2)

Because of the success of such ships, Wijsmuller built a still bigger self-propelled pontoon. They called it the *Mighty Servant*. It had a deck area of 40 by 120 metres and a carrying capacity of 25,000 tonnes. But, in contrast with their predecessors, the *Mighty Servant* series will be equipped with loading gear: derricks with a hoisting capacity of 250 tonnes. This means that such ships are no longer a pure pontoon: they are moving into the 'heavy-lift' class of ship, which we shall be discussing shortly.

The 'heavy-lift' ship

Let us return to the possibilities open to the project manager and his team, created by the growing scope and capability of the shipping industry. The 'heavy-lift' ship, fitted out with derricks – called 'heavy booms' by the sailors – is also growing in size and capacity. Early in 1983 the heavy-lift ship *Jumbo Challenger* was handed over to its owners, Jumbo Shipping. This ship was fitted out with two derricks having a joint lifting capacity of 1,000 tonnes. This is quite remarkable once one knows that Jumbo Shipping started in 1955 with a coaster, the *Stellanova*, which had a 'heavy boom' of only 12 tonnes.

Now the Jumbo Shipping fleet totals 11 units. all sailing under the Dutch flag. This ranks the company amongst the largest of its kind in the world. All the ships are relatively small, with lengths varying from 75 to 110 metres. Partly as a result of this their behaviour at sea is excellent. They move smoothly with the long ocean waves and they hardly pitch. This characteristic is particularly significant to the construction industry, since it makes possible the safe transportation of vulnerable and delicate equipment by sea. In addition, their small size brings flexibility in use: in particular, their slight draught enables them to deliver their cargo to construction sites that are inaccessible to the normal freighters.

The dock vessel

This is yet another design. The ship is indeed built like a dock: hence its name. Dock vessels owe their success to their versatility. The cargo can, for instance, be driven aboard over the collapsible door of the dock, which then serves as an access ramp. The cargo can also sail aboard. The vessel is then sunk until the water has risen about 5 metres above the floor of the dock. This is the ideal method for the transport of floating construction equipment, such

Figure 21.1 The 'Happy Mammoth'
The reactor here seen aboard the 'Happy Mammoth' weighs 615 tonnes. It is destined for an oil refinery in Tjilatjap, Indonesia. This picture shows very clearly the characteristics of the modern dock vessel. (Photograph by courtesy of Mammoet Transport BV, Amsterdam)

as dredgers. The dock vessel is usually equipped with portal cranes, which make it possible to hoist cargo aboard in the 'normal' way. These vessels are usually made highly manoeuvrable, with adjustable propellors and bow thrusters. Typical of such vessels is the *Dock Express 20*, owned by Dock-Express Shipping BV, in which the Rotterdam-based shipowners Van Ommeren have a major stake. The *Dock Express 20* measures 127.5 by 20.2 metres and has a carrying capacity of 15,000 tonnes. Its two 600-tonne portal cranes make it possible to take modules up to 2,000 tonnes on board with the aid of specially designed bogies moving along the crane track.

Another company very active in this field is Mammoet Transport, since 1981 a Ned-Lloyd subsidiary. They have two ships of this type, the *Happy Mariner* and the *Happy Mammoth*. This latter, with two portal cranes, has a lifting capacity of about 640 tonnes. In Figure 21.1 we see the *Happy Mammoth* en route to Indonesia with a reactor vessel weighing more than 600 tonnes on board.

But it seems that no one is resting upon his laurels.

The latest development

Mammoet now have on hand a new heavy-lift vessel with a series of striking characteristics. With a length of 145 metres and a beam of 28 metres this will be the biggest ship of its kind. The 20-metre-wide stern ramp will have a maximum capacity of 2,500 tonnes. This is sufficient for a 2,000-tonne module and its transport vehicle. The deckhouse is at the stern to leave optimal space for cargo and optimal width for the ramp. Two stationary cranes on the starboard side will have a joint lifting capacity of over 1,100 tonnes. Figure 21.2 gives the end elevation of this vessel.

The most remarkable feature of the vessel is that it is also fitted out for the transport of containers. The reason for this is that such heavy module carriers almost always make single trips, usually from an industrialised country to developing countries. In container shipping it seems it is the same: loaded containers on the outward journey and mostly empty containers for return. This can result in empty containers accumulating at certain ports, it being too expensive for the large and fast container vessels to stop off and pick up such small parcels. Ned-Lloyd, the parent company of Mammoet, often have to cope with such problems. The obvious solution is a ship without a return cargo, such as the 'heavy-lift' ship. Hence the adaption of this latest ship of the type for container traffic as well. This also means that cargo can be found for the ship during slack periods in the 'heavy-module' market.

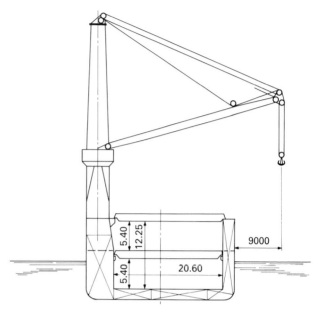

Figure 21.2   The latest 'heavy-lift' vessel
This end elevation gives the main dimensions of the vessel. It has a total
capacity of 6,700 sq metres on the three decks, and can carry over 1,000
containers. A load up to 1,000 tonnes can be lifted over the side. (Drawing by
courtesy of Mammoet Transport BV, Amsterdam)

Let's go skidding along

Another problem confronting the project team is the movement of
modules over short distances, usually with very little room for
manoeuvre. Typical of this is the transfer of drilling platforms and
the like from the yards where they are made to the seagoing
pontoons that are to take them to their final location. For instance,
a 2,800-tonne module built at the IHC Yard in Slikkerveer, The
Netherlands was first jacked up and then placed on a track of
Teflon blocks. It was then skidded along the track onto the
pontoon. Such skidding systems are under continuous development, with the objective of moving ever heavier units.
   A somewhat more refined approach is by using what is called
the water skate. The water skate is operated by Lifting Services
International, a division of Taylor Woodrow Construction Limited. Each water skate consists of a lifting and manoeuvring pad
using water under pressure from a standard commercial water

Figure 21.3 The water skate system
Four deck sections were moved by this method, as illustrated here, from the fabrication area to the quayside loadout position. The sections were fabricated by De Lattre Levivier at Quai de Radicatel, near Le Havre, France, at the mouth of the River Seine. They were fabricated for the oil company Elf Aquitaine, being destined for West Africa. (Photograph by courtesy of Lifting Services International)

pump. There is a load-bearing pallet with a separate skirt fixed to its underside. When water under pressure is passed through the skate it acts as a hydraulic jack, the skirt having the same function as that on a hovercraft. When on hover a certain amount of water escapes and this reduces friction in operation.

The number of water skates used depends on the load. Four skates would be used for a load of, say, 200 tonnes, whilst 40 would be used to move 2,000 tonnes. In this latter case water would be pumped at the rate of 36,000 litres/minute at a pressure of 6 Bar. Figure 21.3 shows a typical application, transferring a deck section for an offshore platform. The water skates cannot really be seen in such an overall view of the operation, but the pump hoses are visible to the left of the unit in the photograph.

Up hill and down dale

At times heavy loads and modules have to be moved through towns, and even across mountains. The problems of transport through urban areas are such that a high degree of specialisation and detailed route study is always required. But seldom has a transport project through a city called for so much preparatory work as when Mammoet were called upon to move a 759-tonne module from the factory of SN Constructions Metalliques de Provence, near Dunkirk in France, to Dunkirk Harbour, for shipment. The module was required for a drilling platform being built near the Shetland Islands for the oil company Conoco. The overall dimensions were 38 by 10 by 15 metres.

In this particular case at least 150 lamp-posts, a bus stop and traffic signs had to be removed to allow the module to pass. Electric cables hanging over the road had to be uncoupled: footbridges across the road were removed: business came to a halt in the shopping area because the power had to be cut off. Module D-9, transported on a 20-axle platform trailer with a capacity of over 1,000 tonnes, pulled by three Mammoet tractors, became the centre of attention. Many Dunkirkers turned out to see the heaviest load ever to go along a public road passing through their town, as illustrated in Figure 21.4, for it was a Saturday. On Sunday the module was loaded onto the Docklift 1, now renamed *Happy Mariner*, one of the fleet of dock vessels operated by Mammoet referred to earlier.

But though it was so big, that module only had to be moved some six kilometres. Move a load over a distance of 1,000 km and you have a very different problem. This problem does not involve

Figure 21.4. A 759-tonne module in the centre of Dunkirk
Here we see the module, mounted on a 20-axle platform trailer, with a capacity of over 1,000 tonnes, on its way to the harbour in Dunkirk, Belgium. (Photograph by courtesy of Mammoet Transport BV, Amsterdam)

251

such heavy loads, but the preparatory work can be even more complex, because of the total time then taken. Any delay in the programme – and one can easily happen – can often be disastrous. Transformers, turbines, and diesel engines are typical of items that have to be moved over the public transport system with the minimum of disruption to normal traffic. Europe has a substantial advantage here, because of its extensive and well-maintained canal system. For instance, Stork-Werkspoor Diesel BV of Amsterdam had to deliver two of their 18-cylinder TM410 Engines, weighing in all about 100 tonnes, to Linz in Austria. The equipment went from Amsterdam to Nuremberg by barge, then on to Regensburg by road, 120 km of autobahn. Then it was transferred once again to a barge, which took it all the way to Linz, where the final distance by road was only about 2 km.

The movement was handled by the firm Arminger-Wels of Austria and took a total of 19 days. Because of the large number of bridges that had to be negotiated, seeing that shipment was largely by canal, a great deal of research was required before transport could be effected. In some cases it was only a matter of centimetres. Figure 21.5 shows one of the engines being transferred from barge to a lowloader for further transport by road.

The impact of project management

The ever-growing capacity of the transport industry to ship larger and larger loads has the obvious result that more and more work is being carried out at the fabricators' yards, and less and less by the construction teams on site. But the burden on the project manager and his team has probably increased. The project manager has not only to consider the need to modularise sections of a process plant. He has to analyse why it is being done, what advantages are to be gained by doing it, what extra costs are involved, where the modules are to be built and whether the site can be accessed and the modules installed. Extra costs are involved in fabrication: are they justified by the savings in time and other benefits that could accrue to the project?

Since the construction of modules is usually contracted out as a complete package, it is obviously very important that a very detailed and precise specification is drawn up, that will minimise design changes once the contract has been let. Whilst improvements in time and hence cost are the primary motivation for the 'module' approach to plant design, there can also be real indirect benefits at construction sites where labour is at a premium or

Figure 21.5 *En route* to Linz, Austria
Here we see one of the Stork TM 410 Engines being offloaded from the barge M.S. *Ulrike* on to a low-loader. (Photograph by courtesy of Stork-Werkspoor Diesel BV., Amsterdam)

where environmental conditions are such that it is advantageous to keep construction labour to a minimum. (1) The platforms in the North Sea are a typical case where both these factors apply to the full. Offshore work, especially in the harsh environment of the North Sea, has brought about a great development in the design skills associated with modularisation, especially in the British construction industry. The 'spin-off' into other areas where modularisation can be of benefit is now being seen.

References

1   Laverton, A.B.E., 'The modular concept in plant design and construction', paper presented for the Institution of Chemical Engineers at the University of Surrey, Guildford, on 22 March 1984. (Copies are available from Matthew Hall Engineering Ltd, London.)
2   Brolsma, J.U., 'Spectacular developments in transporting heavy objects by sea have created new specialism', *Rotterdam Europoort Delta*, 1983, no.2, pp.19–22.
3   Editorial: 'New route to low-density polyethylene', *Chemical Engineering*, 3 December 1979, pp.80–85.
4   Article: 'Chementator', *Chemical Engineering*, 8 October 1979, p.49.

22 Communications worldwide

Communications are vital whatever the activity. Is it any wonder, then, that we not only introduced this subject in our very first chapter under the heading 'The importance of communication' but reverted to it once again in Chapter 8, when the subject was 'Project management'? That time the relevant section was headed 'Communications the link' – and they are! The only link! Yet whilst communications in industry are vital they remain poor. Peter Drucker 'hit the nail on the head' when he said bluntly that, despite the wealth of experience behind us and the marvellous facilities offered by all the latest techniques, some of which we are going to examine later, we *still* do not know what to say, when to say it, how to say it or even to whom to say it!

You think we are exaggerating. You think we are 'making a mountain out of a mole hill'. All right: let us quote the very first paragraph of a book on the subject of communications between employees:(1)

> We've been communicators for a million or more years. But we're still not very good at it. Husbands and wives still misunderstand each other *a dozen times a day*. In industry there's often less communication among the team doing a job than there was between a pack of our grunting ancestors round a trapped mastadon. And with the exception of a host of interpreters, the European Parliament shows little advance on the Tower of Babel.

The emphasis is ours. We may not agree with the author's assessment of the time span, but even if it is in fact only 6,000 years it is still long enough for us to have learnt to communicate.

Till now, we have been assessing the ability to communicate face to face, on the site, but let us now turn to a consideration of the transmission of data and communication to and from project construction sites.

Project sites in remote areas

A greenfield project site is more than likely to be in a remote area with inadequate transport and communication facilities. The site is selected for its proximity to the source of the raw material, since it is usually cheaper to process raw materials where they are found, rather than where they are used.

Just to illustrate let us take a typical project site in a developing country such as India. Once, back in the 1960s, one of us was directing an iron ore beneficiation project at Barsua, near Rourkela, from a head office in Bombay. We knew right from the start that communication with the site and the transmission of data such as drawings and documentation could be a serious problem. Therefore we went so far as to investigate this problem in detail even before preparing our bid, because of its probable impact on both cost and the time to completion. To establish what might happen, we set up what might be called a 'pilot project'. A telephone would not be available on site, but even if it had been available it would have been almost impossible to use, since all calls had to be routed via Rourkela and Calcutta, on the other side of the continent from Bombay. This was in the pre-satellite days, but don't think that things are very much better today. There are still plenty of construction sites around the world that have to get on with the work without a telephone. By the same token, there was no telex facility, since that needed a telephone line. Using our potential client as the 'guinea pig', we arranged for a series of telegrams and letters to be sent in either direction. The result: telegrams took from 3 to 4 days in transit and letters 8–10 days; at least one never reached its destination. This was not really acceptable in relation to a project worth some US$6 million, due for completion within 18 months and carrying heavy penalties for delays in completion. It was decided that the only solution would be to provide a daily courier service between the project site and the head office in Bombay. So the appropriate cost provisions were made in the tender. Following contract award this service proved to be of inestimable value, the travel time between the site and the head office being overnight.

The communications revolution

Let us now move from the ridiculous to – we hope! – the sublime. What is being termed in the popular press 'the communications revolution' is apparently now with us. Words like 'satellite' and 'fibre optics' are becoming household words, at least in the industrialised countries of the world. It seems that at the root of it all lies the existence of a television screen in most households in such countries. Till now, the TV, or the 'idiot box' as it is often called, has been for the reception of TV programmes broadcast over the airways. But apparently that is all going to change. Plans are afoot to make the screen come alive in many new and useful ways. News, travel and other information is already available to those with the necessary additional equipment but soon, it is said, there will be electronic shopping, banking and the like. A domestic satellite receiving dish is envisaged on every roof, with the appropriate receiver/decoder. The decoder is the device that ensures that you pay for what you see and nobody else sees what they shouldn't see. The satellite signal is broadcast in a virtually unbreakable code, which requires an electronic key to turn the signal into a viewable picture, a key that is constantly changing. Each individual subscriber would have his own number, which the DBS (Direct Broadcast by Satellite) system recognises (if the subscription has been paid) and uses to allow the decoder at home to make sense of the signal. This system of encoding and decoding is the key to all the developments in this area that are now being foreseen. But these systems are already working on a commercial scale in the construction industry.

A satellite network

The Bechtel organisation, who operate in the construction field worldwide, have five large offices spread across the United States from coast to coast. Each office now has its own satellite dish antenna. Figure 22.1 shows the dish installed on the roof of the company's home office at 50 Beale Street, San Francisco. Once again, those involved become almost lyrical as they describe the system. Under the headline 'New satellite fosters space age savings' a write-up in *Bechtel News*, the employee newspaper, started out:

Figure 22.1 Space Age communication
The 18-foot dish antenna on the roof of Bechtel's Fifty Beale Street building in San Francisco. The dish weighs some 5,000 lbs., and was lifted disassembled by helicopter. Using a helicopter to ferry materials was US$30,000 cheaper than using a crane. (Photograph by courtesy of Bechtel, San Francisco)

Phone calls rocketing through space may seem like a page out of a NASA operations manual to some people. But at Bechtel that scenario has become a cost-effective reality with the inauguration this month [May 1983] of the company's new satellite-based domestic communications network.

The rooftop antenna dish is aimed at a satellite that serves the US domestic market only. The system is leased by Bechtel from Satellite Business Systems (SBS) and ties the five offices together for voice and data communications. Video and image transmissions are also possible by this system but are not currently used by Bechtel.

The SBS satellite used is 22,400 miles up in space over the Equator, almost directly south of Houston and it stays stationary in that position. The primary satellite so used is known as SBS1, which was launched in November 1980. But the system is also linked to SBS3, which went into orbit in 1982 with the space shuttle *Columbia*. This satellite comes into use automatically if for any reason SBS1 stops functioning.

We referred in Chapter 1 to the inventive imagination of Arthur Clarke, the world's most celebrated science fiction writer. We said then that he has seen many of his wildest dreams turned into reality. The communications satellite is an outstanding example. Back in 1945 an article of his in *Wireless World* gave an exact description of three earth satellites in high orbit (22,000 miles) relaying TV and radio messages to the entire globe. The satellites were envisaged travelling at the earth's own speed of rotation, some 7,000 miles per hour, so that they would hover motionless over the planet. Twenty years later this 'dream' came true: the satellite *Early Bird* was in orbit 22,300 miles above the Equator. His only cash reward for his inventive genius was a small payment for an article entitled 'How I lost a billion dollars in my spare time'.(2)

The savings

It is estimated by Bechtel that the savings in communications cost by the use of the satellite system will be somewhere between 10 and 20 per cent. To quote once again:

Initially, we'll be able to cut costs by routing most long distance phone calls and computer data transmissions via satellite. We will save more as telex, facsimile and Wang-

to-Wang word processor transmissions are phased into the
system.

Whilst calls between the five Bechtel offices will go from building
to building directly by satellite, a long distance call to others goes
via the satellite to the Bechtel office nearest the final destination.
Then it goes further via the normal telephone system. All this is
completely automatic, the switching system selecting the least
expensive route by using the satellite network to the maximum.
The more the satellite is used, the less calls cost.

Outside the US, the normal public facilities come into operation, using terrestrial or undersea cable and satellite transmission
media as may be appropriate. Finally the phone rings on the
jobsite – if the local system is working!

That brings us right back to earth once again, and to the
problems that the project manager and his team have to face day
in, day out, in the field in relation to communications.

Lucky and unlucky days

When we turn to consider the subject of communications in the
context of construction projects worldwide we have to meet yet
another challenge. At a typical project site the workforce may well
come from a number of different countries. This is true not only in
the Near and Far East, but also in Europe, with the one exception
of the UK, still very insular in this respect. Those responsible for
placing the construction contracts look for the contractor offering
to carry out the work at the lowest cost, irrespective of that
contractor's location. This brings us up against the language
barrier once again, and literal translation just does not help as
much as you might think. We have much-publicised instances of
this from the international forum at the United Nations, where
misunderstandings arise even when communication is assisted by
simultaneous translations of the highest order of accuracy. This is
especially true in connection with colloquialisms. An Englishman
there once spoke of something being 'out of sight, out of mind',
only to learn later that the translators had told his audience that he
had been speaking about an 'invisible idiot'!

Cultural differences between countries only make for further
misunderstanding. For instance, in some countries, such as Japan,
there are 'lucky' and 'unlucky' days. Did you ever try to catch a
flight, or get married, on a 'lucky day'? A lot of people do. This
may seem, at first glance, to be a matter of private superstition,

but in Japan it applies to companies as well. As a result, even important Japanese companies will request delivery of new business equipment on a particularly lucky day.

Then, too, there is the matter of gestures. The same gesture can mean a very different thing in one country as compared to another – sometimes even entirely the opposite. We touched on this subject briefly in Chapter 8, in the section 'Communications the link', seeing this as one of the problems that can confront the project manager. The problem goes very deep. Psychologists tell us that every position and movement of the body has a 'language meaning' and there are several books on the subject. Then, too, some gestures are unique to a particular culture. The project manager should be informed on this if he is to avoid unnecessary problems at the construction site. Here are a few examples:(3)

	Gesture	*Meaning*
1	Person sitting, index finger to the temple, other fingers curled under:	In US: He is smart In Europe: He is stupid
2	Vertical movement of the head (nod):	In Greece and Turkey: No Elsewhere: Yes
3	Thumbs up:	US and Western Europe: all right (OK) Sardinia and N. Greece: an insult (up yours!)
4	A ring formed with finger and thumb (OK sign as used by astronauts):	Southern Italy: You arse-hole France and Belgium: You are worth nothing

So, yet another field for careful study by the project manager and his team.

Information galore!

Today, in the construction world, there is a wealth of information available, part of the 'information explosion' that has occurred over the past twenty years or so. The *right* information is the most valuable but often most difficult to acquire. Information *per se* is so abundant and often so conflicting that it may well be of very little value. How then are we to get the right information and where shall we look for it? Unfortunately there is no magic answer to this question.

There are a number of surveys of the construction industry published by the technical journals. Perhaps one of the most comprehensive surveys of this type is that published annually in the US by the magazine *Engineering News Record* under the title *Top 400 Contractors*. This does not list individual contracts, but presents the volume of business done. The survey published in 1984, relating to the 1983 awards, was the twenty-first in the series, but it is confined to US contractors only. It does, however, include their foreign contracts. We present in Figure 22.2 an extract from

Rank	Firm	Business volume (in $ millions) Total	Foreign	Ranking in earlier years 1982	1981	1980	1979
1	Bechtel Group, Inc. San Francisco, Cal.	13,810	7,884	4	4	1	1
2	Kellogg Rust, Inc. Houston, Texas.	8,500	5,000	1	5	5	5
3	Parsons Corp. Pasadena, Calif.	6,628	4,161	5	3	3	7
4	Raymond Inter., Inc. Houston, Texas.	3,212	321	6	19	11	–
5	Stearns-Catalytic, Denver, Colo.	3,119	791	7	18	24	17
6	Foster Wheeler Corp. Livingston, NJ	2,980	2,103	10	9	5	16
7	Fluor Corp. Irvine, Calif.	2,605	1,193	2	2	4	2
8	Lummus Crest Inc. Bloomfield, NJ	2,460	1,720	9	6	7	4
9	Ebasco Services, Inc. New York, NY	2,072	54	12	10	8	6
10	Brown & Root, Inc.	2,059	769	14	1	2	1

Source: Engineering News Record; Extracted from the Annual Surveys of the 'Top 400 Contractors' in the US, published in April of each year.

Note: Rankings are not strictly comparable because of acquisitions and mergers that take place from time to time.

Figure 22.2   The 'Top Ten'
To this listing of the 'Top Ten' for 1983 we have added their ranking for the previous four years.

this survey, showing the position of the 'top ten'. To demonstrate the way in which the fortunes of individual firms in the construction industry vary from year to year we have added the ranking for the previous four years.

This same journal, *ENR*, publishes a similar survey for design firms. These surveys reflect the changing emphasis in the work undertaken by construction contractors in the US – there is a steady movement from 'construction' to 'design-construct', then to 'construction management' and more recently to 'program management'. The latter term is used to describe contractors who undertake to oversee 'megaprojects', costing many billions of dollars and lasting for ten years or more. A typical example is a US\$45 billion project at Jubail, Saudi Arabia, scheduled to take some 15 years to complete.(4) Bechtel are the 'program managers' for this project.

The ENR survey has led, naturally enough, to mention of the 'Billion Dollar Club'. This is a term used by the journal to describe those firms whose annual contract awards exceed US\$1 billion. The number of such firms in the 'club' changes from year to year, as illustrated below:

Year	No. of members of '\$b club'	Top contractor	Contracts awarded US\$ billion	
			Total	Foreign
1980	29	Bechtel Group	10.6	8.5
1981	29	Brown & Root	10.6	2.6
1982	24	Kellogg Rust	8.2	5.0
1983	23	Bechtel Group	13.8	7.9

It should be noted that the above table refers only to US construction firms, as does Figure 22.2. We estimate that worldwide the number of firms with contracts of US\$1 billion or more totalled about 60, including the US firms cited above.

This *ENR* Survey does *not* list individual projects. This is, however, done by a number of journals, notably *Chemical Engineering* and *Hydrocarbon Processing*. The data presented by *Chemical Engineering* relate to the US only, but those in *Hydrocarbon Processing* are worldwide. The listings relate mostly to contracts awarded and therefore appear far too late for contractors looking for potential business. The search for new business can best be done by gaining intelligence at first hand, via 'news' from the jobsites or the use of sales agents and correspondents. Such advance information is vital to the pursuit of potential business.

The best source, though expensive, is the Data Banks. We will mention just two, one from each side of the Atlantic, as typical of the several that are available. The journal *Chemical Engineering*, published by McGraw-Hill, issues a 'Construction Alert Report'. This is reputed to be a comprehensive listing of future chemical process industry construction activity in the US and Canada. Describing it as an 'essential tool', the magazine proclaims:

> If your competitors subscribe to this service ... they're getting *more* information faster on ... construction activity than you are.

Across the Atlantic a British database, the *Chemical Age* 'Project File', claims to 'alert companies to new projects in the early planning stage'. The information is stored on a computer and is claimed to be updated continuously.

Getting hold of 'as-built' data

In recent years more and more emphasis has been placed upon the creation and storing of 'as-built' drawings, so that plants can be modified after startup with the minimum of trouble. But the creation of the 'as-built' records demands intensive effort as the plant is being built and quite often the records are incomplete. With older plants, the records, even if made, could well have disappeared into the archives. Not only that, but the maintenance staff can well make alterations that they fail to record as the years pass by.

One solution to this problem which we thought most interesting was the use of 'photogrammetry', till now a map-making tool. The science of photogrammetry is concerned with the abstraction of positional information from photographs and has been adapted with success to the provision of 'as-built' data. Perhaps it is best to illustrate the way it works by a practical example.(5) ICI's Organic Division in the UK proposed the complete repiping of six reactors and eight measuring vessels on one of their plants, together with the installation of four new items of equipment. It took three days to obtain 15 stereo pairs of photographs, with a survey of the necessary ground control points, at a total cost of £1,100 (US$1,500). The information gained from the photographs, when interpreted, included:

1 Nozzle positions and orientations on the reactors.
2 Existing pipeslot positions and the position of the pipes therein.
3 Break in positions on mains.

The accuracy of these measurements was checked at random against measurements taken on site with a tape, and the maximum difference was found to be 5 mm, but differences as small as 1 or 2 mm were not uncommon. A novel approach, but undoubtedly of great value, especially with plants that have been in operation for many years.

References

1 Bland, M., *Employee Communications in the 1980s,* Kogan Page, 1983, 163 pp.
2 Clarke, Arthur, 'Profit of the Space Age', *Readers Digest,* Indian ed., April 1969, pp.130–44.
3 Ekman, P., Friesen, W.V. and Bear, J., 'The International Language of Gestures', *Psychology Today,* 18, pp.64–9, May 1984.
4 Kharbanda, O.P., 'Process Plant Industry – a Profile', *Chemical Weekly* (India), pp..81–2, 29 May 1984.
5 Klement, U.R. and Bracewell, P.A., *The retrieval of as-built plant information using photogrammetry,* published by Imperial Chemical Industries PLC, UK, 22 pp.

23 The computer revolution

Computers have drastically transformed the business and management world over the past ten years or so and the construction industry has not been exempt. The transformation has been so rapid that we think it may well be called a 'revolution'. In fact, it has happened so fast that it has even taken the experts – shall we call them 'computerists'? – by surprise. We ourselves are no experts, even although we do not hesitate to use computerised tools whenever we can do so with effect – with the effect of saving time.

Contractors and computers

A survey among contractors has shown that around 60 per cent of contractors use a computer in the course of their business.(1) However, the main use has been found to be for accounting purposes. Also, when it comes to the use of the computer in relation to construction activities, much of the use has been due, it seems, to the need to 'keep up with the Joneses'. To quote:(2)

> Over the past five or six years, contractors bought computers because their peer group bought them. They didn't really know what computers could do for them.

The utility of computers to facilitate the work of construction is not doubted. For example, we are told that, by acquiring a small business computer and an operator for it, a housing developer has been able to handle a sevenfold increase in his workload in one year. Such a tremendous increase over such a short space of time could not have been handled manually, but once again it is the accounts side of the business that is being facilitated, rather than the administration of the construction work itself.

System selection

Such success is by no means universal. The selection of the appropriate system is a difficult yet vital choice. The system adopted must suit the specific requirements, which have therefore to be spelt out very clearly and precisely beforehand. That may be thought to be stating the obvious, but such an approach is rarely adopted first time round. Whilst this point is basic to success, it is so little appreciated that it needs to be constantly emphasised. The normal approach is to acquire a computer and then start to consider the problem of its use. But this is, in fact, to 'put the cart before the horse'. The decision with respect to the purchase of the computer should come last, not first. The first step is to set out one's requirements, seeking expert advice. The next step is to establish the type of software best suited to those requirements. Only then should the computer market be surveyed, looking for the machine that can best handle the software and the related requirements as to scope and use. So fundamental is this approach that a number of books have been written devoted to this one aspect: the choice of computers for management purposes. (See, for instance, Ref.3, relating to the small business.)

Just to illustrate the complexity of the approach to the choice (or design) of software and then the computer, we present in Figure 23.1 a table detailing the various steps that could be involved in the selection of a system for engineering design – just one aspect of the work undertaken by the contractor. You will remember the three main phases into which his project work is divided – design, procurement and construction. Notice the number of parties it is recommended should be involved: the client, or owner, the engineering contractor himself, the computer vendor and the software house.(4) The table presents the various stages in order of precedence, and the aspect of computer selection comes low on the list.

We are told (5) that computers are now considered to be 'just another tool or item of equipment'. The approach to its selection should therefore be no different. The objective is to select the right piece of equipment (a computer) to meet the specific requirements. Further, a good computer system has two basic requirements: the right hardware (the computer) and the right

Function	Client	Eng'r. Contrac.	Comp. Vendor	Programming House or Systems House
Preliminary job description	1	.....	.....	.....
Determination of bidder list	2	1	.....	.....
Writing of specification	2	1	.....	.....
Issuing specification	.....	1	.....	.....
Receiving proposals	.....	1	.....	.....
Bid tabulation	.....	1	.....	.....
Vendor selection	1	2	.....	.....
Final computer input selection	2	1	.....	.....
Generate work statement-hardware	2	1	1	.....
Generate work statement-software	2	1	1	.....
Scan table	.....	1	.....	.....
Alarm table	.....	1	.....	.....
Log format	2	1	.....	.....
Display generation	2	1	.....	.....
Material balances	2	1	.....	.....
Heat balances	2	1	.....	.....
Sequencing control	2	1	.....	.....
Manual data input	2	1	.....	.....
Special interface	2	.....	1	•
Special interface programs	.....	.....	1	•
Computer startup	2	1	1	.....
Eqpt. constraint determination	1 or 2	.....	2 or 1	2 or 1
Eqpt. dynamic response	1 or 2	.....	2 or 1	2 or 1
Math model determination	1 or 2	.....	2 or 1	2 or 1
Model updating	1 or 2	.....	2 or 1	2 or 1
Optimizing	1 or 2	.....	2 or 1	2 or 1
Control	1 or 2	.....	2 or 1	2 or 1

1 = Primary responsibility
2 = Secondary responsibility
• Optional responsibility

Note: Client always functions as a reviewer in addition to other assigned primary responsibilities

Figure 23.1 Proposed division of responsibility
This table lists the various steps seen to be necessary in setting up a process design system utilising a computer. (With acknowledgements to L.Skaggs, see Ref.4)

software (the application programs). It is, after all, only another project and should be treated as such. Projects can be a disaster (as we saw in Part 4) or a success (Part 5). The installation of a computer and its systems can also be a disaster: there is no guarantee of success. We have seen more than one such disaster in our time. So approach your 'computer project' properly, as you would any other project.

Let us see the method of approach. There are three basic guidelines governing the choice of a computer system, namely:

1 Define your problem: the need you have which you believe a computer could satisfy.
2 Decide whether your computer is going to be 'in house', or whether you will use a service bureau. Costs have dropped so sharply that quite small companies can now justify the purchase of their own computer.
3 Evaluate the volume of work. This dictates the type of hardware to be purchased.

With respect to that last point, the basic choice these days is between microcomputers, which use floppy disks and mini- and mainframe computers, that employ hard disks. Hard disk systems can cater for more data and can be connected to many more terminals.

Software the key

Any computer system, large or small, comprises three separate parts:

> Hardware
> Software
> Support

All are important, but it is the software that is crucial to success. Not so long ago the hardware vendors supplied the software together with their hardware in a single package. This left the purchaser with no choice. However, after a court ruling in the USA in respect of the firm IBM, who operated in this way, that the sale of both hardware and software in a *single package* was a restrictive trade practice, the market has become much more open. The sale of software is now much more the domain of independent software houses that provide software packages tailored to specific needs. Such houses usually specialise in one particular field, such as project management, construction management, accounting, and so on. When it comes to the purchase of software, the rules apply that one would apply to any other piece of equipment. The appropriate questions must be asked and satisfied. Is the system proven? Is it flexible? Does it have all the applications required? How many installations are already in operation? The more often a system has been installed, the more reliable one can expect it to be. It is in day-to-day operation that the 'bugs' are found and removed.

Construction control systems

The construction of any and every project involves a large number of separate activities that have to be carried out in sequence or in parallel to ensure timely completion. The organisation of these activities can be quite complex and as they are carried out an enormous amount of information is generated that has to be collected and collated if the contractor is to know what is happening and apply any corrective measures that may be required. This administrative exercise can be considerably simplified through the use of computerised construction information reporting (CIR) systems. Typical of those available is that described as being employed by Foster Wheeler, one of the leading contractors.(6)

In such integrated control systems the project site is linked with the various 'home office' locations, terminals on site being wired back to a computer in one of those 'home offices'. This facilitates fast and complete reporting, analysis and feedback. Within hours of the close of the work-week not only the project manager at the site but also the project director at the home office can have a complete printout, showing not only what has happened during the week, but also the cumulative picture to date in respect of every area of field cost, together with any other data considered relevant. All these detailed requirements have, of course, to be built into the relevant software system. Review of such data promptly, immediately after the event, allows management to discover the trend in time to take corrective action where necessary, as we demonstrated in Chapter 8, in the section 'The trend is everything'. A project left to itself can only go in one direction – upwards. Both costs and the time taken grow ... and grow. Uncontrolled growth leads to disaster, as we saw in the four case studies taken in Part 4. Foster Wheeler, whose use of an integrated, computerised project control system we have taken as an example, are members of the 'billion dollar league' in the contracting industry, as we saw in Chapter 22 (Figure 22.2) and were one of the pioneers in this field.(6) They claim that their investment has paid off well. The system they adopted has enabled them to continuously monitor and direct their available resources, thus helping them to live within the budget and schedule set for each of their projects. The chief objectives of their CIR System are:

1 Weekly dissemination of the management plan, including level of supervision.
2 Weekly reporting on the status, promptly at the end of each week.
3 Availability of information at site and at the home office, at all levels.

The microcomputer

The impact of microcomputers on construction management has

been studied in some depth, and some valuable findings are the result.(7) The study we refer to provides the background to the use of computers for project management, demonstrating the limitations of the mainframe computer and the rising potential of the microcomputer. The latter are compact enough to be installed at site on the desk of the project manager or cost controller and should be used once the size of project justifies it. The speed of processing means that the results are available when they are most needed – almost immediately after the event – provided always that the input has been entered promptly. The desktop facility can be also be used interactively: the user can ask questions and get answers. This is a real breakthrough, since at that point the computer has become a genuine tool of management, and is no longer the status symbol it used to be.

The application and use of microcomputers falls into three main categories:

1 Well-established applications, such as a payroll, ledger, cash flow and project planning, saving routine work.
2 Applications requiring careful study and continuous reappraisal of data, such as materials control, plant control, site performance and evaluation, with forecasting and resource scheduling.
3 Applications justifying the purchase of a microcomputer because of the savings in time that result, such as clerical routines, parametric estimating, document scheduling.

You 'takes your choice'

A Site Activity Analysis Computer Package has been developed (8) that evaluates design alternatives by measuring on-site labour expenditure and from that deriving site productivity. This is expected to help in the evaluation of alternative design and management strategies at a very low cost.

The application of computers has also been extended to the standardisation of construction specifications, thereby greatly increasing the productivity of engineers and designers.(9)

Another valuable tool in tracking progress, schedule and budget status on construction projects is the IBSM, or Integrated Budget and Schedule Monitoring program, developed by Engineering Science Inc., of Georgia, USA.(10) The IBSM program provides the following facilities:

Project planning
Task outline and scheduling, and budgeting
Projected expenditure curves
Monitoring schedule and budget status

For a more detailed discussion of the potential of this particular approach, see Reference 11. It is said that, with proper management control and sound use of the flow of information, substantial savings are possible.

Inflation poses problems of its own to the construction contractor and computer programs have been developed to overcome these.(12) With hyper-inflation, such as is encountered in Mexico and the Latin American countries, the computer program is extremely effective, because it becomes the impartial arbiter of cost. All estimates and contract award sums are recorded in terms of, for instance, 'today's peso', this being from then on constantly updated by the use of an index figure, which is available from published data. This means that the contractor is not penalised because of inflation and can be assured of fair compensation, invoices being calculated for payment by assessing the percentage of work completed and then applying the inflation factor.

Japan starts late but catches up fast!

This is not the first time that we have taken Japan as an example. The secret of the success of Japan seems to lie in the fact that 'self-reliance', which we saw to be a powerful factor in India (Chapter 18), has never been a Japanese dogma. It is hardly a dogma the Japanese could adopt, depending as they do on the outside world for most of their basic needs, including energy and other basic raw materials. In addition Japan has been quick to import the latest technology in a variety of fields, such as optics, electronics, chemicals manufacture and the like. The Japanese people seem able to absorb the technology, adapt it to their own specific requirements and then go on to improve it. The end result is the export of hardware based on technology without equal elsewhere in the world.

Let us take a few examples of this in relation to the application of computers by Japanese construction companies. Remember that their written language is very different to that used by the rest of the world. Nevertheless –

● Shimizu Construction developed a six-step computer-aided

design system for their architects. The design time on some high-rise buildings was cut by up to 40 per cent. The 'in-house'-developed graphics-based software can operate in either English or Japanese.

- Ohbayashi-Gumi have developed programs which, in conjunction with purchased software, provide an integrated design system that enables their planners to model city blocks and incorporate new buildings.
- Taisei invested in 150 engineers to write software for three years on end, so that they could catch up with their competitors. Their planning, preliminary design and estimating system cuts the cost of preparing proposals by some 90 per cent!
- Takenaka Komuten plan, estimate and prepare final designs using the computer. Other software packages provide management data to their executives through desktop terminals. A solids-modelling capability is under development for use with a microcomputer.

The turnover of these companies runs into billions of dollars and they would without doubt qualify for the 'billion dollar club', were that extended beyond the United States.

Robotisation

Robotisation in relation to construction in the field is very, very new – but as you might expect from what we have just said, it has surfaced in Japan. Armed with its world lead in the field of electronics, Japan has gone ahead fast with the development of jobsite robots, pressurised by a shortage of workers.(13)

But before we look at what Japan is doing here, let us be clear as to what constitutes a true robot. The Japanese Industrial Robot Manufacturers Association – yes, the state of the art in Japan is such that it warrants an 'Association' – list six categories of robot, ranging from the man-operated manipulator to playback robots and 'intelligent' robots that can determine movement by senso- and recognition functions. In the US robots are defined as –

those machines that weld energy and intelligence ... that can extract information from the environment with its actions.

Since a construction site is an environment under constant change a robot designed to operate on a construction site needs much greater 'intelligence' if it is to have the same degree of autonomy as it would have on the factory floor, where the operating environment is stable. Such robots have therefore to have a much greater load and force range if they are to be useful. These more stringent requirements have been met, for we find robots operating in the field in Japan. Typical applications include:

Beam spraying
Automated concrete distributors
Fully automatic drill jumbos
Fully automatic rock drilling systems
Untended mucking system
Rolling stock and manipulator arm

The beam sprayer, the first item on our list, can spray beams in a structure roughly 20 per cent faster than a skilled worker. Micro-computers control the sprayer's manipulator arm and rolling stock. This paint-spraying robot is on sale at around US$10,000. The last item, which is a modification of the first, has been designed for use on high-rise buildings, and was used with success on 40-storey Headquarters Offices for Toshiba, constructed on the Tokyo waterfront. The contractor on that particular project, Shimizu, have invested some US$400,000 in research and the development of this particular device, but have no intention whatever of putting it on the market. We do not need to tell you why!

The chronic labour shortage in Japan has driven these contrac-tors to the strategy of robotisation. Shimizu are considered to be the 'pace setter' in this field but they have not worked alone. They have joined hands with some other contractors and machinery manufacturers in a cooperative research and development effort. Japan's Ministry of Construction have also launched a US$2 million research project on the use of robots in design, construc-tion and maintenance.

It is apparent from the work done so far that robots are ideal for work in areas where man cannot go, such as on the bottom of the ocean or inside a 10 inch pipe. This thought reminds us that in Britain the Water Research Centre, working in collaboration with

British manufacturers, have developed a range of remotely operated cutting tools for work inside pipes. Whether these can be classified as 'robots' depends, as we said earlier, on the definition you give that word.

Summing up, let us quote from a paper dealing with productivity:(14)

> Computer technology and robotics are revolutionising productivity. But no matter how sophisticated they may become, it's people who use the tools and not the other way around.

This sounds a warning to which we do well to take heed. The machine will never be a substitute for commonsense. We still have to deal with people. Thus, for instance, despite three-dimensional computerised draughting, such as is available via CAD, models still have a role to play. Even if not now needed for pipework design, they are still needed for the simple souls (still the great majority) who cannot visualise a three-dimensional setup from a two-dimensional drawing.

References

1 Report: *Equipment Guide News*, August 1983, p.3.
2 'Special Computer Report', *Engineering News Record*, 212, 31 May 1983, pp.45-58.
3 Smith, R.R., *The small computer in small business – A Guide to selection and use*, Stephen & Green Press, 1981, 143 pp.
4 Skaggs, L., 'Contractor eyes process computer', *Hydr. Proc.*, 57, Feb. 1978.
5 Article: 'There is a lot of work involved in selecting and installing a good computer system', *Equipment Guide News*, April 1983.
6 Bromberg, I., 'CIR – Construction control system – Construction Information Reporting computerised control system for the process plant industry', *Eng. & Proc. Econ.*, 1, 1976, pp.113-22. Mr Bromberg wrote as an employee of Foster Wheeler.

7   Trimble, G., 'Construction management and the impact of micro-computers', paper presented at the 7th Internet World Congress on Project Management, Copenhagen, September 1982.

8   Hall, B.O. and Stevens, A.J., 'Variability in construction – Measuring it and handling it', paper presented at the 7th Internet Congress on Project Management, Copenhagen, September 1982.

9   Carroll, C.R. Jr, 'Construction development by computer', *National Development,* October 1982, pp.79–89.

10 Mitchell, N.B. Jr, 'Computerised Project Management' *National Development*, August 1982, pp.53ff.

11 Burstein, D. and Stasiowski, F., 'Project Management for Professionals', *Whitney Library of Design*, 1982.

12 King, P.M., 'Cost Control on Construction Projects', *National Development*, Sept. 1982, p.105ff.

13 Report: 'Japan takes early lead in robotics', *Engineering News Record,* 211, 21 July 1983, pp.42–5.

14 Goodes, M.R., 'Dollars and a sense of productivity', paper presented at the 6th IE Manager's Seminar in New Orleans on 12 March 1984, sponsored by the American Institute of Industrial Engineers, reprinted in *Cost Engineering*, 26, no.4-A, July 1984, pp.1ff.

24   Where do we go from here?

Well, our present journey now nears its end. We have looked at international construction from many points of view. We have seen that wherever man has lived, he has been busy constructing things. We began by looking at some of the marvels of construction in the past – the 'seven wonders' of the ancient world. We thought that it could be a fitting end to look at some modern marvels of construction.

Wonders of today's world

A recent article (1) selected what that particular writer considered to be the most spectacular construction projects, from a list of 107 projects in 26 countries. He thought that these projects, which excluded military constructions, were those most likely to make the past two decades the greatest for construction in modern times. We list and describe them briefly below. The choice is his, not ours.

Snowy Mountains Scheme
For our first project we go to Australia. The Snowy Mountains Scheme takes water that originally flowed east down to the Tasman Sea without it being utilised and diverts it through a system of tunnels so that it now flows west, providing irrigation to land previously desert. The scheme consists of 9 large dams, ten power stations, some 100 miles of tunnels and 80 miles of aqueducts. It cost in all roughly US$600 million (probably US$3 *billion* at 1984 values).

The work of construction employed people from 30 countries. A complete radio network linked the construction sites and supplies to remote camps were delivered by parachute. A special immigration programme was set up by the Australian Government to attract technicians and labourers for the project. This scheme, they say, is now helping to transform the face of the 'land with a big thirst'.

Rance Tidal Works

Now we go to France. This is a dream come true: electrical power from the ocean's tides. On the coast of Brittany, near St Malo, the tides of the Atlantic Ocean are amongst the strongest in the world, as high as 44 ft. A dam half a mile long has been constructed across the river Rance, with the associated power station. This, the first tide-driven station in the world, has a capacity of 550mkWh per year. A specially designed turbine harnesses the power of both the incoming and outgoing tides – the normal turbine spins in one direction only. The system is so ingeniously designed that at night, when power demand is low, it pumps water into a reservoir instead of producing power. Thus the water level behind the dam is raised, giving extra power availability when the tide starts running out. The potential is enormous. The UK is already considering a similar scheme (the Severn Barrage), to take advantage of the tidal bore up the River Severn Estuary.

The Delta Works

Now The Netherlands, or Holland, as it is more popularly known – although Holland was once but one of what is now twelve provinces. We have already looked at some aspects of the Delta Works in Chapter 19. Spanning more than 30 years (1953 to 1985), the ultimate cost has been the subject of vigorous debate, but no-one doubts the benefits that will result. We will try to sum it all up with two brief quotations:(2)

> Never before has such a project, practically in open sea and often exposed to adverse weather conditions, been attempted.

> Daring projects like this ask for new technologies and special solutions. The experience gained is invaluable.

This gigantic project has drawn the attention of hydraulic engineers around the world. Canada and the USSR now have projects for which the expertise and experience of the Dutch hydraulic engineers has been sought, so its benefits do not stay in The Netherlands.

New York Narrows Bridge

This engineering marvel was the world's most costly bridge when it was built in 1963 for over US$325 million. That would be around US$1.5 billion today (1984). It spans the Narrows at the entrance to New York Harbor, so that all ocean liners entering New York pass under it. It is a landmark easily spotted by plane passengers as they fly into New York. With the world's longest suspension span, 4,260 ft from tower to tower, the bridge hangs 228 ft above the shipping channel. The double-decked central span, carrying twelve traffic lanes, was the heaviest ever built, four steel cables, themselves weighing 39,000 tons, holding a dead weight of 84,000 tons plus a live load of 10,000 tons from the traffic that roars across. No wonder these cables require huge anchorages, solid monoliths of concrete and steel, each weighing 400,000 tons (heavier than the Empire State Building). The bridge is so large that the towers, though perfectly perpendicular to the earth's surface, are 5 inches farther apart at the top than at the base because of the curvature of the earth.

Mont Blanc Tunnel

This road tunnel between France and Italy runs 6,000 ft below ground and is 12 km long. Numerous problems were encountered during construction, delaying the completion of the project by more than a year. One blast broke open a glacier-fed stream which spurted icy water at the rate of 11,000 gallons/minute. The French had 5 fatalities. The Italians also lost five men in a digging operation, whilst they lost another three when a huge avalanche swept down on their workers' camp. What did it take? Completed in August 1962, it took six years and in all 18 lives to build, US$60 million in money, 10 million manhours and 3 million pounds of explosive.(3) But at the end of it all we have a miracle of engineering, the longest vehicular tunnel in the world, which redrew the roadmap of Europe.

The invisible trade

The export of construction services is a legitimate and growing trade, but it is termed an 'invisible export'. We remember that one of us once had to tender, in the late 1960s, for an important construction contract. We were in India; the project was in Qatar. It was a fertiliser factory, and we had to send 600 construction workers, with the usual complement of foremen, supervisors and engineers. The total value of our part of the project was some US$10 million in those far off days, but all the equipment and materials were being supplied by others. Our contribution was 'labour only'. We had to convince the Indian Government and the other authorities involved that this was indeed exporting something from India, and so deserving of the appropriate export benefits. We succeeded, but it was not easy, since it was the very first contract of this type won by an Indian construction company.

Since then the construction industry has come a long way, both in India and worldwide. Such 'invisible exports' are not only recognised by governments, but coveted. The International Engineering and Construction Industries Council (IECIC) seek to regulate this trade, which till now has been ignored, they say, by the US Government in particular.(4) The IECIC is composed of the American Consulting Engineers Council, the Associated General Contractors of America, the National Constructors Association and the American Institute of Architects – consultants and contractors sitting on the same side for once! There are similar organisations in many other countries active in the international field with such services, since they are now recognised to be a most valuable generator of export earnings. It is felt, despite the work already done, that there is a need for clearer and more direct communication between industry and government to foster this trade.(4) They should 'join hands' to 'assemble a comprehensive data base', in order to formulate the appropriate national legislation and governmental policies.

The energy syndrome

The economic wellbeing of the world at large has been very dependent upon the price of oil for a great many years now, with the result that big fluctuations in the price of oil have had a most disturbing effect. In Figure 24.1 we illustrate the movement in the average oil price since 1970 and give a most hesitant view of the future.(5) The two considerable upsurges in price, in 1973 and 1979, have made it apparent that from then on industrial development was to be linked to the availability of energy. The cheaper that energy, of course, the more scope there would be for development. First on the ground in all such development is, of course, the construction industry. That industry is involved throughout, both in the initial development of the energy resource, and in all the consequences that flow from it.

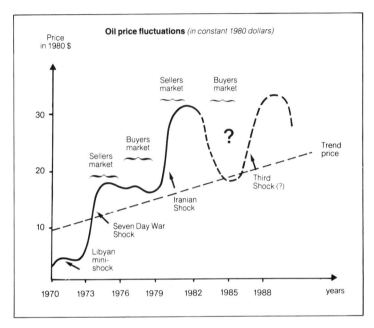

Figure 24.1   Oil price fluctuations
This diagrammatic presentation of oil price fluctuations over the past decade is chiefly of interest because it emphasises the view of an expert that uncertainty still lies ahead. (Published by courtesy of Compagnie Française des Pétroles, Paris)

When we look at the development of energy resources, we see that utilisation does not and cannot take place overnight. The development is inevitably spread over several decades, whether the source be an oilfield, a nuclear reactor or – as we shall see shortly – the sun. Such development also calls for investment, largely through the construction industry, running into billions upon billions of dollars. These two factors call for rigorous planning, based on carefully established projections. Unfortunately, with the world now in turmoil, this is no longer possible.

Looking back, we see that until 1970 world energy growth was so continuous, despite such handicaps as the slump years of the

1930s, that forecasters felt entitled to define and follow a number of empirical laws. There was the law of the economy of scale, which led to a steady growth in the size of refineries, of tankers, of electric power plants and of the manufacturing plants that depended upon the facilities that were thus provided. There was also the law of periodic doubling: in particular the law of decennial doubling, brought into vogue by electrical engineers in relation to the growth of their power stations. Oil followed that law for more than 70 years. Between 1900 and 1973 world oil consumption increased on average by a little more than 7 per cent per annum. Thus it doubled seven times in succession, every ten years, rising from 20 million to more than 2,800 million tonnes per year. Such laws make forecasts easy.

But all of a sudden, and to the great surprise of all the economists, that set of concepts collapsed almost overnight. There was economic upheaval, triggered it seems by the oil crisis of 1973, and given further impetus by a second crisis in 1979. In addition, the law of the economies of scale came up against a wall: there were also diseconomies of scale that had gone unnoticed, chiefly because all the attention was upon the plant alone, rather than on both the plant and its place in the infrastructure. We have discussed this subject in some detail elsewhere (6), so we will not go into any more detail now. Suffice it to say that one significant consequence was the search for diversification into other sources of energy. The possibilities in relation to the wind, the tides and the sun began to be examined seriously. Much trust had been placed in nuclear energy as an alternative source, but at about the same time that source too began to be suspect, as we have outlined in Chapter 13. To illustrate the scene, we give in Figure 24.2 a diagrammatic illustration of the way in which the various energy sources have each, in turn, risen to pre-eminence over the past 100 years or so, together with a forecast for the next fifty years.(7) As you will see from the reference at the end of this chapter, (8) this diagram is from a most authoritative source. As we study its message, it becomes apparent that a very serious place indeed is given to the use of solar energy from the year 2000 on.

But what does all this mean to the construction industry?

Teaching an old dog new tricks

What it means, above all, is that the construction industry is going to have to cope in the near future with a very different type of

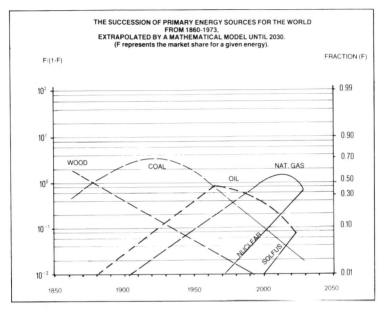

Figure 24.2 World primary energy resources
Here we have an extrapolation by Michel Grenon (4) of the phasing of primary
energy sources, worldwide, for the next fifty years. Note that solar energy is
expected to grow markedly in importance and significance. (Published by
courtesy of Compagnie Française des Pétroles, Paris)

construction work to that with which it has till now been familiar.
It has taken the industry all of thirty years, via the nuclear power
plant developments, to become expert in establishing 'clean
conditions': in being able to follow and demonstrate the history of
every item from manufacture to final placing on site. This latter
experience proved invaluable as the operating conditions in processing plants, offshore and undersea installations became ever
more onerous and the same criteria had to be applied there – until,
as we saw in Chapter 17, with the Statpipe Project, the materials
engineer could assert that with his computer he could 'locate the
pipe at any stage from mill to seabed'. Everything relevant about
every piece of pipe, every item of equipment, was on record.

We saw from Figure 24.2 that the expectation of the expert is
that solar energy will become a substantial reality. The construction industry will therefore have to learn and apply yet another set
of installation techniques, and perhaps find themselves constructing vast installations in the arid, sun-ridden deserts rather than in

and under the oceans, as they are having to do at the moment to recover gas and oil.

It has already begun to happen.

The sun and sugar

We like to bring you, whenever possible, specific case histories to illustrate the point we wish to make. We are fortunate to be able to do this in relation to the developing use of solar energy, having had access to a report on the prospects for solar repowering at Pioneer Mill Co. Ltd in the Hawaiian Islands.(9)

An advanced conceptual design for a solar repowering facility has been prepared, with funding provided by the US Department of Energy (DOE) Solar Repowering Program. The design involves the addition of a solar central receiver steam supply system to the sugar factory operated by the Pioneer Mill Co. Ltd, located on the west coast of Maui in the Hawaiian Islands, adjacent to the town of Lahaina.

The Pioneer Mill facility was chosen not only because of its location, but because it was a cogeneration facility. That is, the company generates electric power over and above its own requirements, to make economic use of the bagasse, a residue from the sugar cane, which it uses as fuel. The surplus electric power is fed to the Maui Electric Company. There is a long history of cooperation between the sugar plantations and the Hawaiian utilities, and the various plantations on Maui currently provide some 30 per cent of the island's annual electrical generation.

The economic need lies in the fact that the State of Hawaii depends upon imported oil for over 90 per cent of its electric power, and a renewable energy resource, such as the sun, may well be the only option for the future. The report, which was prepared in 1982, demonstrated that the proposed facility, if proceeded with, could be operational by 1987 and would then serve to demonstrate that similar solar repowering systems could achieve a wide commercial application, bringing with them significant savings in the critical and costly fuels from oil.

The solar facility

This solar project is now well in hand. Construction in the field should begin in late 1984, for completion in late 1986. The project is currently estimated to be costing some US$ 40 million. The solar facility will provide steam to the existing turbines in the power house. The solar receiver generates around 41,000 kg/hr of steam at a pressure of 7.31 MPa (1,060 psia) and 435°C. and the net added electrical generation is some 14,500 MWhe.

The solar facility itself consists of a total of 1,020 heliostats, comprising a collector system that mirrors solar radiation onto a central receiver. The array of heliostats is pictured in Figure 24.3. The receiver system consists of an elevated steam generator on a tower, 80 metres above the ground. Figure 24.4 is a photograph of a standard production model heliostat, currently being manufactured at the rate of 5,000 heliostats per year. Each heliostat, which has to be moved continously so that the mirrors direct the rays of the sun onto the receiver throughout the day, weighs more than 2 tonnes – two tonnes that have to move slowly but surely in harmony with the movement of the sun across the sky.

The motion of the mirrors is computer-controlled. It will be appreciated that each heliostat is in a different position relative to the receiver, so that each heliostat has to be individually controlled via the computers and is fitted with a microprocessor to interpret the signals received from the computers. The array covers in all an area of some 55 acres (220,000 sq. metres). Of the total estimated cost of US$40 million, the collector system we have just described is estimated to cost some US$25 million. We leave you to visualise the complexities of construction. What is so significant in our view is that whilst the concept as such is simple enough it could only be brought to economic reality once microcomputers were available at low prices.

All this is, inevitably, but a foretaste of the future. Quite obviously, the next step will be to consider building such a facility, far greater in size, in a remote area where the sun will for ever shine from a cloudless sky.

Photovoltaics – technology from space

The system of winning energy from the sun that we have just considered in some detail involves directing the heat of the sun onto a vessel which then generates steam. But another part of this same dream – energy from the sun – involves the direct conversion of solar radiation into electricity using devices that theoretically

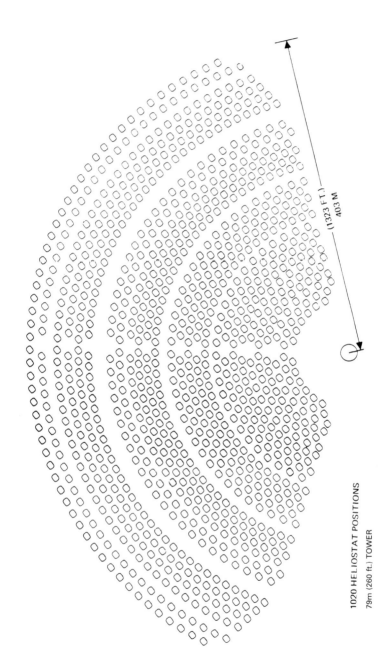

1020 HELIOSTAT POSITIONS

79m (260 ft.) TOWER

(1323 FT.)
403 M

Figure 24.3 Heliostat field at Maui – plan view
This a diagrammatic layout of the 1020 heliostats designed to provide solar energy at the Pioneer Mill Facility on Maui in the State of Hawaii. (Reproduced by courtesy of Bechtel Group, Inc., San Francisco, Cal., USA)

Figure 24.4   A third generation heliostat
This is a view of the ARCO Power Systems Third Generation Heliostat, standing some 7.44 metres high and having having a total reflective area of some 60 sq. metres. (Photograph by courtesy of the Atlantic Richfield Oil Company)

cannot wear out. This is via photovoltaics, at present an industry in the making. Whilst the concept goes back to 1839, when the work of the physicist Antoine Becquerel made it possible, thanks to the invention of the selenium cell, the first really usable photovoltaic cells (silicon cells) date back to 1954.(10)

Currently installed solar photovoltaic cells have an annual production of around 3,000 million tonnes of oil equivalent (Mtoe) per year, but the industry producing them is doubling every year. They present the potential for energy self-sufficiency: a few square metres on the roof of one's house or a few hectares in the desert is a dream that is not far from reality. Today such schemes are technically feasible – a 1MW photovoltaic plant is already operational in California and another 16MW plant is under construction. But the capital investment is exorbitant. The outlay is about US$12 per watt, whereas the average nuclear power plant costs only about US$1 per watt. So, despite the low running costs, photovoltaics are not yet competitive. However, the technology has made the present adventures into space possible. The first applications emerged about twenty years ago with the development of artificial satellites. Solar electricity is still the preferred means of ensuring continuous energy supplies to these satellites, particularly all those forming part of telecommunications systems, such as we described in Chapter 22. Here the objective is to secure high yields with very great reliability, virtually irrespective of the problem of cost. For use on earth, however, cost becomes of paramount importance.

Whilst today photovoltaics find application in small and medium-sized units, from a few watts to a dozen kilowatts, the industry is developing very rapidly and it may not be too long before the construction industry will have to consider the design and construction of fields of photovoltaic cells, arrayed very similarly to the heliostats we pictured in Figure 24.3.

We began this chapter by looking at a few modern 'wonders' that had made a most beneficial contribution to the wellbeing of mankind in a number of very different ways. That was the construction industry of yesteryear. Twenty years on from now, will someone be writing in somewhat similar vein of a solar facility in the Sahara? Or even in space? Or will the construction industry be busy rebuilding after the holocaust?

References

1 Wharton, Don, 'Wonders of Tomorrow's World', *Readers Digest,* Indian ed., April 1963, pp.127–34.
2 De Jonge, H.F. and Smulders, A., 'Eastern Scheldt storm surge barrier', *SWD Review,* no.23, February 1983, pp. 9–16. The *SWD Review* is the house magazine of Stork-Werkspoor Diesel of Amsterdam.
3 Rankin, A., 'The Great Mont Blanc Tunnel', *Readers Digest,* US ed., May 1966, pp.207–16.
4 Hodge, R.J., 'Design/Construction Exports: IECIC's Role', *Business America,* 1 Nov. 1982, pp.24–5.
5 Stoffaes, C., 'The price of oil inflation', in the house journal *Total Information,* no.95, 1983, pp.8–24. (This journal is published from Paris by Compagnie Française des Pétroles.)
6 Kharbanda, O.P. and Stallworthy, E.A., *How to learn from project disasters*, Gower, Aldershot, Hants., UK, 1983, 273 pp. See Chapter 15, 'Small is beautiful'.
7 Grenon, M., 'Oil and Fossil Energies', in the house journal *Total Information*, no.95, 1983, pp.2–7.
8 Michel Grenon, writer of Ref.7, is the author of numerous books on energy policies including *Le Nouveau Pétrole* (The New Oil), Hachette, 1973 and *La Pomme Nucléaire et l'Orange Solaire* (The Nuclear Apple and the Solar Orange), Robert Laffont, 1978.
9 Report: 'Advanced conceptual design for solar repowering at Pioneer Mill Co. Ltd.', May 1982, prepared by Bechtel Group, Inc., San Francisco, Cal., USA.
10 Rodot M., Bianchi J.P. and Peter, F., 'Photosynthesis and photovoltaic cells: two related methods of using light from the sun', *Total Information*, no.97, 1984. (Compagnie Française des Pétroles, 5 Rue Michel-Ange, 75781 Paris Cedex 16.)

Epilogue

We share the enthusiasm of E.E.(Gene) Halmos for the construction industry. He once wrote:(1)

> Construction has been an honored profession throughout history. Without it, Rome could not have created a world empire, without it the Pyramids would have been impossible, without it the modern world of swift communications and interchange of goods and services would be unthinkable.
>
> Construction men – however rough and unemotional they may appear – really have an enduring, all-consuming love affair with their profession. They think it, talk it, dream it. The daily challenge that it presents is a never-ending lure to all of them.
>
> True love is often inarticulate when it attempts to explain the object of its devotion.

Nevertheless, Mr Halmos wrote a book about it, and we have now got to the end of this one. He has pointed out the complete dependence of our modern world upon the work of the construction industry. We have sought, as he does, to demonstrate that whilst that industry is building for the present it is also shaping the *future*. The construction industry is responsible for much innovation: innovation that has been and still is the fruit of the necessities of the industry and its continuing ability to meet the challenges it faces.

The poetry of construction

Nowhere is this more apparent than when construction takes place in the open sea. Sometimes the ultimate achievement is very visible, as with the Delta Works in Holland, of which a Dutchman has written:(2)

> Never before has such a project, practically in the open sea and often exposed to adverse weather conditions, been attempted ... Daring projects like this ask for new technologies and special solutions. The experience gained is invaluable.

Sometimes the work done is largely invisible, as with the submarine pipeline from Bombay High in India or the Statoil pipeline project being built for Norway. One of the project engineers on that latter project became really lyrical in his description of the largely invisible:(3)

> It snakes along the ocean floor like a mammoth sea animal, with tentacles of pipe and concrete. The man-made arms and legs of it ... make their way onshore and off, as if caught in a metamorphosis between land and ocean.

But seen or unseen, the contribution that the construction industry has made to our general wellbeing is still there. For instance, a report on the work of the construction industry in the North Sea (4) says that whilst the North Sea is the world's 'most demanding testbed' it nevertheless offers a 'unique shop window for companies to show their skills and capabilities'.

Without 'construction' the world as we know it would not be. Construction is an international industry but it does not and cannot stand alone. The construction industry is concerned with 'projects' – projects large and small. A project is a non-routine, one-off exercise, and each project is different from the next, with its own specific parameters of both time and cost.

Proper project management

For the proper execution of projects we need project management and project managers. The concept has been there from time immemorial, but the increasing complexity of projects, especially over the last forty years or so, has resulted in the development of project management as a technique in its own right. A project has a beginning and an ending and project management should begin at the beginning and continue to the very end, bitter or sweet.

The standard method of dividing up a project is to speak of three main phases, once it has been approved – design, procurement and construction. Design and procurement support and lead to construction. In this book we have looked at the construction industry worldwide and seen that as the techniques of construction have developed over the years the construction engineer has done much designing on his own account, developing or causing to be developed a great variety of ingenious machines to facilitate his work.

But we have come, as we have said, to the end of our story. We have sought to bring you the fascination it holds for us – and we can each now look back over more than three decades of continuous activity in the industry. Truly, we have also tried to bring to you some of the lessons that have to be learnt if one is to be effective, contributing to success stories rather than to disasters. But you will *not* make a success of your job or your project unless you enjoy your work: so we have indeed tried, by letting you see not only the grinding detail but the completed project, to imbue you with some of our enthusiasm.

The project manager leads a project management team, and either in this book or elsewhere (5)(6) we have told many parables to help in demonstrating that they are indeed a *team*. We have compared their efforts to climbing a mountain or fighting a battle; we have likened the project manager to the conductor of an orchestra, the pilot of a plane, the captain of a ship. May we now make one last comparison. Let us conclude by saying that what they are also doing is *painting a canvas*. The project manager, the design engineers, the procurement and construction personnel are the ones who actually *paint* that canvas. The cost control engineers, the planning engineers, the cost accountants provide the frame which enables the painting to be clearly seen and properly evaluated for what it is. So, for instance, if the project manager and his team do not think and practise cost control, then *costs* will not be controlled and the painting will be a mess, however elegant the frame. That is, expounding the parable, however sophisticated the cost control techniques, however many cost control engineers have been busy on the project.(7)

Of course, the *real conclusion* is the operating, functioning installation, built at an economic cost, doing what it was planned that it should do. If that end result has indeed been achieved, it should not be seen as a matter for pride. Rather should it have been a humbling experience. So many awkward things could have happened – but they didn't. Many things did indeed go wrong, most often due to ignorance or lack of foresight – but sometimes it really was just bad luck. The end result would never have been achieved but for the cooperation of a multitude of people doing humdrum, routine jobs. They all played their part. And with the players each playing their part construction will go from strength to strength.

References

1   Halmos, E.E., *Construction: a way of life – a romance,* first published by Westminster Communications and Publications, Washington DC, 1979, but now available from Mr E.E. Hamlos. PO Box 259, Poolesville, MD 20837, USA.
2   De Jonge, H.F., 'Eastern Scheldt Storm Surge Barrier', *Diesel & Gas Power Worldwide,* September 1982.
3   Moore, S., 'Up from the deep', *Fluor Magazine*, vol. XL, no. 2, 1983.
4   'The North Sea: a springboard for British industry', a report commissioned by Shell UK Limited, and available from Shell-Mex House, London, WC1.
5   Kharbanda, O.P. and Stallworthy, E.A., *How to learn from project disasters – true life stories with a moral for management*, Gower, Aldershot, UK, 1983.
6   Stallworthy, E.A., and Kharbanda, O.P., *Total project management – from concept to completion,* Gower, Aldershot, UK, 1983.
7   Kharbanda, O.P., Stallworthy, E.A. and Williams, L.F., *Project cost control in action,* Gower, Aldershot, UK, 1980.

Index